GROWING AND PRESERVING

YOUR OWN

FRUITS AND VEGETABLES

GROWING AND PRESERVING YOUR OWN FRUITS AND VEGETABLES/

Edited by
George Fitzley, ed /

JONATHAN DAVID/PUBLISHERS
MIDDLE VILLAGE, N. Y. 11379

GROWING AND PRESERVING YOUR OWN FRUITS AND VEGETABLES

Growing Vegetables in the Home Garden was issued in 1972 as United States Department of Agriculture Home and Garden Bulletin No. 202; *Home Canning of Fruits and Vegetables* was revised in 1965 as Home and Garden Bulletin No. 8; *Home Freezing of Fruits and Vegetables* was revised in 1966 as Home and Garden Bulletin No. 10; *How to Make Jellies, Jams and Preserves at Home* was revised in 1974 as Home and Garden Bulletin No. 56; *Making Pickles and Relishes at Home* was revised in 1970 as Home and Garden Bulletin No. 92; Chapter 1 is adapted from *The Home Fruit Planting*, by M.B. Hoffman (New York State Extension Bulletin 913, revised 1974); and *Disease and Insect Control in the Home Orchard*, revised in 1972 by James L. Brann and Phil A. Arneson.

Photographs courtesy W. Atlee Burpee Co., Warminster, Pa., and Stark Bro's Nurseries, Louisiana, Mo.

Library of Congress Cataloging in Publication Data

Fitzley, George, 1938-
  Growing and preserving your own fruits and vegetables.

  1. Fruit-culture. 2. Vegetable gardening.
3. Fruit—Preservation. 4. Vegetables—Preservation.
I. Title.
SB355.F54   634   75-4569
ISBN 0-8246-0198-X

Printed in the United States of America

Publisher's Note

This book combines five previously published pamphlets by the United States Department of Agriculture: *Growing Vegetables in the Home Garden, Home Canning of Fruits and Vegetables, Home Freezing of Fruits and Vegetables, How to Make Jellies, Jams, and Preserves at Home,* and *Making Pickles and Relishes at Home.*

Two pamphlets, in adapted form, published by the New York State College of Agriculture Extension Service have also been included: *The Home Fruit Planting,* by M.B. Hoffman and *Disease and Insect Control in the Home Orchard,* revised by James L. Brann and Phil A. Arneson.

These publications are presented here as a unit in order to be of service to anyone who wishes to grow and preserve his own fruits and vegetables either as a hobby or in order to save money.

Though all chapters in this book have been prepared by experts and are accurate in every respect, it will sometimes be necessary for the reader to turn to local agricultural personnel to ascertain precise information governing their own localities, since this presentation is limited by space and, by its very nature, must be a general presentation.

Readers are encouraged to send away for catalogues prepared by seed companies and nurseries. These catalogues offer a vast amount of useful information as well as suggestions about the varieties of fruits and vegetables available, about planting techniques, and about equipment that can be used to good advantage.

Table of Contents

Growing Fruits in the Home Garden

In several senses, it is more difficult to give general nation-wide information about growing fruits than it is about vegetables. Vegetables, for the most part, are annuals. They progress from seed to fruit in one growing season, and then die. Most types of vegetable crops can be grown in any part of the country. Occasionally, such climatic conditions as a short growing season or extreme heat and cold have to be taken into account, but these limitations can often be offset by artificial means.

With fruit cultivation, the situation is different. Most fruit crops are perennials which require anywhere from two to ten years to bear fruit. In most parts of the country, this means that fruit crops must pass through winter conditions which have the capacity to destroy the plant, or alter its fruit bearing potential. (The word *hardiness* is used to categorize a plant's capacity to withstand seasonal changes.) Because it is impractical to alter climatic conditions for fruits (except for short periods of time), fruit cultivation is a very regional enterprise. Anyone expecting a measure of success will have to turn to state and local agricultural authorities for information peculiar to his area.

The information that follows is very general because it is being addressed to a national audience. Most of the fruits discussed here can be grown in some part of all states. Fruits such as citrus, which are distinctly regional, are omitted.

Growing fruit for home use can be an interesting hobby and a profitable venture. Fruit that is allowed to ripen on the plant is of the best eating and culinary quality. In addition to being appetizing, fruits are classed as protective foods because they contain certain substances essential to good health. These reasons justify a home fruit planting wherever there is a place for it.

Strawberries are one of the first fruits to ripen, followed by raspberries, currants, gooseberries, blueberries, cherries, peaches, plums, grapes, pears, and apples. By properly selecting the kinds and varieties of fruit for the home planting, a succession of fresh fruit of high dessert quality may be available through most of the summer. Surpluses can be canned or frozen for winter use.

This chapter has been adapted from a booklet entitled *The Home Fruit Planting*, by M.B. Hoffman, Professor Emeritus, Cornell University. The section on plant disease was prepared by James L. Brann and Phil A. Arneson.

There are, however, certain limitations and precautions that should be considered carefully when contemplating a planting. The success or failure of a home fruit planting is determined by: (1) the availability of a suitable site and soils, (2) the selection of those fruits and varieties adapted to the locality, (3) pest control, and (4) cultural care.

In some sections of the country, peaches, cherries, and the more tender varieties of other tree fruits do not withstand winter temperatures. Furthermore, tree fruits are exacting in their spray requirements. It is not possible to control insects and diseases on large trees without power-driven spray machinery that would not be justified for a small home planting. This is especially true for apples because both leaves and fruit are attacked by the scab fungus and by a number of insects. Dwarf trees seem to offer some solution to this problem because pest-control treatments can be applied with small hand-operated equipment. Dwarf trees occupy less space and bear at an earlier age than do standard trees on seedling stocks.

The small fruits, such as strawberries, raspberries, blueberries, currants, and grapes offer definite advantages for garden culture. They require a minimum of space for the amount of fruit produced and bear one or two years after planting. Also, it is easier to control pests on these than on tree fruits.

Site and Soil

The site of the home fruit planting is usually determined by circumstances. Nearness to the house is desirable, but if the building is on low ground where frosts are likely to occur, it is better, if possible, to plant on higher ground.

Fruit plants differ from crop plants in that they are perennials and their root systems live in the soil throughout the year. Because fruit plants start their top growth early, a correspondingly early and vigorous root growth is needed to supply the tops with increasing amounts of water. The soil must have, in addition to available water, an adequate supply of air so the roots can "breathe" and thus release the energy that is used by them when they grow and absorb water and nutrients. A soil that is waterlogged or saturated during the spring does not contain the air needed for the proper functioning of the roots of fruit plants. The soil should have enough internal drainage to allow the roots to start unimpaired activity early in the spring and to continue this activity until leaf fall in late autumn. Otherwise, maximum growth and production will not be realized. In obtaining satisfactory performance of fruit plants there is no substitute for a well-drained soil.

Climatic Requirements

Minimum winter temperatures determine the areas in which most fruit plants can be grown with success. Most county agricultural extension services can provide minimum temperature information. However, be aware that temperatures can vary by quite a few degrees within a relatively confined area because of elevation. The chart provided here gives approximate information.

Only the hardiest varieties of apples, such as Yellow Transparent, Duchess, Wealthy, Northwest Greening, and Cortland, can withstand winter temperatures of 30 degrees below zero (-30° F.) or colder, and even these varieties may suffer from winter injury at such temperatures. The less hardy varieties of apples, such as Rhode Island Greening and Northern Spy, and pears can usually

The Approximate Range of Average Minimum Temperatures

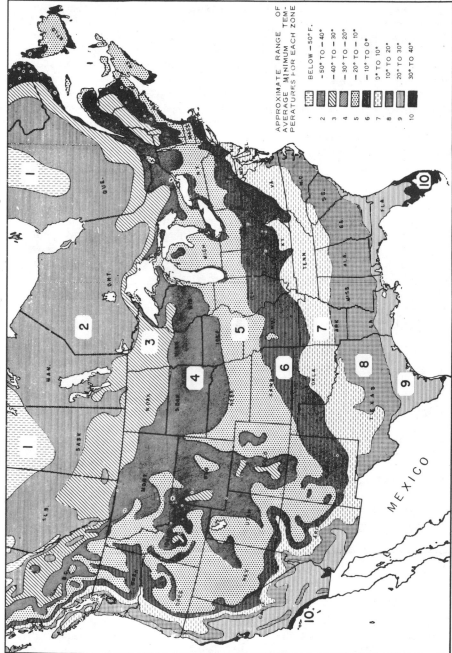

APPROXIMATE RANGE OF AVERAGE MINIMUM TEMPERATURES FOR EACH ZONE

1	BELOW −50° F.
2	−50° TO −40°
3	−40° TO −30°
4	−30° TO −20°
5	−20° TO −10°
6	−10° TO 0°
7	0° TO 10°
8	10° TO 20°
9	20° TO 30°
10	30° TO 40°

withstand winters during which the minimum temperature goes to 25 degrees below zero (-25° F.). Sour cherries and certain plums may suffer winter injury when the minimum temperature goes lower than 20 degrees below zero (-20° F.). A temperature of 20 degrees below zero would also result in damage to the wood of sweet cherry and peach trees, and the flower buds of peaches are usually killed when winter temperatures reach 15 degrees below zero (-15° F.). The exact temperature that the various species of tree fruits withstand varies greatly, depending on the amount of hardiness acquired at the time of the freeze as well as other environmental factors.

Those areas with the coldest winters also have the shortest growing season. The figure on page 67 shows the average date of the last spring frost. The date of the last spring frost in some sections is important because a late frost may injure or kill fruit blossoms, resulting in a loss of the crop. This often happens where frost is frequent after May 10.

Planting Plans

The home fruit planting represents an expenditure in both time and money. Consequently, it should follow a carefully considered plan. The space available and the requirements and preferences of the family serve as a guide in choosing the kinds of fruit and quantities to plant. Thought should also be given to arrangement, spacing, and selection of varieties.

Planting Guide

Fruit	Distance		Bearing age	Approximate yield per mature plant	Ripening period
	Between rows	Between plants			
	Feet	*Feet*	*Years*		
Tree Fruits					
Apple (dwarf)	20	20	5	2 bushels	August to October
Pear (dwarf)	20	20	4	1 bushel	August to September
Peach	20	20	4	2 bushels	August to September
Cherry (sweet)	25	25	7	1 bushel	July
Cherry (tart)	20	20	4	1 bushel	July
Plum	20	20	5	1 bushel	August to September
Small Fruits					
Grapes	10	10	4	8 pounds	September to October
Raspberries	8	3	3	1 quart	July
Blackberries	8	3	3	1 quart	July
Currants	8	3	3	3 quarts	June to July
Blueberries	6	4	4	2 quarts	July to August
Strawberries	3	2	1	1 pint	June

The chart and planting guide may be helpful in drawing a plan that will meet conditions and requirements. It is well to remember that a small planting that receives good care may yield more fruit of good quality than a larger planting that suffers from neglect. Ample space should be allowed for all tree fruits to develop without crowding. This is essential in maintaining a bearing surface low enough for pest control.

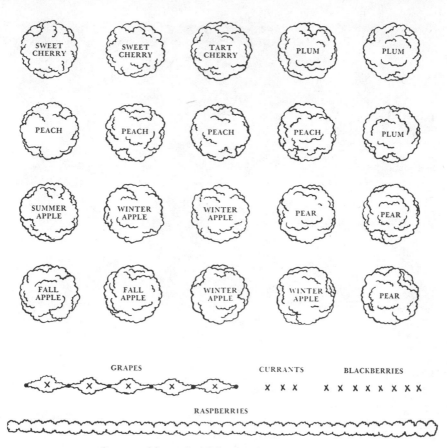

Suggested home fruit planting for family of five

Varieties

Proper evaluation of tree fruit varieties requires many years of observation. The list of standard sorts has been reduced considerably in recent years. Old varieties that are no longer available have been discarded because the tree or fruit, or both, failed in some essential characteristic. New varieties are constantly being introduced, but they require a lengthy test period to establish their true value. When all the characteristics, such as the adaptability of the tree and the use of the fruit have been considered, the standard varieties should prove best for the home planting. Reading commercial catalogues will give you much useful information on available varieties.

Varieties of small fruits can be tested rapidly. There has been much improvement recently in these fruits, resulting in a wider choice of higher quality and more satisfactory kinds than ever before. The varieties suggested here are listed in the order of their season of ripening and should supply fresh fruit throughout the longest period possible in any locality where the particular fruits can be grown. In compiling this list, consideration has been given to adaptability of the various varieties to a wide range of conditions as well as to all those purposes for which fruit is generally used in the home.

A 14-year-old dwarf apple tree on Malling IX rootstock. Apple trees grown on this rootstock begin to bear in the second or third year after planting.

Nursery Stock

If apples and pears are included in the home fruit planting, the use of dwarf trees overcomes the objections to the large size attained by trees of these fruits growing on seedling roots. Dwarf apple trees, which reach a height of only 5 to 6 feet at maturity, are produced by the use of a rootstock known as *Malling IX* or *East Malling IX*. Pears are dwarfed by grafting on quince rootstock. Not all pear varieties grow satisfactorily on quince roots. This can be overcome, however, by first grafting a compatible variety, such as Hardy, on the quince root and, following a year's growth, grafting the desired variety on the Hardy stem. Mahaleb cherry seedlings when used as a rootstock have a dwarfing effect on the Montmorency cherry, although this effect is somewhat less than that of the rootstocks suggested for apples and pears. When buying dwarf trees, it is important to specify the desired variety-rootstock combination.

Though Malling IX has the greatest dwarfing effect on apples, it is not always available. The following chart shows the effect other dwarfing roots will have on apple trees.

Tree Sizes Expressed as a % of Standard Apple Trees According to Rootstock Used

East Malling IX . . . . 30% of standard
East Malling XXVI . . . . 40% of standard
East Malling VII . . . . 50% of standard
Malling—Merton 106 . . . . 60% of standard
Malling—Merton 111 . . . . 70% of standard

Apples
  Summer:
    Lodi*
    Jerseymac

  Fall:
    Paulared

  Winter:
    Cortland
    Delicious
    Golden Delicious
    Idared*

Raspberries (red)
  Heritage
  Taylor*
  Newburgh

Raspberries (black)
  Bristol*
  Huron*

Raspberries (purple)
  Clyde*

Pears
  Clapp Favorite
  Gorham
  Bartlett*
  Bosc

Plum (prune)
  Richard's Early Italian
  French Damson*
  Stanley*
  Green Gage

Plum (Japanese)
  Early Golden
  Shiro

Blackberries
  Darrow*

Currents
  Red Lake*

Gooseberries
  Poorman*

Blueberries
  Blueray
  Bluecrop
  Jersey

Peaches
  Brighton
  Raritan Rose (white)
  Red Haven
  Halehaven*
  Eden (white)
  Redskin

Cherries (sweet)
  Emperor Francis
  Schmidt*
  Windsor

Cherries (tart)
  Montmorency*

Grapes
  Alden
  Himrod
  Buffalo
  Worden*
  Delaware*
  Niagara
  Concord*

Strawberries
  Fletcher
  Catskill
  Sparkle

* Especially satisfactory for canning or other culinary purposes for which the fruit might be used.

Varieties and Pollination

For the fruits of apples, pears, sweet cherries, and some plums to set and develop, there must be cross pollination between two varieties of the same fruit. Certain apple varieties, such as Gravenstein and Rhode Island Greening, are not only self-unfruitful but produce poor pollen which is ineffective in setting fruit of other varieties. To be sure of adequate cross pollination, at least three varieties of apples should be planted; while any two of the recommended varieties of pears, sweet cherries and plums should prove satisfactory for this purpose. The Montmorency cherry, all listed varieties of peaches, and the small fruits are sufficiently self-fruitful to set satisfactory crops with their own pollen.

Nursery stock should be purchased from a reliable firm that specializes in the business. One-year-old whips are best. At this age, they can be transplanted with less mortality and more easily trained to a desirable shape. Fruit trees and plants are often injured through improper care after their arrival from the nursery. If the land is not ready for planting when the stock arrives, it should be unpacked immediately and heeled-in on a well-drained spot. The trees can be set temporarily in a trench about 12 to 18 inches deep. They can be placed close together. The soil should be packed firmly over the roots and mounded so that excess water will drain away during a prolonged rain. Small fruits may be cared for in the same way. Every effort should be made to set the plants in their permanent location before growth starts.

Preparation of the Soil and Planting

The planting of all fruits should be done in early spring as soon as the ground can be suitably prepared and before the plants have started growth. Plowing and thorough disking of the soil are desirable for most fruit plants and quite important for raspberries, strawberries, and other small fruits.

After preparation of the soil, it is helpful to place stakes where each tree is to be located. The distances should be measured with a tape and the stakes sighted for alignment in both directions. When dwarf apple and pear are planted, all fruit trees can be spaced 20 by 20 feet. The sweet cherry would be the only exception to such spacing. Since there is no satisfactory dwarfing stock for sweet cherry trees, they should be spaced about 25 to 30 feet apart to prevent crowding at maturity.

Before the trees are planted, any broken or injured roots should be trimmed off and long, thin, or straggly roots shortened. Unnecessary exposure of the roots to sun and wind before planting may cause the roots to dry out quickly and lessen the chances of successful transplanting. Holes for the trees should be large enough to accommodate the roots in their natural positions. The top soil should be set aside when digging the hole and thrown in first around the roots. It is important that the soil settle under and around the roots to exclude air spaces. Moving the tree up and down carefully as the first few shovelfuls of soil are thrown in helps to accomplish this. As the hole is being filled, the soil should be stamped firmly. Many failures in transplanting are due to insufficient or improper firming of the soil about the roots.

It is usually suggested that trees and plants be set at about the same depth or an inch or so deeper than they stood in the nursery row. Dwarf apple trees on Malling IX and dwarf pear trees on quince roots must, however, always be planted with the union between the variety and the rootstock slightly above ground level. If this is not done, the trees, particularly apple trees on Malling IX, may form their own roots on the variety portion of the stem above the graft union and in such cases the dwarfing effect of the rootstock will disappear and the trees will grow to a large size.

The root system of Malling IX is brittle and trees on this stock may break off when the tops become large enough to offer resistance to a strong wind. This can be prevented by providing supports in the form of a stake or post for each tree. A piece of 2-inch galvanized gas pipe makes a permanent and inconspicuous support when driven into the soil. The support should be about 4 or 5 inches from the trunk and should extend several inches above the lowest scaffold limbs. A durable piece of hemp cord or a heavy wire covered with a section of garden hose serves to fasten the trunk to the support. The tie should always be loose enough to prevent binding or girdling as the trunk increases in circumference.

For setting grapes and bush fruits, it may be convenient to open a furrow with a light plow. The plants can then be set in the bottom of this furrow and the earth drawn about their roots and pressed firmly.

Somewhat more care is necessary in setting strawberry plants. It is important to have the crown of the plant even with the surface of the ground so that the terminal bud, or growing point, is just above the surface. The plant is likely to rot if planted too deep, and, if planted too shallow, the crown and roots may dry out. When the ground is well prepared, strawberries can be set rapidly and satisfactorily with a garden trowel. As with other plants, it is necessary to firm the soil about the roots.

Culture of Tree Fruits

Soil Management

Young trees will not compete successfully with grass and weeds or an established sod. To make normal growth, they need clean cultivation or a mulch system. Cultivation, to be most effective, should begin early before the buds start growth and should be discontinued after the first of July. Following this early period of cultivation a cover crop should be seeded. Buckwheat is often used for this purpose, but a combination of rye and vetch which would live over winter is considered better.

If for any reason the cultivation-cover crop system cannot be followed, equally good results can be obtained by mulching the trees. In fact, dwarf trees seem to respond better to mulching than to cultivation. Mulching is recognized as an excellent soil-conservation practice. The purpose of the mulch is to suppress grass and weeds, conserve moisture, improve soil structure, and contribute fertility as it decomposes. Wheat straw or any kind of waste hay makes satisfactory mulching material.

The mulch should be applied about 6 inches deep. It will soon settle into a mat less than half this thickness. The mulched area should extend from near the tree trunk to a point somewhat beyond the spread of the branches. In young plantings, the row middles or unmulched area can be seeded with bluegrass or a pasture seed adapted to the soil and the locality. This should be mowed two or three times each season and the clippings allowed to remain on the ground. If the grass is tall when cut, it may be raked up and used for mulching under the trees. Grass clippings from the row middles seldom supply enough mulching material for the trees. It will be necessary each year to bring in some additional mulching material to replace that lost through decomposition and to extend the mulched area as the trees grow larger.

Rodent Control

One of the chief objections to the mulch system of culture is that it encourages field mice. These rodents can damage the tree severely by girdling near the base of the trunk. The most practical way to protect young trees from this damage is to enclose the base of the trunk with a cylinder of ¼-inch mesh hardware cloth. Various types of plastic tree guards are also available. This cylinder should be about 6 inches in diameter and extend from several inches below the soil level to the first scaffold branch. Some orchardists have found that mice are discouraged by placing a layer of cinders 4 or 5 inches in depth around the base of the trunk. Baiting the mice runways with poison grain or diced cubes of apples or carrots coated with zinc phosphide reduces the mouse population.

A young apple tree well established by the mulch system of culture and protected from mouse damage by a wire guard.

Fertilization

On most soils it would not be necessary to fertilize fruit trees during the first year after planting because the preparation of the soil and the use of top soil around the roots usually releases and supplies enough nutrients for the first season's growth. Of late, *slow release* fertilizer tablets have been developed which can be put in the hole with the new plant and will feed it for two years without injuring the roots. The need for fertilizer in subsequent years depends on the soil and on the cultural practice. It is important to obtain good annual growth with a dark-green leaf surface. The liberal use of stable manure, when available, generally gives excellent results. The cultivation-cover crop system supplemented with moderate amounts of manure should supply the trees with adequate fertility. Mulching with strawy manure is also satisfactory.

When manure is not available, commercial fertilizers can be used. They will be needed if cultivation or adequate mulching is not employed. A nitrogen fertilizer, such as sodium nitrate or ammonium nitrate, is usually best for tree fruits. If a mixed fertilizer is used, it should contain at least 10 per cent nitrogen. The rate of application varies with the age or size of the trees. Sodium nitrate might be applied at the rate of ¼ pound for each year the tree has been set. A young tree two or three years old requires about ½ pound, while mature trees should receive from 4 to 5 pounds. If ammonium nitrate is used, the rate should be cut in half since it contains twice as much nitrogen as sodium nitrate. Mixed fertilizers would be used at slightly higher rates, depending on the nitrogen analysis. The fertilizer is sown broadcast beneath the outer spread of the branches and somewhat beyond. The best time to make the application is in early spring as the buds begin to show green.

Freshly applied mulch consisting of wheat straw or any other mature non-legume material should be supplemented with the nitrogen treatments for the first two years. After the mulch mats and begins to decompose on the underside, commercial fertilizers may not be needed if the mulch is replenished as needed.

Pruning

Young fruit trees

Young fruit trees should be pruned early during late winter or early spring. It is best to practice very light pruning of dwarf apple and pear trees during the first few years after planting. The principles of pruning dwarfs are the same as for standard trees on seedling roots, but the amount is less because dwarf trees do not grow so large. Dwarf trees should be headed lower than standard trees. The one-year-old unbranched tree should be cut back at planting time to a height of 12 to 18 inches so it will form laterals at a low level. When planting a two-year-old branched tree, two or three well-spaced laterals and a leader are selected for the permanent framework and the other lateral growths are removed. Where many branches that originate close together are left, crowding eventually develops. The lateral branches selected as permanents may be cut back to two-thirds of their original length, although a weaker lateral left because of its desirable location should be cut back less or not at all. The leader or main trunk may be cut back lightly but should be pruned less than laterals in order to maintain its dominance. Other branches will arise from lateral buds on the leader at a higher level. Five or six such well-placed scaffolds make up the framework of the mature tree.

Pruning is a dwarfing process and the branch or limb that is cut most makes the least total growth during the following season. This principle may be applied in maintaining a desired balance between various parts of the tree by pruning more severely those branches that are to be discouraged.

The training and pruning that young cherry trees receive during the first few years have an important bearing on the future framework and length of life of the tree. At planting time, all branches that form narrow angles with the trunk should be removed. If allowed to remain and become a part of the framework, such branches are almost sure to split under a load of fruit or the weight of snow or ice. The bark in narrow-angled crotches is most susceptible to winter killing, which further weakens the branch. Scaffold branches selected for permanents should be equally spaced around the trunk and, where possible, at least 4 to 6 inches apart up and down the trunk. The lowest branch should originate from 16 to 18 inches above the ground level. The way most cherry trees come from the nursery, it is seldom possible to select more than three suitable scaffold branches at planting time. The more vigorous of these may be shortened, but, as with the apple, the main stem or leader should be left longer than any of the scaffolds. Prunes and plums are handled in a similar way.

While the central leader or modified leader system of training is adapted to most kinds of fruit trees, peaches are usually trained to an open center or vase-shaped tree. One-year-old nursery trees are usually from 3 to 6 feet in height with some lateral branching. Laterals that were developed in the nursery row as secondary shoots are generally too weak to make good framework branches. It is best to cut such trees back to a height of 1½ to 2 feet and cut off the laterals to short stubs with one bud at the base. This encourages the growth of strong shoots on the trunk. As soon as the shoots have grown a few inches, usually by the first of June, three or four of the best ones may be selected for the framework branches and the others removed. Equal growth and branching of these shoots results in an open center tree. Occasionally, nursery trees have three or four well-developed laterals at a satisfactory level that can be used as scaffold

A 2-year-old apple tree before pruning (left) and after pruning (right).

A 2-year-old Montmorency cherry tree as it came from the nursery (left). The same tree as that shown on the left after pruning. The top branch is the leader; the lateral branches which were selected are well spaced and form wide angles with the trunk.

Peach tree before pruning (left) and after pruning (right) at planting time. The laterals are cut to short stubs and the top headed back at about 30 inches.

Peach tree before (left) and after (right) selecting shoots for the framework branches. This is called *deshooting*. It would be best to deshoot somewhat earlier before the new growth has developed as much as that indicated in the photograph.

Strong, well-spaced laterals on this nursery tree. These laterals made it unnecessary to cut back to stubs. Four laterals have been selected and the top cut back at about 30 inches.

limbs; then the main stem can be cut back to the proper height and the laterals tipped to uniform lengths.

In subsequent years

For apples, pears, cherries, and prunes, a few corrective cuts will be needed during the next five or six years or until the trees come into bearing. This pruning should be limited to the removal of water sprouts, crossing limbs that rub against a permanent branch, and the prevention of bad crotches and weak unions that would split and ruin the shape of the tree when bearing a crop. A bad crotch is a fork where two branches of equal length and diameter arise at a common point. Generally, one of two such branches can be removed entirely. But, if it seems desirable to save both of them, one should be cut back severely. It will then become smaller and develop as a lateral branch to the unpruned one.

Weak unions are common in some varieties of fruit trees and most varieties of sweet cherries. Often, vigorous shoots grow upright against the trunk or against other branches. To prevent this, limbs that spread out from the trunk at wide angles should be chosen as scaffold limbs and those that tend to grow upright against the trunk should be removed. Only an occasional cut is required for this kind of pruning and it gradually becomes less necessary as the trees come into bearing. Trees that have had proper corrective pruning from the beginning need little if any pruning during their early bearing years. Over-pruning during these formative years delays bearing.

Following the first and second year's growth of the peach tree, the main scaffold branches should be headed back lightly to outward growing laterals. Small shoots crossing in the center may be left since they will bear the first fruits. The

A 3-year-old peach tree before pruning (left) and after pruning (right). The main scaffold limbs were headed back and a moderate amount of fine wood removed.

purpose of heading back scaffolds is to continue the development of an open-center tree that will be low and spreading for convenience in thinning, spraying, and picking. Pruning during the third and fourth years should be as light as possible, removing only any decidedly crowding limbs or low-hanging branches in the center that are becoming heavily shaded, and heading back to outward laterals any of the scaffold limbs that are getting too high or out of balance with the other.

Pruning mature fruit trees

After fruit trees are well into bearing, more pruning of a slightly different nature will be needed to keep them within bounds and to maintain vigor of the fruiting wood. This pruning should consist of heading back branches that are getting out of control and of removing from the inside of the tree small weak wood or other areas that are becoming dense.

Dwarf apple and pear trees, at maturity, often require some heading back of the leader or main branches. Such cuts should be made close to a strong lateral. The height of cherry and plum trees will also need to be controlled. This is accomplished in the same way. In many trees, the leader may be taken out at the origin of a scaffold branch, forming a modified leader tree with a distribution of scaffold limbs which in turn can be headed back to secondary branches.

Most of the pruning, however, should be small cuts devoted to the thinning out of weak wood in thick, shaded portions of the tree. This type of wood, if it bears, produces poorly colored fruit of low quality. Its removal stimulates the vigor of the remaining fruiting wood and facilitates spraying.

Peaches are borne on twigs of the previous season's growth. As the trees at-

An 8-year-old dwarf apple tree on Malling IX rootstock showing early development of many fruit buds before pruning (top) and after pruning (bottom). The pruning consisted of heading back the main scaffold branches to keep the tree within bounds and a light thinning of weaker twigs.

A mature Montmorency cherry tree with a good distribution of scaffold limbs arising from a modified leader which has been cut back to a lateral. Annual pruning consists of a light heading back of scaffolds and moderate thinning of fine wood.

tain full size, rather severe pruning is required to maintain and renew fruiting wood of good vigor throughout the tree and at a low level. Terminal shoot growth of 12 to 15 inches a year is desirable. It is on such growth that the fruit buds are formed and good crops are borne. To obtain this type of growth, cutting back of branches into two- or three-year-old wood is commonly practiced. The cuts should be made to an outward-growing side branch. After heading back all the main branches, it is usually desirable to thin out about a third of the previous season's shoot growth. Peach trees of good vigor produce much more fruiting wood than is needed for a full crop. If some of it is not removed, the tree will overbear and then the fruit will be small and wood growth will be weak for the following crop.

Fruit Thinning

Young trees seldom set heavy enough to warrant thinning of the fruit; but after bearing is well established, some attention should be given to this practice. This is especially true with peaches and some varieties of plums, prunes, and apples. When the set is excessive, proper thinning results in larger, better colored and higher quality fruits. Thinning should be done early, from two to three weeks after bloom, if possible.

Where fruits are clustered, all but one fruit in each cluster should be removed. Peach fruits should be from 4 to 8 inches apart, using the wider spacing for the early varieties. Plums and prunes should be thinned so that the fruits are four to five inches apart. The small, insect and disease injured fruit should be removed first.

An excessive set on apples prevents flower-bud formation for the next season and results in alternate bearing or a heavy crop of small sized fruit one year and no crop the next. This is a common occurrence with Golden Delicious and some other varieties. It can be prevented by early thinning. Apples should be spaced from 4 to 6 inches apart, which means one fruit on every third or fourth spur. Thinning actually requires very little time and the improved size, quality and repeat bloom are well worth the effort.

Culture of Small Fruits

Soil Management and Fertilization

Grapes and the bramble fruits, including all raspberries and blackberries, should be cultivated during the spring and early summer, after which weeds or a seeded cover crop may be allowed to grow. During the second and succeeding years, if manure is not available and plant growth is poor, one of the nitrogen fertilizers, such as nitrate of soda, ammonium nitrate, or a mixed fertilizer high in nitrogen, may be used. For grapes, from ¼ to ½ pound of sodium nitrate is suggested for each vine. If the cane growth of brambles is unsatisfactory because of a nitrogen deficiency, 6 pounds of nitrate of soda per 100 feet or row should meet the requirements. Ammonium nitrate is used at one-half these amounts. Fertilizer for grapes and brambles may be scattered broadcast between the rows.

Grass and weeds under the grape trellis may be controlled by mulching. If mulch material is available for this purpose, commercial fertilizer will probably not be needed. While brambles respond to mulching, this practice often results in a late vigorous growth of canes that are susceptible to winter injury. Shallow cultivation during the spring and early summer is the best system of culture for brambles.

Currants and gooseberries, because they are among the hardiest of the deciduous fruits, can be grown quite satisfactorily by mulching. Two bushels of fresh grass clippings placed around each bush annually in the early spring seems to meet all the cultural requirements for these fruits on most soils.

Training and Pruning Grapes

The grapevine is pruned to control the quantity and quality of both wood growth and fruit production. In pruning, it is the aim to leave enough of the best fruiting wood to obtain maximum production of good clusters and to remove the surplus to prevent overbearing and its consequent inferior wood growth. This is *pruning* proper. Pruning is also employed to make well-proportioned vines that are easily managed and kept within definite bounds. This is more correctly termed *training*. Both operations are often referred to as pruning, but the two terms should not be confused.

The grape lends itself to almost any desired system of training or distribution of the bearing surface. For this reason there are many systems. Only one is discussed here; namely, the *Kniffin* system. It is easy to train vines to this system which requires no summer tying and is as well if not better adapted to the home garden than any other system.

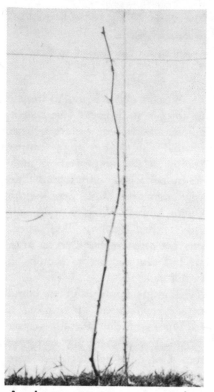

A vigorous young grape vine pruned to form the trunk after the first season's growth.

A trellis is necessary for support and should be erected at planting time or shortly thereafter. The trellis for the Kniffin system has two or three wires (usually No. 9 or No. 10 wire) strung tightly between posts. The lower wire is placed from 2½ to 3 feet from the ground and the upper wire at the 5- or 6-foot level. The posts should be 8 feet long, set 2 feet in the ground, and 20 feet apart. This spacing allows two vines between each two posts. Posts of some durable wood such as locust or cedar are preferred. The end post should be well braced.

A vine trained according to the single-stem, four-cane Kniffin system consists of a single trunk that reaches to just below the top wire. After each annual pruning from two to six canes, bright brown wood of the previous season's growth, are left. These canes arise from spurs or short arms of 2-year wood and extend out on the wires in both directions from the trunk. From buds at the nodes of these canes, leafy shoots grow and bear the clusters of fruit. These shoots in turn become canes the following year. When this fruiting habit of the grape is kept in mind, training and pruning of the vine becomes quite simple.

At planting time, the vine is cut back to two buds. Both buds will likely grow into shoots, in which case the lower or weaker one may be allowed to trail on the ground until its removal the following year. The most vigorous or upper shoot should be supported in an upright position with a stake to keep it straight and prevent breakage. This becomes the permanent trunk, and as growth proceeds it should be tied loosely to the wires of the trellis or the supporting stake until the

A grape vine trained according to the four-cane Kniffin system; unpruned (above) and pruned (below). The one-year prunings from this vine amounted to 1.8 pounds. There were 38 buds left on the vine after pruning.

trellis is constructed. When good growth is obtained, the trunk may be formed the first season. The next spring, it is cut off just below the top wire and tied firmly in place. If growth is not so vigorous the first year, the best cane should again be cut back to two buds and the process repeated to form a trunk.

The first canes to be trained horizontally along the wires arise from lateral buds on the young trunk. After that, canes can usually be selected from basal buds of the previous year's canes or from renewal spurs left for that purpose. An unpruned and pruned vine trained to the single-stem, four-cane Kniffin system is shown.

Once the training system is established the vines must be pruned annually. The amount of wood, or more correctly the number of buds to leave, should be governed by the vigor of the vine. This may vary from 30 to 60 buds. A mature grapevine of moderate vigor limited to 10 feet of trellis space should not ordinarily carry more than 40 buds. The prunings from such a vine should weigh about 2 pounds, which is a good measure of its vigor. No more than 60 buds should be left on the most vigorous vines where the prunings would approximate 6 pounds. Leaving too many buds for the vigor of the vine greatly weakens the growth for the bearing of succeeding crops and the clusters become small, loose and the berries inferior. Since a mature vine before pruning may have several hundred buds, it is apparent that grapes require a rather severe pruning.

The most productive canes should be saved for fruiting. These will be about ¼ inch in diameter with an internode length of 5 to 8 inches. Canes of small diameter and short internodes or those that taper rapidly are unproductive and should be discarded. By watching the vines closely, the amateur can soon learn to balance the amount of pruning with growth and production.

The productivity of the canes on the lower wire is not as high as the canes on the upper wire. If more than four canes are needed to obtain the proper bud number, the extra one or more canes should be put on the top wire. On vines that are low in vigor and cannot support the buds on four canes, the bottom canes may be shortened to spurs until vine vigor is restored.

With canes placed in a horizontal position, the shoots toward the end of the cane usually make the best growth. To have productive canes originate close to the trunk, two-bud spurs should be left in such positions. Shoots will arise from these renewal spurs and serve as fruiting canes the next year. In this way, the vine is kept in bounds.

Because the grape has a long productive life and is on its own roots, it is possible to renew old vines that have gotten out of bounds and trail for great distances. The pruning that can be done the first year will consist of limiting the vine to a few new canes originating as close to the trunk as possible. A good vigorous sprout coming up from the root or at a low level on the trunk should be retained and tied to the wires of the trellis for the purpose of renewing the old trunk. This sprout is handled like a young vine, and, after several years, the old trunk can be cut away entirely. A vine that fails to send up a sprout or sucker may be cut off at the ground to force such growth. Of course, in such a case, immediate fruit production is sacrificed.

Occasionally, someone wants to grow grapevines on arbors, porches, and elsewhere to furnish shade as well as fruit. In such instances the same principles of pruning are followed although the method of training must be modified. The principal difference is the amount of old wood left, the number of buds retained, and the distribution of the fruiting canes. Usually, the trunk is longer, and in some instances, it is desirable to leave short permanent arms coming from the

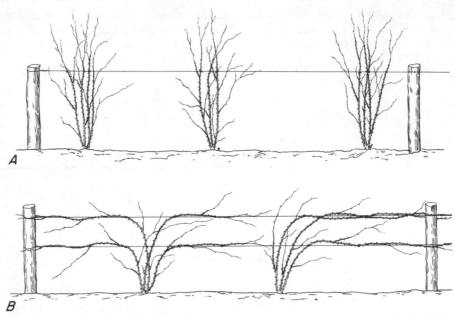

Trellises for blackberries: *A*, train erect plants to a one-wine trellis; *B*, train trailing plants to a two-wine trellis.

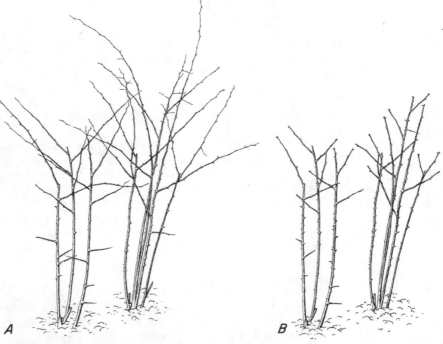

An erect raspberry plant: *A*, before pruning; *B*, after pruning.

30 **GROWING AND PRESERVING ...**

A hill of vigorous red raspberry canes pruned to a height of 5 feet and supported by a stake.

A purple raspberry plant after spring pruning. The lateral growths which resulted from tipping the previous summer have been shortened and the weak canes eliminated.

trunk. More fruiting canes and spurs, and consequently more buds, may be kept than would be desirable on a vine confined to less space, because such arbor vines in a favorable environment eventually develop a larger root system and trunk. It therefore has more capacity. In other words, when grown for the purpose of shade, the trunk of the vine is carried to the necessary height, and permanent lateral arms and yearling canes are trained in such a way that the shoots bearing the foliage will cover the arbor to the best advantage. Even then, the necessary renewal pruning should be given annually for best results.

Typical fruit clusters of blackberries: *A*, trailing varieties; *B*, erect varieties.

Pruning Brambles and Bush Fruits

For bramble fruits, the two-year-old fruiting canes should be removed as soon as the harvest is completed. These canes are of no further use and tend only to spread disease to the new shoots. The old canes should be cut off close to the ground.

Black raspberries, purple canes, and blackberries respond to summer pinching of the new shoots. The tip ends of the shoots are pinched off when they have reached a height of from 18 to 24 inches, which is usually in early June. When the shoot is pinched back, it stops growing at the end and the buds on the side push out to form lateral branches. Plants treated in this way are lower and more self-supporting.

Red raspberries produce suckers freely and for this reason are commonly grown in hedge rows about 2½ feet in width. Sprouts appearing in the row middles should be destroyed, or the patch will become a thicket of weak canes. The new shoots of red raspberries should not be summer-pinched, because laterals forced by this treatment are subject to winter killing. Before growth starts in early spring, the unbranched canes are cut back to a height of about 3 to 4 feet. The weakest canes should be removed. In plantings where cane growth is exceptionally vigorous, red raspberries may be kept in hills and supported by a stake. This leaves vigorous canes and takes advantage of their greater fruiting capacity. It also simplifies picking.

In the spring, black raspberries, purple canes, and blackberries are pruned to shorten the lateral branches that developed as a result of summer pinching. The laterals on blackcaps and purple canes are cut back to 5 or 6 inches; those on blackberries are left from 10 to 12 inches. The weak, spindling canes are cut out entirely.

The pruning of currants and gooseberries is governed by the fact that 2- and 3-year-old wood is the most fruitful. In pruning, therefore, branches older than four years are cut out at the ground, as are the weakest of the young shoots.

Care of Strawberries

The ground for strawberries should be thoroughly prepared by working it to a fine mellow condition to a depth of 6 to 8 inches. A liberal application of rotted compost or a high-grade garden fertilizer, thoroughly incorporated in the soil at the time it is prepared, should meet the fertility requirement of strawberries on most soils.

Early spring is the best time to set strawberry plants. They should be set as soon as the ground can be prepared. The plants become established and start growth quickly during the cool days of late April or early May when there is usually a good supply of moisture. Early planting also encourages the formation of early runner plants that are more productive and bear better quality fruit than those formed in late summer.

Only well-grown healthy stock should be planted, and only those plants that were formed from early runners the previous season are worth consideration. A trowel or dibble is a handy tool for setting strawberry plants in well-prepared soil. The holes should be large enough to accommodate the roots without doubling or wadding them together. The plants should be set firmly and at the same depth as they previously grew. When the crown is set too high, the plants may dry out; and when set too deep, the mortality will likely be high.

Frequent but shallow cultivations or hand hoeings are needed to maintain a fine surface mulch and to destroy the weeds that would take moisture and nutrients from the plants. Cultivation should be started soon after the plants are set and repeated every ten days or two weeks, or after every rain, until weeds are under complete control and enough runner plants have set to form the matted row.

Some of the buds within the crowns of the newly set plants are flower buds that were formed the preceding fall. When the plants begin growth, these buds push out stems that terminate in flower clusters. All flowering stalks should be carefully pinched off as they appear, preferably before the blossoms open. The untimely development of flowers and fruits decreases the vigor of the plants and retards runner production. The more frequently the new planting is de-blossomed, the better the results will be.

Runners from the parent plant take root and form new plants, and these in turn send out runners to form more plants. In this way the matted row develops. It is the most practical system for training strawberries and is well adapted to the home garden. The one fault of the matted-row system as commonly practiced is that too many plants may form. This is especially true in a favorable growing season. Many of these plants are produced late in the season, are small, and have little capacity to bear, yet they use soil moisture and nutrients that retard the development and reduce the production of other plants. Some of the late formed plants might be regarded as "strawberry weeds."

A little attention to spacing and thinning of runner plants during the summer usually increases yield and a high-quality fruit. The early plants can be spaced by covering the runners with a little soil just back of the leafy tip so that they will strike root about 6 or 7 inches apart. From four to six plants per square foot are enough and any excess should be removed. The width of the matted row should be confined to about 2 feet by cutting off runners beyond these bounds. Much of this can be accomplished while hoeing and weeding the planting.

The strawberry planting needs to be mulched as an insurance against winter injury. If plants are unprotected, the low winter temperatures may kill the fruit buds and cause injury to the roots and tissues of the crown. Mulch, if not removed too early, delays bloom in the spring and in this way affords protection against a late spring frost. Part of the mulch left on the rows during harvest helps to conserve moisture, to smother weeds, and to keep the berries clean.

Wheat straw or marsh hay are ideal mulch materials. Oat straw, rye straw, or leaves are often used but are considered inferior to clean wheat straw.

The mulch should be applied sometime during the first three weeks of November, depending on the section. By this time, the plants have usually been exposed to several frosty nights, growth has been retarded, and the hardening processes have set in. A light frost will not injure the plants, but they should be protected before temperatures reach 15° to 18° F. The mulch should be spread uniformly over the planting. If, however, there is a scarcity of material, the tops of the rows should be mulched rather than the middles. Usually a mulch about 2 inches in thickness, when settled, gives ample protection. This requires about 15 pounds of dry straw per 100 square feet.

The following spring, when an inspection of the plants shows new leaf growth or a slight yellowing of the foliage, the mulch should be opened over the rows. From one-half to two-thirds of a heavy mulch needs to be forked off the plants and tramped down in the row middles. The plants will grow up through that which remains. In removing mulch, the aim is to leave some of the material

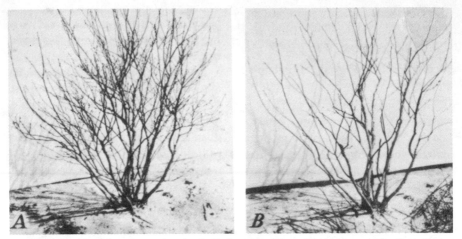

Four-year-old blueberry bush: A, Before pruning; B, after pruning. Pruning reduced the fruit buds by about 75 percent. In very fertile soils, a large number of fruit buds might be left for a heavier crop.

around the base of the plants in order to keep the berries clean and conserve moisture.

After the first crop is harvested, it is customary to keep the planting intact for a second one. When good care has been practiced, one has only to pull out weeds as they appear and add a little mulch over the rows for protection during the next winter. It is seldom advisable to save the planting for a third crop.

Blueberry Culture

Blueberries are more specific in their cultural requirements than are other small fruits. The natural habitat of the high-bush blueberry is usually the lowland swamp or hammock where relatively moist, acid (pH 4.0 to 5.0) soil conditions prevail with a shallow, year-round water table. The shrub has a shallow, fibrous root system that grows largely in the leaf mold and humus layer above the water table. Thus, this natural habitat supplies a maximum of both oxygen and moisture throughout the root zone.

Recent nutritional work with blueberries has shown that this plant grows vigorously even at pH 6.5, if the soil is well aerated and the necessary nutrients are maintained in an available form. On the other hand, they may fail to grow at pH 4.5 with inadequate aeration and nutrients. As compared with other fruit plants, blueberries seem to have a relatively low requirement for potassium, calcium, and phosphorus, and a high requirement for iron, manganese, and possibly magnesium. They respond vigorously to nitrogen and apparently absorb nitrogen in the ammonia form more readily than in the nitrate form.

Most soils with a pH value of 5.5 to 6.0 are fairly well supplied with calcium, but are low in available iron and manganese and the nitrogen is likely to be largely in the nitrate form. In addition, many of these soils have a clay texture, are somewhat poorly aerated, and are subject to drying near the surface in summer. These may be the principal reasons why blueberries usually fail on soils of this type.

Such soils may be modified to meet better the requirements of blueberries if one wishes to grow them in the home fruit planting. Where the land is level and

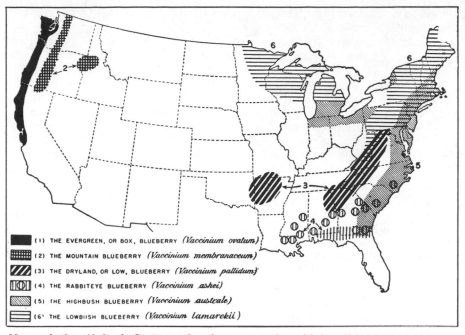

(1) THE EVERGREEN, OR BOX, BLUEBERRY *(Vaccinium ovatum)*

(2) THE MOUNTAIN BLUEBERRY *(Vaccinium membranaceum)*

(3) THE DRYLAND, OR LOW, BLUEBERRY *(Vaccinium pallidum)*

(4) THE RABBITEYE BLUEBERRY *(Vaccinium ashei)*

(5) THE HIGHBUSH BLUEBERRY *(Vaccinium australe)*

(6) THE LOWBUSH BLUEBERRY *(Vaccinium lamarckii)*

Map of the United States, showing areas in which wild blueberries are extensively harvested.

internal drainage is slow, the row on which the plants are set should be ridged about 18 to 24 inches high. The ridge needs to be about 2 feet wide, which means that the rows must be spaced 7 to 8 feet apart in order to afford enough top soil to construct the ridges. The reason for planting on ridges composed mainly of top soil is to furnish the best possible drainage and provide a medium open and porous enough in texture to encourage growth of fine, fibrous roots.

High or sloping ground with good internal drainage need not be ridged. It is important, however, that the soil be well supplied with organic matter for the retention of moisture and nutrients. Nitrogen is held against loss from leaching, and some other nutrients are maintained in a more available form by organic matter. Organic materials may be added in the form of peat, sawdust, muck, compost, straw, or wood chips. Such materials may be raked or otherwise incorporated into the soil before planting.

An acid soil is desirable. A soil pH of 4.0 to 5.2 should exist for the prevention of iron deficiency and the maintenance of nitrogen in the ammonia form. Under acid-soil conditions well supplied with organic matter, nitrates are converted into ammonia nitrogen that is freely utilized by blueberry plants. As the soil becomes less acid, above pH 5.5, nitrifying organisms predominate and ammonia nitrogen is converted into nitrate nitrogen that is used to a lesser extent by the plants and is easily leached from the soil. Thus, it becomes more difficult to maintain adequate nitrogen for the plants.

Loam soils not normally acid enough for blueberries (pH 5.5 to 6.5) may be improved by the addition of 5 pounds of sulfur per 100 square feet. This should be worked into the soil the year before the planting is made. Sulfur should be applied very sparingly, if at all, after the plants are established. Ammonium sulfate has an acidifying effect on the soil. In many cases, the use of ammonium sulfate as a fertilizer together with a heavy organic mulch will be enough and will eliminate any need for sulfur.

If mulching material is scarce, shallow tillage may be used to control weeds and grass. Blueberry roots are near the surface and are therefore easily destroyed by tillage. A heavy mulch combined with hand weeding is preferred to any form of cultivation. Mulching is desirable to maintain a good structure of the surface soil so that water will penetrate freely as well as to prevent heaving of the plants and subsequent root injury in the early spring. Sawdust is one of the best mulching materials, although other materials may be used with beneficial results. Any kind or age of sawdust may be used and applied whenever convenient. From 3 to 6 inches of mulch should be maintained, the amount of annual renewal depending on the rate of decomposition.

Where a mulching system is used, nitrogen will probably be the only fertilizer element needed and this should be in the ammonium form. Ammonium sulfate is the best choice. If ammonium sulfate cannot be obtained, ammonium nitrate may be used. Fertilizer is not used at planting time, but the following year ammonium sulfate should be applied at the rate of 1 to 2 ounces per plant in early May and again in mid-June. The rate should be increased as the plants grow older until mature plants, from five to six years of age, receive from ½ to ¾ pound annually, depending on their size. In applying the fertilizer, scatter it uniformly over the surface of the mulch from ½ to 3 feet from the center of the bush, exercising care to prevent any deposit on the foliage.

The requirements of blueberry plants for other nutrients, such as potassium, phosphorus, calcium, magnesium, and the like, are very low and adequate quantities are usually present in most soils, especially under a mulch system of culture. In very acid sandy soils, a complete fertilizer and possibly dolomitic lime (calcium and magnesium) may prove beneficial, but the dolomitic lime should not be applied to soils above pH 5.0.

Iron deficiency, indicated by a chlorotic condition of the young leaves, is usually caused by a lack of soil acidity. It may be temporarily corrected by a foliage spray of 1 per cent ferrous sulfate or the incorporation of ferrous sulfate in the soil. In soils not acid enough for blueberries, the soil applications are soon converted to unavailable forms and the leaf symptoms are again evident on the new growth.

Blueberries suffer considerable damage from an extended drought. A good supply of moisture should exist throughout the shallow-root zone until well after the harvest. A prolonged dry spell during and following harvest greatly reduces fruit-bud formation for the next crop. About 1 inch of rain each week during July and August is required by a mature planting. Any deficit in rainfall during this period should be made up by irrigation. This can be accomplished in the home planting by attaching a suitable sprinkler to the garden hose and applying the water in late evenings when evaporation is at a minimum.

The fruit of the blueberry is produced on wood of the previous season's growth. Strong shoots from the base of the plant or vigorous laterals from the older canes produce the best berries. Little or no pruning is required the first two or three years, but older bushes, if not properly pruned, overbear and produce large quantities of small, worthless berries. Bearing branches close to the ground should be removed as well as dead and broken branches. Dense areas of weak, twiggy growth should be thinned by cutting back to vigorous side shoots. Occasionally old, weak canes, which produce no strong laterals, are cut out in favor of younger shoots that will grow more vigorous fruiting branches.

Disease and Insect Control in the Home Orchard

Success in growing fruit depends on effective control of insects and diseases. A successful control program is based on recognition of the common diseases and insects, selection of effective pesticides, proper timing of pesticide sprays, and thorough coverage of fruit and foliage with the spray mixture.

Spraying Equipment for the Home Orchardist

The commercial fruit grower, because of the size of his operation, can afford to buy large equipment that does an efficient and effective job of covering his orchards. Even with these large motor driven machines, growers find it necessary to apply approximately 400 gallons of dilute spray per acre (10 to 15 gallons per tree) to obtain satisfactory control of the various insect and disease pests.

The home orchardist with a few fruit trees is at a disadvantage when it comes to obtaining equipment that will do a satisfactory job of spraying his trees.

In most cases, he is restricted largely by cost to hand operated sprayers or those operated by small electric or gasoline motors. The capacity of these machines is small, the pressure is low and the energy he must expend to do an effective job is considerable. Yet, the home owner fights the same pests often on the same size trees as the commercial grower. It has been shown time and again that failure of home owners to get adequate control of pests on their fruit trees can be generally attributed to (1) failure to apply enough material to cover the trees completely, (2) failure to make applications on time and (3) failure to continue the spray program late enough into the summer.

Common Insects and Diseases

Apple scab, one of the most common diseases of apple, is easily recognized by the olive-green spots on the fruit and foliage. The young spot or lesion has indefinite margins, but, within two or three weeks, the margins become distinct and the entire lesion appears valvety or suede-like. Severely infected leaves may be dwarfed, cupped or curled and may drop prematurely. Fruits infected during the early season may be severely deformed or may drop by early June.

The organism that causes scab winters in the dead leaves on the ground. Primary infections occur during rainy periods from the time green tissue appears in the spring through the end of June.

Secondary infections arise from the fungus spores (seeds) that are produced by primary infection lesions on the leaves and fruit of the current season. These spores are spread by rains and cause new infections all through the summer. Thus, good scab control early in the season makes control in the late summer easier. Weekly applications of captan or a multi-purpose spray mixture from the time the buds show green in the spring through mid-June are usually sufficient. But, additional applications at 12-14 day intervals will be necessary if early season infections are not controlled.

Rust diseases of apple (apple rust, hawthorn rust and quince rust) are caused by fungi that complete part of their life cycle on the red cedar and part on apple, hawthorn or quince. Apple and hawthorn rusts produce bright orange-colored spots on the leaves. Both apple and quince rust infect the fruit; the apple rust spots are orange, while the quince rust spots are sunken and dark green. Infections of these fungi occur during rainy periods in early spring from green tip through petal fall. The rust diseases can be controlled by applying protective sprays from the green tip through the petal fall stages. In areas where rust diseases are prevalent, ferbam should be added to the basic multipurpose mixture in these sprays.

Powdery mildew of apple is caused by a fungus that winters in the dormant buds. Leaves emerging from infected buds are covered by a white fungus growth. Secondary spread of the disease to other leaves and buds occurs from the time the bud forms in late June. To control this disease, add Karathane (25 percent W.P., 1 tablespoon per gallon) to the multipurpose mixture in all sprays from green tip through third cover spray.

Fire blight blossom and twig infections may be serious on pear trees and some varieties of apple. The bacteria that cause the disease winter in diseased cankers on the trees and are disseminated by wind-blown rain, insects and pruning tools. Fire blight usually attacks the blossoms, but spread may be very rapid during the late spring and summer.

This disease can be controlled by pruning and spraying. Infected twigs and branches should be cut off and burned in late winter. The cuts should be made at least six inches below the dead area. Pruning tools should be disinfected between cuts in a 10 percent Clorox solution to avoid spreading the disease to other branches if pruning is done after March 15. Blossom blight on the trees can be controlled by spraying three times with Bordeaux mixture (copper sulfate, 2 tablespoons plus spray lime, 6 tablespoons per gallon) or streptomycin, 100 parts per million. Make spray applications when a fifth of the blossoms are open, when two-thirds of the blossoms are open and when all are open.

Sucking insects, such as pear psylla, aphids, leaf hoppers and plant bugs must be controlled as they help spread fire blight.

Peach leaf curl is caused by a fungus that winters as tiny spores on the twigs and bud scales of the peach tree. As the leaf buds open in the spring, the spores germinate and cause leaf infections. Infected leaves become thickened and curled or crinkled and have a yellowish and reddish color. Diseased leaves drop off later. Peach leaf curl is easily controlled by one spray of ferbam (2 tablespoons per gallon) any time in the dormant period before the buds begin to swell or open.

Brown rot of stone fruits is a fungus disease that attacks peaches, plums, cherries and nectarines. The fungus winters in infected twigs or fruits that have remained on the tree or dropped to the ground. In rainy periods during the spring and summer, spores are liberated and attack the blossoms and fruit. Brown rot is controlled by the captan in the multipurpose spray mixture when used according to the schedule given at the end of this chapter.

Black knot of plum is a fungus disease characterized by black, rough, cylindrical enlargements on the twigs. The knots may be two to four times the diameter of the twigs and up to 8 inches long. Black knot is controlled by pruning in winter or early spring. Infected twigs and small branches should be pruned 4 inches below the knot, removed from the planting and burned. Knots may be eradicated from desirable branches by removing the visible knotty tissue. When used in a seasonal spray schedule, captan will control the disease if pruning and other sanitation practices are followed.

Plum curculio is a small beetle, about ¼-inch long, which attacks all orchard

Fruit infected by quince rust (left) and cedar apple rust (right).

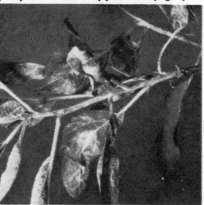

Apple scab lesions on fruit (left) and primary powdery mildew infection on apple terminal (right).

Peach leaf curl symptoms on leaves.

fruit crops. The insect emerges from hibernation in the spring when the fruit is exposed (petal fall on apples and shuck split on stone fruits). The female deposits eggs in the fruit. A small crescent-shaped scar is made by the female at the time of egg laying. The larvae bore into the fruit where they feed. Infested fruits drop to the ground during June; the larvae enter the soil, pupate and emerge as adults in August. If eggs are not deposited in the cut made by the female or if the larva dies before reaching the seed, the fruit may not fall. In such cases, the typical crescent-shaped curculio scar develops and persists through harvest. The adults sometimes feed on the fruit in the fall before cool weather forces them into hibernation.

Control measures are directed against the adult beetles in the period from petal fall until 21 days after petal fall. Three sprays of the multipurpose mixture spaced seven to ten days apart starting at petal fall will control this insect.

European apple sawfly is an apple pest. The adult sawfly inserts eggs into the calyx cup (sepals of the apple flower) during full bloom and at petal fall. The larvae tunnel under the skin in a characteristic spiral pattern. In a few days they move to a second and later even to a third apple where they bore into the seeds. These latter fruit fall to the ground where the larva completes its development by pupating in the soil. The fruit originally infested remains on the tree and the spiral tunnels develop into ugly scars often causing the fruit to be misshapen.

European apple sawfly adults can be controlled by a prompt petal fall application of the multipurpose spray mixture. Any delay in applying the petal fall spray will permit this insect to cause additional damage.

Codling moth is the common worm found in apples. Control measures are directed against the adults before oviposition and against the larvae which hatch from eggs deposited on the fruit and foliage. The first eggs normally hatch 18 to 21 days after the petals have fallen. Sprays of the multipurpose mixture applied every 10 days throughout the summer will control this insect.

Apple maggot is the most destructive of all insects that attack apples and plums. It is commonly called the railroad worm because of the brownish trails or tracks the larvae or maggots leave as they bore into the flesh of the fruit. Maggot flies (picture-winged flies slightly smaller than a housefly) emerge from the soil from the middle of June through the middle of August, and feed for about one week before the female deposits eggs *under* the skin of the apple with a needlelike ovipositor. Upon hatching, the maggots or larvae bore through the fruit. In heavy infestations many larvae may be found in a single fruit reducing it to a pulpy mass of brown trails. In certain varieties the fruit may become knobby or dimpled as the inner tissue is destroyed. Infested fruits fall to the ground prematurely, allowing the larvae to leave the fruit and enter the soil where they pupate until the following year. The spray schedule used against the codling moth also will control the apple maggot flies while they are feeding on the foliage. However, the interval between sprays should not be longer than 10 days, or the residue on the fruit and leaves will not be heavy enough to kill the flies. For adequate protection against the apple maggot, control of the flies must be maintained from the last week in June through the first of September.

Picking up and destroying fallen apples at weekly intervals from early August through harvest kills the larvae within the fruit and reduces the potential for maggot injury the following year.

Aphids or plant lice present on apple trees are principally of two species, the *rosy aphid* and the *green apple aphid*. Both species cause the leaves to become twisted and rolled. Rosy aphids do most of their damage early and cause the

Egg laying and feeding scars of the plum curculio (upper left). Fire blight has wilted and killed terminals and blossoms on this branch (upper right). European apple sawfly injury on mature apples (lower left). Black knot infection on plum branch (lower right).

Healthy apple on left. Apples deformed by rosy apple aphid on right.

Oriental fruit moth injury to peach twigs (upper left). Second brood codling moth adult on fruit. Note frass from first brood larval entrance on left and new second brood entrance on right (upper right). Typical injury caused by apple aphid (lower left). Pear leaves and fruit showing black sooty mold growing on honey dew exuded by pear psylla (lower right).

Cherry fruit fly maggot injury to cherries.

Typical sites and injury by peach tree borer.

fruit of certain varieties to become dwarfed and deformed. A fungus growing in the honey-dew secreted by the aphids may cause black smut spots on the fruit and foliage. The rosy aphid should be controlled by a spray of malathion applied in the ½ in. green or pink spray. Green apple aphids may also be controlled by the malathion applied in the post bloom and/or summer sprays.

Mites are responsible for the bronzing of leaves of many fruit trees. Two species, the European red mite and the two-spotted mite, are most commonly found. The European red mites' eggs winter on trees. The eggs can be killed by spraying with 2 percent superior dormant oil emulsion (5 tablespoons per gallon) at the tight cluster stage. Usually the malathion in the multipurpose spray mixture will suppress both species of mites when used in the complete seasonal spray program. Kelthane (35 percent WP, 2 tablespoons per gallon) may be added to the spray mixture to give greater assurance of mite control. Kelthane alone in a separate spray may be used if infestation becomes heavy.

Pear psylla is the most common insect on pears. When uncontrolled, it may cause early defoliation of the tree and loss of the crop. The nymphs secrete honeydew which turns black, as does that of aphids. The pre-bloom and petal fall sprays are the most important in controlling this insect.

Peach tree borers attack peach trees and other stone fruits. Two species, the peach tree borer and the lesser peach tree borer, feed on the cambium or inner bark of the tree. The adults of both species are clear winged moths and both deposit eggs on the bark of the trees. The peach tree borer larvae enter the tree within 12 inches of the ground level and bore into the cambium; the lesser peach tree borer larvae attack the branches and limbs of the tree. The borers of either species can be detected by gummy exudate mixed with a sawdust-like material that is secreted from the burrows. Gum secretions also can be caused by other injuries to the tree. Positive diagnosis of borers can be made by cutting away the bark and looking for the larvae in their burrows. Both species of borers are controlled by the malathion in the spray mixture. To control the peach tree borer effectively, however, the trunk and lower branches must be thoroughly drenched.

Oriental fruit moths produce two or more broods each year. The first brood attacks the young terminals of peach trees, burrowing into them for several inches causing the leaves to wilt. The second and third broods attack the fruit. The young larvae enter the fruit at the point of attachment to the stem, frequently leaving no external evidence. A preventive program must be followed for control. The six-spray program at the end of this chapter is designed to control all three broods.

Cherry fruit flies are closely related to the apple maggot and have a similar life cycle. Emergence of the adult flies begins about June 1 and continues for about one month. The insecticides in the multipurpose spray mixture control the fruit flies and plum curculio on cherries if used according to the schedule given.

Selection of Effective Pesticides

No one pesticide will control all insects and diseases that attack fruit trees. In recent years, however, a number of low hazard, effective materials have been developed which can be used in combination. The basic multipurpose spray mixture which has been very effective is a combination of captan, malathion and methoxychlor. Captan is a fungicide that controls the major diseases, and malathion and methoxychlor are insecticides that control the major fruit insects.

Carbaryl (Sevin), one of the newer and less hazardous insecticides, also controls the major fruit pests. However, if used on apples within three weeks of petal fall it thins the crop by causing some of the fruit to fall. It does not have this effect on the other tree fruits.

Therefore, carbaryl (Sevin) may be substituted for malathion and methoxychlor in the summer sprays or it may be used to supplement the multipurpose spray mixture. It should not be used on apples before the third cover unless the crop needs thinning. Under certain conditions other pesticides may be added to the basic spray mixture to control specific insects or diseases. These special pesticides and rates are discussed under the specific pests.

Home fruit growers may purchase one-package, multipurpose fungicide and insecticide mixtures at farm and garden supply centers. If one-package mixtures are not available, the individual components may be purchased and mixed by the home orchardists.

Timing and Applying Pesticide Sprays

The development of orchard pests is closely correlated with the development of the tree. Therefore, spray applications are timed according to tree development which can be more readily observed than the pests themselves.

The greatest disease activity occurs during pre-bloom and bloom. Diseases are usually spread during rainy periods, and sprays should be applied prior to or within 12 hours following the beginning of a rain.

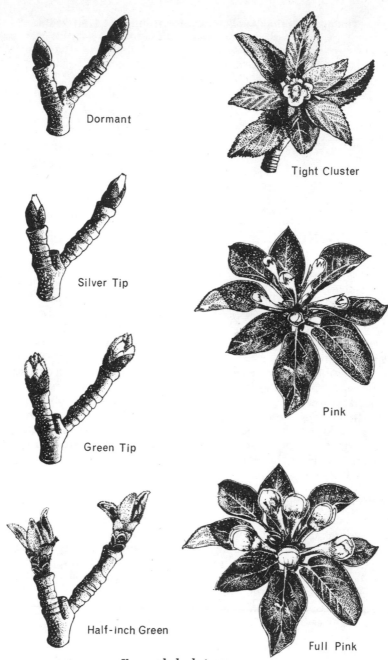

Dormant

Tight Cluster

Silver Tip

Pink

Green Tip

Half-inch Green

Full Pink

Key apple bud stages.

Insects are most active during warm weather with occasional rains. Sprays to control insects must be applied at approximately 10-day intervals throughout the season beginning at petal fall. Spray applications of insecticides during bloom are unlawful and should be avoided to prevent killing bees. The fungicide

Photographs of insect injuries by Gertrude Catlin, drawings of apple bud stages by Joseph A. Keplinger, N.Y.S. Agricultural Experiment Station, Geneva.

Timing of Spring Applications for Control of Fruit Pests.

Stage of Tree Development*	Apples	Pears	Peaches	Plums	Cherries
Dormant..................			Ferbam		
Green-tip.................	Captan only				
½-inch green.............	Captan or oil-ferbam		Oil	Oil	Oil
Pink.....................	MP†	MP	MP	MP	MP
Bloom‡...................	Captan	Bordo	Captan	Captan	Captan
Petal Fall................	MP	MP	MP	MP	MP
First Cover...............	MP	MP	MP	MP	MP
Second Cover.............	MP	MP	MP	MP	MP
Third Cover..............	MP	MP			MP
Fourth Cover.............	MP		MP	MP	MP
Fifth Cover..............	MP				
Sixth Cover..............	MP	MP	MP		
Seventh Cover............	MP	MP			

* Bloom: When blossoms are open.
  Petal fall: When three-quarters of the petals have fallen.
  First to Seventh Cover: Sprays at 10-day intervals starting 10 days after petal fall.
‡ *Insecticides must not be applied during bloom.*
  Fungicides may be applied if necessary.
† MP: Multi-purpose spray mixture

Captan (50% WP)	2 tablespoons per gallon of water
Malathion (25% WP)	2 tablespoons per gallon of water
Methoxychlor (50% WP)	3 tablespoons per gallon of water

  Carbaryl (Sevin) (50% WP) at 3 tablespoons per gallon of water may be substituted for the malathion and methoxychlor in the summer sprays or used as a supplement in the multi-purpose spray mixture.
  Carbaryl (Sevin) will tend to thin apples if applied within 3 weeks of petal fall.

captan may be applied safely during bloom to protect against diseases that develop at this time.

Sprays should be applied under conditions that favor thorough coverage of all fruit and foliage. This will usually be early in the morning or in the evening when wind velocity is low and the humidity high. Concentrate on spraying the top of the tree. If the tops are thoroughly covered very little spray will need to be directed at the lower limbs. The tree should be sprayed until some of the mixture starts to drip from the leaves. Adequate coverage is greatly simplified by heading the tree back, by following annual pruning practices or by planting dwarf fruit trees.

Key Apple Bud Stages

For the control of certain pests, spray treatments are often applied before bloom. To time these applications precisely for optimum control, it is necessary to understand and recognize the key pre-bloom apple bud stages. The accompanying diagram illustrates and gives the names of these bud stages as adopted by New York State and many other areas in 1965. Since the older names are sometimes still used they are given in parentheses.

Description of bud stages:
Dormant: Buds essentially dormant.
Silver Tip: Buds swollen and bud scales separated to expose some light gray tissue and tips.
Green tip: Fruit buds broken at tips and showing about 1/16" green.
Half inch green (delayed dormant): about ½" of green tissue projecting from fruit buds.
Tight cluster (pre pink): Blossom buds exposed but tightly appressed, stems short.
Pink: All blossom buds in cluster pink, stems fully extended.
Full pink: Petals in blossom buds elongated, 1-3 days before open bloom.

Growing Vegetables in the Home Garden

This publication is intended for country-wide distribution. Any gardener using it also needs local information, especially on the earliest and latest safe planting dates for vegetables and any special garden practices and varieties that are best for his location. Gardeners may get local information and advice from their State agricultural experiment stations and county agricultural agents.

Selecting a Site

A back yard or some other plot near your home in full sunlight is the most convenient spot for a home vegetable garden. However, poor drainage, shallow soil, and shade from buildings or trees may mean the garden must be located in an area farther from the house.

In planning your garden, consider what and how much you will plant. It is better to have a small garden well maintained than a large one neglected and full of weeds. Diagram the garden rows on paper and note the length you wish to assign to each vegetable. Use a scale of a selected number of feet to an inch. Then you can decide how much seed and how many plants to buy.

Consider also the possibility of working your vegetables in plots in front of your shrubbery. Many vegetables are ornamental in appearance. Some vegetables can be grown in your flower beds; others can be grown entirely in containers.

The amount of sunlight your garden gets must also be considered. Leafy vegetables, for example, can be grown in partial shade but vegetables producing fruit must be grown in direct sunlight.

Protecting the Garden

The garden should be surrounded by a fence sufficiently high and close-woven to keep out dogs, rabbits, and other animals. The damage done by stray animals during a season or two can equal the cost of a fence. A fence also can serve as a trellis for beans, peas, tomatoes, and other crops that need support.

This chapter was prepared by Robert E. Wester, Agricultural Research Service, Northeastern Region, U.S. Department of Agriculture.

In most sections of the country, rodents of various kinds damage garden crops. In the East, moles and mice cause much injury. Moles burrow under the plants, causing the soil to dry out around the roots. Mice either work independently or follow the burrows made by moles, destroying newly planted seeds and young plants. In the West, ground squirrels and prairie dogs damage vegetable gardens. Most of these pests can be partially controlled with traps.

Soil, Drainage, and Sunshine

Fertile, deep, friable, well-drained soil is necessary for a successful garden. The exact type of soil is not so important as that it be well drained, well supplied with organic matter, retentive of moisture, and reasonably free of stones. The kind of subsoil also is vitally important. Hard shale, rock ledges, gravel beds, very deep sand, or a hardpan under the surface soil is likely to make the development of high-grade garden soil extremely difficult or impossible. On the other hand, infertile soil that has good physical properties can be made productive by using organic matter, lime, commercial fertilizer, and other soil improving materials.

Good drainage of the soil is essential. Soil drainage may often be improved by installing agricultural tile, digging ditches, and sometimes by plowing deep into the subsoil. The garden should be free of low places where water might stand after a heavy rain. Water from surrounding land should not drain into the garden, and there should be no danger of flooding by overflow from nearby streams.

Good air drainage is necessary to lessen the danger of damage by frost. A garden on a slope that has free movement of air to lower levels is most likely to escape late-spring and early-autumn frost damage.

A gentle slope of not more than 1½ percent facing in a southerly direction helps early crops get started. In sections that have strong winds, a windbreak of board fence, hedge, or trees on the windward side of the garden is recommended. Hedges and other living windbreaks should be far enough away from the garden to prevent shade or roots from interfering with the garden crops.

The garden should get the direct rays of the sun all day if possible. Some crops can tolerate partial shade, but no amount of fertilizer, water, or care can replace needed sunshine. Even where trees do not shade garden crops, tree roots may penetrate far into the soil and rob crops of moisture and plant food.

Damage to garden crops by tree roots may be largely prevented by digging a trench 1½ to 2 feet deep between the trees and the garden, cutting all the tree roots that cross the trench. Then put a barrier of waste sheet metal or heavy roofing paper along one wall of the trench and refill it. This usually prevents root damage for several years.

Preparing the Soil

Good soil for growing vegetables must be protected by proper cultivation, use of organic matter, maintenance of soil fertility, and control of plant pests. Properly prepared soil provides a desirable medium for root development, absorbs water and air rapidly, and usually does not crust badly.

Tillage practices do not automatically create good garden soil. Tillage is needed to control weeds, mix mulch or crop residues into the soil, and to alter soil structure. Unnecessary tillage increases crusting on the soil surface, and if the soil is wet, tillage compacts it.

Fertility requirements differ between long and short growing seasons and among soil types. In almost every State, the Extension Service will test soils and provide fertilizer recommendations.

Plant pests compete with garden crops and impair their growth. These pests include weeds, insects, fungi, bacteria, viruses, and nematodes. They must be controlled or the garden will not succeed. However, chemical controls must be used carefully to prevent damage to neighboring crops or subsequent crops. When mechanical and chemical controls do not work, crops that are resistant to the pests should be planted in the area for a season or two.

The time and method of preparing the garden for planting depend on the type of soil and the location. Heavy clay soils in the northern sections are frequently benefited by fall plowing and exposure to freezing and thawing during the winter, but when the garden is cover-cropped, it should not be plowed until early spring. In general, garden soils should be cover-cropped during the winter to control erosion and to add organic matter. Gardens in the dryland areas should be plowed and left rough in the fall, so that the soil will absorb and retain moisture that falls during the winter. Sandy soils, as a rule, should be cover-cropped, then spring-plowed. Whenever there is a heavy sod or growth of cover crop, the land should be plowed well in advance of planting and the soil disked several times to aid in the decay and incorporation of the material. Land receiving applications of coarse manure either before or after plowing should have the same treatment.

Soils should not be plowed or worked while wet unless the work will certainly be followed by severe freezing weather. Sandy soils and those containing high proportions of organic matter—peats and mucks for example—bear plowing and working at higher moisture content than do heavy clay soils. The usual test is to squeeze together a handful of soil. If it sticks together in a ball and does not readily crumble under slight pressure by the thumb and finger, it is too wet for plowing or working. When examining soil to determine if it is dry enough to work, samples should be taken both at and a few inches below the surface. The surface may be dry enough, but the lower layers too wet, for working. Soil that sticks to the plow or to other tools is usually too wet. A shiny, unbroken surface of the turned furrow is another indication of a dangerously wet soil condition.

Fall-plowed land should be left rough until spring, when it may be prepared by disking, harrowing, or other methods. Spring-plowed land should be worked into a suitable seedbed immediately after plowing. Seeds germinate and plants grow more readily on a reasonably fine, well-prepared soil than on a coarse, lumpy one, and thorough preparation greatly reduces the work of planting and caring for the crops. It is possible, however, to overdo the preparation of some heavy soils. They should be brought to a somewhat granular rather than a powdery-fine condition for planting. Spading instead of plowing is sometimes advisable in preparing small areas, such as beds for extra-early crops of lettuce, onions, beets, and carrots.

Organic Matter

Organic matter improves soil as a growing medium for plants. It helps release nitrogen, minerals, and other nutrients for plant use when it decays. A mulch of partially rotted straw, compost, or undecomposed crop residue on the soil helps keep the soil surface from crusting, retards water loss from the soil, and keeps weeds from growing.

Practically any plant material can be composted for use in the garden. Leaves, old sod, lawn clippings, straw, and plant refuse from the garden or kitchen can be used. Often, leaves can be obtained from neighbors who do not use them or from street sweepings.

The purpose of composting plant refuse or debris is to decay it so that it can be easily worked into the soil and will not be unsightly when used in the garden. Composting material should be kept moist and supplied with commercial fertilizer, particularly nitrogen, to make it decay faster and more thoroughly.

The usual practice in building a compost pile is to accumulate the organic material in some out-of-the-way place in the garden. It can be built on open ground or in a bin made of cinder blocks, rough boards, or wire fence. The sides of the bin should not be airtight or watertight. A convenient time to make a compost pile is in the fall when leaves are plentiful.

Making a new compost pile.

In building the compost pile, spread out a layer of plant refuse about 6 inches deep and add one-half pound or one cupful of 10-10-10, 10-20-10, or 10-6-4 fertilizer to each 10 square feet of surface. Then add 1 inch of soil and enough water to moisten but not to soak it. This process is repeated until the pile is 4 to 5 feet high. Make the top of the pile concave to catch rainwater.

If alkaline compost is wanted, ground limestone can be spread in the pile at the same rate as the fertilizer.

The compost pile will not decay rapidly until the weather warms up in spring and summer. In midsummer, decay can be hastened by forking over the pile so moisture can get to parts that have remained dry. The compost should be ready for use by the end of the first summer.

For a continuing supply of compost, a new pile should be built every year.

Compost ready for use in the garden.

Compost can be used as a mulch, or worked into flower beds and the vegetable garden.

When properly prepared and thoroughly decayed, compost is not likely to harbor diseases or insects. If the compost is used in soil where an attempt is made to control plant diseases, or if it is mixed with soil used for raising seedlings, the soil should be disinfected with chemicals recommended by your county agricultural agent or State agricultural college.

Commercial Fertilizers

Commercial fertilizers may be used to advantage in most farm gardens, the

Using a soil-compost mixture under and around plants in the garden.

composition and rate of application depending on locality, soil, and crops to be grown. On some soils with natural high fertility only nitrogen or compost may be needed. The use of fertilizers that also contain small amounts of copper, zinc, manganese, and other minor soil elements is necessary only in districts known to be deficient in those elements. State experiment station recommendations should be followed. Leafy crops, such as spinach, cabbage, kale, and lettuce, which often require more nitrogen than other garden crops, may be stimulated by side dressings. As a rule, the tuber and root crops, including potatoes, sweetpotatoes, beets, carrots, turnips, and parsnips, need a higher percentage of potash than other vegetables.

The quantity of fertilizer to use depends on the natural fertility of the soil, the amounts of organic matter and fertilizer used in recent years, and the crops being grown. Tomatoes and beans, for example, normally require only moderate amounts of fertilizer, especially nitrogen; whereas onions, celery, lettuce, the root crops, and potatoes respond profitably to relatively large applications. In some cases, 300 pounds of commercial fertilizer may be sufficient on a half-acre garden; in other cases, as much as 1,000 to 1,200 pounds can be used to advantage.

Commercial fertilizers, as a rule, should be applied either a few days before planting or when the crops are planted. A good practice is to plow the land, spread the fertilizer from a pail or with a fertilizer distributor, then harrow the soil two or three times to get it in proper condition and at the same time mix the fertilizer with it. If the soil is left extremely rough by the plow, it should be harrowed once, lightly, before fertilizing. For row crops, like potatoes and sweetpotatoes, the fertilizer may be scattered in the rows, taking care to mix it thoroughly with the soil before the seed is dropped, or, in the case of sweetpotatoes, before the ridges are thrown up.

Application of the fertilizer in furrows along each side of the row at planting time does away with the danger of injury to seeds and plants that is likely to follow direct application of the material under the row. The fertilizer should be placed so that it will be 2 to 3 inches to one side of the seed and at about the same level as, or a little lower than, the seed.

The roots of most garden crops spread to considerable distances, reaching throughout the surface soil. Fertilizer applied to the entire area, therefore, will be reached by the plants, but not always to best advantage. Placing fertilizer too near seedlings or young plants is likely to cause burning of the roots. The fertilizer should be sown alongside the rows and cultivated into the topsoil, taking care to keep it off the leaves so far as practicable.

Heavy yields of top-quality vegetables cannot be obtained without an abundance of available plant food in the soil. However, failure to bear fruit and even injury to the plants may result from the use of too much plant nutrient, particularly chemical fertilizers, or from an unbalanced nutrient condition in the soil. Because of the small quantities of fertilizer required for short rows and small plots it is easy to apply too much fertilizer. The chemical fertilizers to be applied should always be weighed or measured. Table 1 shows how much fertilizer to apply to each 50 or 100 feet of garden row or to each 100 to 2,000 square feet of garden area.

If it is more convenient to measure the material than to weigh it, pounds of common garden fertilizer, ammonium phosphate, or muriate of potash, may be converted roughly to pints or cups by allowing 1 pint, or 2 kitchen measuring cups, to a pound. For example, table 1 gives 0.25 pound for a 100-pound-per-

Measurement	Weight of fertilizer to apply when the weight to be applied per acre is—			
	100 pounds	400 pounds	800 pounds	1,200 pounds
Space between rows, and row length (feet):	*Pounds*	*Pounds*	*Pounds*	*Pounds*
2 wide, 50 long ------------	0.25	1.0	2.0	3.0
2 wide, 100 long ------------	.50	2.0	4.0	6.0
2½ wide, 50 long -----------	.30	1.2	2.4	3.6
2½ wide, 100 long ----------	.60	2.4	4.8	7.2
3 wide, 50 long ------------	.35	1.4	2.8	4.2
3 wide, 100 long ------------	.70	2.8	5.6	8.4
Area (square feet):				
100 -----------------------	.25	1.0	2.0	3.0
500 -----------------------	1.25	5.0	10.0	15.0
1,000 ---------------------	2.50	10.0	20.0	30.0
1,500 ---------------------	3.75	15.0	30.0	45.0
2,000 ---------------------	5.00	20.0	40.0	60.0

acre application to 100 square feet. This would call for about ¼ pint, or ½ cup, of fertilizer. ground limestone weighs about 1-1/3 times as much as the same volume of water; therefore, measured quantities of this material should be about one-fourth less than those calculated as equivalent to the weights in the table. For example, ¾ pint of ground limestone weighs about 1 pound. Ammonium sulfate and granular ammonium nitrate are much lighter, weighing about seven-tenths as much as the same volumes of water; therefore, volumes of these substances calculated by the foregoing method should be increased by about one-third.

Liming

Lime, ground limestone, marl, or ground oyster-shells on garden soils serves a threefold purpose: (1) to supply calcium and other plant nutrients; (2) to reduce soil acidity; (3) to improve the physical character of certain heavy soils. As a rule, asparagus, celery, beets, spinach, and carrots are benefited by moderate applications of lime, especially on soils that are naturally deficient in calcium. Dolomitic limestone should be used on soils deficient in magnesium. Most garden vegetables do best on soils that are slightly acid and may be injured by the application of lime in excess of their requirements. For this reason lime should be applied only when tests show it to be necessary. In no case should the material be applied in larger quantities than the test indicates. Most garden soils that are in a high state of fertility do not require the addition of lime.

With good drainage, plenty of organic matter in the soil, and the moderate use of commercial fertilizers, the growth requirements of nearly all vegetables may be fully met. The local garden leader, county agent, or State experiment station can supply information on soil tests that can be made for each locality. (Samples of soil should not be sent to the U.S. Department of Agriculture.)

Lime, when needed, is spread after plowing and is well mixed with the topsoil by harrowing, disking, or cultivating. Burned lime or hydrate lime should not be applied at the same time as commercial fertilizers or mixed with them, because loss of nitrogen is likely to result, thus destroying part of the plant nutrient value. As a rule, lime should be applied in the spring, because some of it may be washed from the soil during winter. Any of the various forms of lime, such as hydrated and air-slacked lime, may be used but the unburned, finely ground, dolomitic limestone is best. Fifty-six pounds of burned lime or 74 pounds of hydrated lime is equivalent to 100 pounds of ground limestone. Finely ground oystershells and marl are frequently used as substitutes for limestone. Lime should not be used on land that is being planted to potatoes unless the soil is extremely acid, because very low soil acidity increases the development of potato scab.

Choosing Garden Tools

Very few tools are necessary for a small garden. It is better to buy a few simple, high-grade tools that will serve well for many years than equipment that is poorly designed or made of cheap or low-grade materials that will not last. In most instances, the only tools needed are a spade or spading fork, a steel bow rake, a 7-inch common hoe, a strong cord for laying off rows, a wheelbarrow, and a garden hose long enough to water all parts of the garden. A trowel can be useful in transplanting, but it is not essential. If the soil is properly prepared, plants can be set more easily with the hands alone than with a trowel.

For gardens that are from 2,000 to 4,000 square feet, a wheel hoe is very useful because it can be used for most work usually done with a common hoe and with much less effort. The single-wheel type is probably the easiest to handle and best for use as an all-purpose wheel hoe. Other styles are available and may be used if preferred.

The cultivating tools, or attachments, for the wheel hoe should include one or more of the so-called hoe blades. They are best for weeding and are used more than the cultivator teeth or small plow usually suplied with a wheel hoe.

For gardens over 4,000 square feet, a rotary garden tiller is useful in preparing the soil for planting and controlling weeds.

Many gardeners who do little or no farming have the choice of hiring equipment for gardenland preparation or buying their own. Equipment for hire too often is unavailable when needed, so that a favorable season for planting may be missed. Country gardeners, in increasing numbers, are turning to small farm and garden tractors for land preparation, cultivation, lawn mowing, and hauling sprayers in gardens and orchards. Those who garden every year and who have large homesteads usually find this equipment a good investment. The size and type of equipment needed depend on the amount of work to be done, the contour of the land, and the character of the soil. For cultivating and other light work a 2- to 3-horsepower tractor is used. If plowing or other heavy work is involved, a larger tractor is desirable. Modern outfits of this size are well adapted to cultivating small areas. A medium-size tractor suitable for cultivating a large garden can also be used for plowing.

The rotary tiller, which is capable of preparing light to medium soils for planting in one operation, has been widely adopted by gardeners who have such soils. In the hands of a careful operator and on land that is not too hard and heavy and is reasonably free from stones, roots, and other obstructions, this machine has many desirable features. It can be adjusted to cultivate very shallowly or to plow the soil and fit it for planting. Tools such as sweeps may be attached, thereby adapting the machine to straddle-row cultivating.

Use of well-adapted implements in preparing garden land greatly lessens the work required in cultivating. Clean, sharp, high-grade tools greatly lessen garden labor. For larger gardens, a wheel-type hand fertilizer distributor, a sprayer or duster (preferably a wheelbarrow-type power sprayer), and a seed drill are generally profitable. Minor tools include two pointed iron stakes and weeders.

If sufficient water is available, irrigation equipment is necessary in many areas and highly desirable in nearly all gardens. Furrow application requires careful planning and laying out of the garden area and precise handling of the soil to insure even distribution of water. Overhead pipes with nozzles at short intervals, temporary lines of lightweight pipe with rotating sprinklers, and porous hose laid along the rows are extensively used. The most common practice is to use a length or two of garden hose, with or without sprinklers, fed by faucets on temporary or permanent lines of pipe through the garden.

In winter, when there is little heat from the sun, little water is used by plants so irrigation is not needed in most areas. However, in summer, rainfall is usually inadequate and irrigation is essential for maximum production.

Arranging the Garden

No one plan or arrangement for a garden can suit all conditions. Each gardener must plan to meet his own problem. Careful planning will lessen the work of gardening and increase the returns from the labor. Planting seeds and plants at random always results in waste and disappointment. Suggestions for planning a garden are here presented with the idea that they can be changed to suit the individual gardener.

The first consideration is whether the garden is to be in one unit or in two. With two plots, lettuce, radishes, beets, spinach, and other vegetables requiring little space are grown in a small kitchen garden, and potatoes, sweet corn, pumpkins, melons, and other vegetables requiring more room are planted in a separate patch, as between young-orchard-tree rows or in other areas where conditions are especially suitable for their culture.

The cultivation methods to be employed are important in planning the garden. When the work is to be done mainly with a garden tractor, the site and the arrangement should be such as to give the longest practicable rows. On slopes of more than 1½ percent, especially on light-textured soil, the rows should extend across the slope at right angles, or on the contours where the land is uneven. The garden should be free from paths across the rows, and turning spaces of 10 to 12 feet should be provided at the ends. The rows for small-growing crops may be closer together for hand cultivation than for cultivation with power equipment.

Any great variation in the composition of the soil within the garden should be taken into consideration when deciding on where to plant various crops. If part of the land is low and moist, such crops as celery, onions, and late cucumbers should be placed there. If part is high, warm, and dry, that is the proper spot for early crops, especially those needing a soil that warms up quickly.

Permanent crops, such as asparagus and rhubarb, should be planted where they will not interfere with the annual plowing of the garden and the cultivation of the annual crops. If a hot-bed, a coldframe, or a special seedbed is provided, it should be either in one corner of, or outside the garden.

Tall-growing crops should be planted where they will not shade or interfere with the growth of smaller crops. There seems to be little choice as to whether the rows do or do not run in a general east-and-west or in a general north-and-south direction, but they should conform to the contours of the land.

Succession of Crops

Except in dry-land areas, all garden space should be kept fully occupied throughout the growing season. In the South, this means the greater part of the year. In fact, throughout the South Atlantic and Gulf coast regions it is possible to have vegetables growing in the garden every month of the year.

In arranging the garden, all early-maturing crops may be grouped so that as soon as one crop is removed another takes its place. It is desirable, however, to follow a crop not with another of its kind, but with an unrelated crop. For example, early peas or beans can very properly be followed by late cabbage, celery, carrots, or beets; early corn or potatoes can be followed by fall turnips or spinach. It is not always necessary to wait until the early crop is entirely removed; a later one may be planted between the rows of the early crop—for example, sweet corn between potato rows. Crops subject to attack by the same diseases and insects should not follow each other.

In the extreme North, where the season is relatively short, there is very little opportunity for succession cropping. In dry-land areas, inter-cropping generally is not feasible, because of limited moisture supply. Therefore, plenty of land should be provided to accommodate the desired range and volume of garden crops.

Late Summer and Fall Garden

Although gardening is commonly considered mainly as a spring and early-summer enterprise, the late-summer and fall garden deserves attention too. Second and third plantings of crops adapted to growing late in the season not only provide a supply of fresh vegetables for the latter part of the season but often give better products for canning, freezing, and storing. Late-grown snap and lima beans and spinach, for example, are well adapted to freezing and canning; beets, carrots, celery, and turnips, to storage. In the South, the late-autumn garden is as important as the early-autumn one.

Selecting Seed

Except in special cases, it pays the gardener to buy seed from reputable seedsmen and not to depend on home-grown supplies. Very fine varieties that do extremely well in certain areas have been grown for long periods from locally produced seed, and such practices are to be commended, provided adequate measures are taken to keep the strains pure.

Vegetables that are entirely, or readily, cross-pollinated *among plants of their kind* include corn, cucumbers, melons, squash, pumpkins, cress, mustard, brussels sprouts, cabbage, cauliflower, collards, kale, kohlrabi, spinach, onion, radish, beet, and turnip. Those less readily cross-pollinated are eggplant, pepper, tomato, carrot, and celery. Beans, peas, okra, and lettuce are generally self-pollinated, but occasionally cross-pollinated, lima beans sometimes rather extensively. Because sweet corn will cross with field corn, it is unwise to save sweet corn seed if field corn is growing in the same neighborhood. Hybrid sweet corn

TABLE 2.—*Quantity of seed and number of plants required for 100 feet of row, depths of planting, and distances apart for rows and plants*

Crop	Requirement for 100 feet of row		Depth for planting seed	Distance apart		
				Rows		Plants in the row
	Seed	Plants		Horse- or tractor-cultivated	Hand-cultivated	
			Inches	*Feet*		
Asparagus	1 ounce	75	1 -1½	4 -5	1½ to 2 feet	18 inches.
Beans:						
Lima, bush	½ pound		1 -1½	2½-3	2 feet	3 to 4 inches.
Lima, pole	½ pound		1 -1½	3 -4	3 feet	3 to 4 feet.
Snap, bush	½ pound		1 -1½	2½-3	2 feet	3 to 4 inches.
Snap, pole	4 ounces		1 -1½	3 -4	2 feet	3 feet.
Beet	2 ounces		1	2 -2½	14 to 16 inches	2 to 3 inches.
Broccoli:						
Heading	1 packet	50- 75	½	2½-3	2 to 2½ feet	14 to 24 inches.
Sprouting	1 packet	50- 75	½	2½-3	2 to 2½ feet	14 to 24 inches.
Brussels sprouts	1 packet	50- 75	½	2½-3	2 to 2½ feet	14 to 24 inches.
Cabbage	1 packet	50- 75	½	2½-3	2 to 2½ feet	14 to 24 inches.
Cabbage, Chinese	1 packet		½	2 -2½	18 to 24 inches	8 to 12 inches.
Carrot	1 packet		½	2 -2½	14 to 16 inches	2 to 3 inches.
Cauliflower	1 packet	50- 75	½	2½-3	2 to 2½ feet	14 to 24 inches.
Celeriac	1 packet	200-250	⅛	2½-3	18 to 24 inches	4 to 6 inches.
Celery	1 packet	200-250	⅛	2½-3	18 to 24 inches	4 to 6 inches.
Chard	2 ounces		1	2 -2½	18 to 24 inches	6 inches.
Chervil	1 packet		½	2 -2½	14 to 16 inches	2 to 3 inches.
Chicory, witloof	1 packet		½	2 -2½	18 to 24 inches	6 to 8 inches.
Chives	1 packet		½	2½-3	14 to 16 inches	In clusters.
Collards	1 packet		½	3 -3½	18 to 24 inches	18 to 24 inches.
Cornsalad	1 packet		½	2½-3	14 to 16 inches	1 foot.
Corn, sweet	2 ounces		2	3 -3½	2 to 3 feet	Drills, 14 to 16 inches; hills, 2½ to 3 feet.
Cress Upland	1 packet		⅛- ¼	2 -2½	14 to 16 inches	2 to 3 inches.
Cucumber	1 packet		½	6 -7	6 to 7 feet	Drills, 3 feet; hills, 6 feet.
Dasheen	5 to 6 pounds	50	2 -3	3½-4	3½ to 4 feet	2 feet.
Eggplant	1 packet	50	½	3	2 to 2½ feet	3 feet.
Endive	1 packet		½	2½-3	18 to 24 inches	12 inches.
Fennel, Florence	1 packet		½	2½-3	18 to 24 inches	4 to 6 inches.
Garlic	1 pound		1 -2	2½-3	14 to 16 inches	2 to 3 inches.
Horseradish	Cuttings	50-75	2	3 -4	2 to 2½ feet	18 to 24 inches.
Kale	1 packet		½	2½-3	18 to 24 inches	12 to 15 inches.
Kohlrabi	1 packet		½	2½-3	14 to 16 inches	5 to 6 inches.
Leek	1 packet		½-1	2½-3	14 to 16 inches	2 to 3 inches.
Lettuce, head	1 packet	100	½	2½-3	14 to 16 inches	12 to 15 inches.
Lettuce, leaf	1 packet		½	2½-3	14 to 16 inches	6 inches.
Muskmelon	1 packet		1	6 -7	6 to 7 feet	Hills, 6 feet.
Mustard	1 packet		½	2½-3	14 to 16 inches	12 inches.
Okra	2 ounces		1 -1½	3 -3½	3 to 3½ feet	2 feet.
Onion:						
Plants		400	1 -2	2 -2½	14 to 16 inches	2 to 3 inches.
Seed	1 packet		½-1	2 -2½	14 to 16 inches	2 to 3 inches.
Sets	1 pound		1 -2	2 -2½	14 to 16 inches	2 to 3 inches.
Parsley	1 packet		⅛	2 -2½	14 to 16 inches	4 to 6 inches.
Parsley, turnip-rooted	1 packet		⅛- ¼	2 -2½	14 to 16 inches	2 to 3 inches.
Parsnip	1 packet		½	2 -2½	18 to 24 inches	2 to 3 inches.
Peas	½ pound		2 -3	2 -4	1½ to 3 feet	1 inch.
Pepper	1 packet	50-70	½	3 -4	2 to 3 feet	18 to 24 inches.
Physalis	1 packet		½	2 -2½	1½ to 2 feet	12 to 18 inches.
Potato	5 to 6 pounds, tubers		4	2½-3	2 to 2½ feet	10 to 18 inches.
Pumpkin	1 ounce		1 -2	5 -8	5 to 8 feet	3 to 4 feet.
Radish	1 ounce		½	2 -2½	14 to 16 inches	1 inch.
Rhubarb		25-35		3 -4	3 to 4 feet	3 to 4 feet.
Salsify	1 ounce		½	2 -2½	18 to 26 inches	2 to 3 inches.
Shallots	1 pound (cloves)		1 -2	2 -2½	12 to 18 inches	2 to 3 inches.
Sorrel	1 packet		½	2 -2½	18 to 24 inches	5 to 8 inches.
Soybean	½ to 1 pound		1 -1½	2½-3	24 to 30 inches	3 inches.
Spinach	1 ounce		½	2 -2½	14 to 16 inches	3 to 4 inches.
Spinach, New Zealand	1 ounce		1 -1½	3 -3½	3 feet	18 inches.
Squash:						
Bush	½ ounce		1 -2	4 -5	4 to 5 feet	Drills, 15 to 18 inches; hills, 4 feet.
Vine	1 ounce		1 -2	8 -12	8 to 12 feet	Drills, 2 to 3 feet; hills, 4 feet.
Sweetpotato	5 pounds, bedroots	75	2 -3	3 -3½	3 to 3½ feet	12 to 14 inches.
Tomato	1 packet	35-50	½	3 -4	2 to 3 feet	1½ to 3 feet.
Turnip greens	1 packet		¼- ½	2 -2½	14 to 16 inches	2 to 3 inches.
Turnips and rutabagas	½ ounce		¼- ½	2 -2½	14 to 16 inches	2 to 3 inches.
Watermelon	1 ounce		1 -2	8 -10	8 to 10 feet	Drills, 2 to 3 feet; hills, 8 feet.

should not be saved for seed. The custom of saving seed from a choice watermelon is safe, provided no citrons or other varieties of watermelons are growing nearby. Likewise, seed from a muskmelon is safe, even though it was grown side by side with cucumbers. Beans do not readily cross and their seed also may be saved. Cabbage, kohlrabi, kale, collards, broccoli, and cauliflower all intercross freely, so each must be well isolated from the others if seed is to be saved.

Seeds should be ordered well in advance of planting time, but only after the preparation of a garden plan that shows the size of the plantings and the quantity of seed required. Table 2 shows the quantity of seed required for a given space, but allowance should be made for the possible need of replanting. Crops and varieties that are known to be adapted to the locality should be selected. The agricultural experiment station of each State, county agricultural agents, and experienced gardeners are usually able to give advice about varieties of vegetables that are adapted to the area. Standard sorts of known quality and performance are usually the best choice.

Disease-resistant strains and varieties of many important vegetables are now so generally available that there is little reason for risking the loss of a crop through planting susceptible sorts. This phase of the subject is treated in detail under the individual crops.

Some seeds retain their vitality longer than others. Seeds may be divided into three groups as follows: (1) Comparatively short-lived, usually not good after 1 to 2 years—corn, leek, onion, parsley, parsnip, rhubarb and salsify; (2) moderately long-lived, often good for 3 to 5 years—asparagus, beans, brussels sprouts, cabbage, carrot, cauliflower, celery, kale, lettuce, okra, peas, pepper, radish, spinach, turnip and watermelon; and (3) long-lived, may be good for more than 5 years—beet, cucumber, eggplant, muskmelon, and tomato.

Starting the Plants

Table 2 gives in general the proper depth of planting for seed of the various vegetables, the quantity of seed or number of plants required for 100 feet of row, and the correct spacing of rows and of plants within the row. Special planting suggestions are given in the cultural hints for the various garden crops.

Earliness, economy of garden space, and lengthening of the growing season may be obtained by setting the plants of many vegetables instead of sowing the seed directly in the garden. Moreover, it is almost impossible to establish good stands from seed sown directly in place in the garden with delicate plants, such as celery, under average conditions.

In the warmer parts of the United States, practically all vegetable plants may be started in specially prepared beds in the open with little or no covering. In the temperate and colder regions, if an early garden is desired, it is essential that certain crops, such as tomatoes, peppers, eggplant, early cabbage, cauliflower, and early head lettuce, be started indoors, in hotbeds, or in coldframes. Occasionally onion, beet, cucumber, squash, and melons are started under cover and transplanted.

Starting Plants in the House

Seeds can be germinated and seedlings started in a box, pan, or flowerpot of

One-half-inch furrows made with a jig.

Clear plastic film gives a flat, even, subdued light and holds the moisture.

soil in a window. In addition to having at least 6 hours of direct sunlight each day, the room must be kept reasonably warm at all times.

Washed fine sand and shredded sphagnum moss are excellent media in which to start seeds. Place a layer of easily drained soil in the bottom of a flat and cover this soil with a layer—about three-fourths inch thick—of either fine sand or sphagnum moss. Press the sand or moss to form a smooth, firm seedbed.

Then, using a jig, make furrows in the seedbed one-half inch deep. Water the sand or moss thoroughly and allow it to drain.

Sow seeds thinly in the rows and cover the seeds lightly with a second layer of sand or moss. Sprinkle the flat, preferably with a fine mist, and cover the flat

Seedlings with first true leaves ready for transplanting.

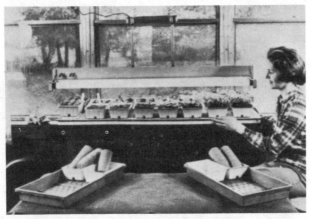

Starting plants under fluorescent light opposite a window.

with a sheet of clear plastic film. The plastic film diffuses and subdues the light and holds moisture in the soil and air surrounding the seeds. Plastic films offer advantages over glass coverings in that they are light in weight and are non-shattering.

Place the seeded and covered flat in a location that is reasonably warm at all times and has 6 hours of direct sunlight each day. The flat will require no further attention until after the seedlings have developed their first true leaves. They are then ready to transplant to other containers.

It is seldom possible to keep the transplanted plants in house windows without their becoming spindling and weak. For healthy growth, place them in a hotbed, coldframe, or other place where they will receive an abundance of sunshine, am-

Soil pellets, left to right, unmoistened, moistened with emerging seedling, and lettuce plant ready to plant in the garden.

Growing early plants in a glass coldframe located on the south side of the house. Some heat is applied from the basement window.

ple ventilation, and a suitable temperature.

Strong, vigorous seedlings can be started under 40-watt fluorescent tubes. These tubes should be 6 to 8 inches above the seedlings. Temperatures should be about 60° F. at night and 70° during the day. Best results are obtained if the fluorescent fixture is next to a window to increase the amount of light reaching the young plants.

Soil pellets are the simplest and easiest method for starting plants and are readily available from garden supply stores and other sources. Soil pellets are a well-balanced synthetic soil mixture and are free of soilborne diseases and weeds.

Special Devices for Starting Plants

In determining the type of equipment for starting early plants, the gardener must consider the temperature and other climatic conditions in his locality, as well as the nature of the plants to be started. Hardy plants, such as cabbage, need only simple inexpensive facilities, but such heat-loving, tender seedlings as peppers and eggplant must have more elaborate facilities for successful production. In the warmer parts of the United States, and in the well-protected locations elsewhere, a coldframe or a sash-covered pit on the sunny side of a building usually suffices. In colder sections, or in exposed areas elsewhere, some form of artificial heat is essential. Where only a little protection against cold damage, at infrequent intervals, is needed, a coldframe in which a temporary bank of lamps can be placed may be sufficient. The hotbed, lean-to, or sash greenhouse heated by manure, pipes, flues, or electricity are all widely used, the choice depending on conditions. A comparatively small plant-growing structure will provide enough plants for several gardens, and joint efforts by a number of gardeners will usually reduce the labor of producing plants.

The plant-growing structure should always be on well-drained land free from danger of flooding. A sunny, southern exposure on a moderate slope, with trees, a hedge, a board fence, or other form of windbreak on the north and west, makes a desirable site. Plenty of sunshine is necessary.

Hotbeds and other plant-growing devices require close attention. They must be ventilated at frequent intervals, and the plants may require watering more than once daily. Convenience in handling the work is important. Sudden storms may necessitate closing the structure within a matter of minutes. Plant growing at home should not be undertaken by persons obliged to be away for extended periods, leaving the plant structure unattended.

A tight well-glazed structure is necessary where the climate is severe; less expensive facilities are satisfactory elsewhere.

Covers for hotbeds and coldframes may be glass sash, fiber glass, plastic film, muslin, or light canvas.

In the moderate and cooler sections of the country, standard 3- by 6-foot hotbed sash is most satisfactory. Even this requires supplementary covering with canvas, blankets, mats, or similar material during freezing weather. The amount of covering is determined by the degree of heat supplied the structure, the severity of the weather, and the kind of plants and their stage of development. Farther South, where less protection is necessary, a muslin cover may be all that is needed and for only a part of the time.

Many substitutes for glass as coverings for hotbeds and coldframes are on the market. The most widely used substitutes are various kinds of clear plastic film. Some of these have a life-span of only one season, and others a lifespan of 3 to 5 years.

Clear plastic film transmits as much light as glass in the visible range, and more than glass in the ultraviolet and infrared ranges.

The film comes as flat sheets (on rolls) and in tubular form. Flat-sheet film is used for tacking onto wooden frames; the tubular form is used for enclosing metal tubular frames with a tight double layer of film.

Large plant hoods made from semicircular aluminum or galvanized steel pipe and fitted with a sleeve of tubular plastic film make excellent coldframes or seasonal row covers. When used in this way, a double layer of plastic film provides an air space that insulates against 4° to 7° of frost temperature change.

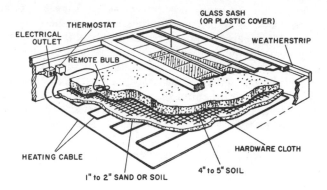

An electrically heated glass hotbed with thermostatic control is ideal for the home gardener.

Electrically heated plant beds are ideal for the home gardener, provided electric rates are not too high. The beds may be built any size. Because they are equipped with thermostatic control, they require a minimum of attention. It is now possible to buy frames—completely equipped with heating cables, switches, and thermostats—ready to assemble and set in position. Fill the frames with soil or plant boxes and connect to a source of current. Small frames may be removed at the end of the season and stored; larger frames are usually treated as a permanent installation. For more detailed information, see USDA Leaflet 445, Electric Heating of Hotbeds.

Hardening Plants

Plants should be gradually hardened, or toughened, for 2 weeks before planting in the open garden. This is done by slowing down their rate of growth to prepare them to withstand such conditions as chilling, drying winds, shortage of water, or high temperatures. Cabbage, lettuce, onion, and many other plants can be hardened to withstand frost; others such as tomatoes and peppers cannot. Withholding water and lowering the temperature are the best ways to harden a plant. This may be done in a glass or plastic coldframe.

About 10 days before being planted in the open ground, the young plants in beds or flats are blocked out with a large knife. Blocking, or cutting the roots, causes new roots to form quickly near the plants, making recovery from transplanting in the open easier. Blocking also makes it easier to remove the plants from the bed or flat with minimum injury.

Southern Grown Plants

Vegetable plants grown outdoors in the South are shipped to all parts of the country. They are grown cheaply and usually withstand shipment and resetting very well. They may not always be as good as home-grown plants, but they save the trouble of starting them in the house or in a hot-bed. Plants of beets, brussels sprouts, cabbage, cauliflower, lettuce, onions, peppers, and tomatoes are extensively grown and shipped; tomato, cabbage, and onion plants make up the bulk of the shipments. The plants are usually wrapped in bundles of 50 each and shipped by either mail or express. Tomato and pepper plants are packed with a little damp moss around the roots, but onion and cabbage plants are usually packed with bare roots. Shipments involving large numbers of bundles are packed in ventilated hampers or slatted crates and usually are sent by motor-truck or rail express. Shipments by air mail and air express are increasing.

The disadvantages of using southern-grown plants are the occasional delays in obtaining them and the possibility of transmitting such diseases as the wilt disease of the tomato, black rot of cabbage, and disorders caused by namatodes. State-certified plants that have been carefully inspected and found as free of these troubles as can be reasonably determined are available. Southern-grown plants are now offered for sale by most northern seedsmen, by mail-order houses, and often by local hardware and supply houses.

Transplanting

The term "transplanting" means shifting of a plant from one soil or culture medium to another. It may refer to the shifting of small seedlings from the seedbed to other containers where the plants will have more space for growth, or it may mean the setting of plants in the garden row where they are to develop for the crop period. Contrary to general belief, transplanting does not in itself stimulate the plant or make it grow better; actually growth is temporarily checked, but the plant is usually given more space in which to grow. Every effort should be made during transplanting to interrupt the growth of the plant as little as possible.

Plants started in seed flats, flowerpots, and other containers in the house, the hotbed, the greenhouse, or elsewhere should be shifted as soon as they can be handled to boxes, flowerpots, plant bands, or other containers where they will have more room to develop. If shifted to flats or similar containers, the plants should be spaced 2 or more inches apart. This provides room for growth until the plants can be moved to their permanent place in the garden. Most gardeners prefer to place seedlings singly in flowerpots, paper cups with the bottoms pierced for drainage, plant bands, berry boxes, or other containers. When the plants are set in the garden, the containers are carefully removed.

Soil for transplanting should be fertile, usually a mixture of rich topsoil and garden compost, with a very light addition of a commercial garden fertilizer.

Moistening the seedbed before removing the seedlings and care in lifting and separating the delicate plants make it possible to shift them with little damage to the root system and with only minor checks to their growth. Plants grown singly in separate containers can be moved to the garden with almost no disturbance to the root system, especially those that are hardened for a week or two before being set outdoors. Plants being hardened should be watered sparingly, but just before they are set out, they should be given a thorough soaking.

Plants grown in the hotbed or greenhouse without being shifted from the seedbed to provide more room and those shipped from the South usually have very little soil adhering to the roots when they are set in the garden. Such plants may require special care if transplanting conditions are not ideal; otherwise, they will die or at least suffer a severe shock that will greatly retard their development. The roots of these plants should be kept covered and not allowed to dry out. Dipping the roots in a mixture of clay and water helps greatly in bridging the critical transplanting period. Planting when the soil is moist also helps. Pouring a half pint to a pint of water, or less for small plants, into the hole around the plant before it is completely filled is usually necessary. A starter solution made by mixing ½ pound of a 4-12-4 or 5-10-5 commercial fertilizer in 4 gallons of water may be used instead of plain water. It is usually beneficial. Finally, the freshly set plants should be shaded for a day or two with newspapers.

Plants differ greatly in the way they recover from the loss of roots and from exposure to new conditions. Small plants of tomatoes, lettuce, beets, cabbage, and related vegetables are easy to transplant. They withstand the treatment better than peppers, eggplant, and the vine crops. When started indoors and moved to the field, the vine crops should be seeded directly in berry baskets or containers of the same size that can be transferred to the garden and removed without disturbing the root systems. Beans and sweet corn can be handled in the same manner, thereby often gaining a week or two in earliness.

Planting the Garden

One of the most important elements of success in growing vegetables is planting or transplanting each crop at the time or times that are best for the operation in each locality. Temperatures often differ so much between localities not many miles apart that the best planting dates for some one vegetable may differ by several days or even 2 weeks.

TABLE 3.—*Some common vegetables grouped according to the approximate times they can be planted and their relative requirements for cool and warm weather*

Cold-hardy plants for early-spring planting		Cold-tender or heat-hardy plants for later-spring or early-summer planting			Hardy plants for late-summer or fall planting
Very hardy (plant 4 to 6 weeks before frost-free date)	Hardy (plant 2 to 4 weeks before frost-free date)	Not cold-hardy (plant on frost-free date)	Requiring hot weather (plant 1 week or more after frost-free date)	Medium heat-tolerant (good for summer planting)	except in the North (plant 6 to 8 weeks before first fall freeze)
Broccoli	Beets	Beans, snap	Beans, lima	Beans, all	Beets
Cabbage	Carrot	Okra	Eggplant	Chard	Collard
Lettuce	Chard	New Zealand spinach	Peppers	Soybean	Kale
Onions	Mustard	Soybean	Sweetpotato	New Zealand spinach	Lettuce
Peas	Parsnip	Squash	Cucumber	Squash	Mustard
Potato	Radish	Sweet corn	Melons	Sweet corn	Spinach
Spinach		Tomato			Turnip
Turnip					

Vegetable crops may be roughly grouped and sown according to their hardiness and their temperature requirements. A rough timetable for planting some of the commoner crops is shown in table 3, based on the frost-free dates in spring and fall. The frost-free date in spring is usually 2 to 3 weeks later than the average date of the last freeze in a locality and is approximately the date that oak trees leaf out.

The gardener naturally wants to make the first planting of each vegetable as early as he can without too much danger of its being damaged by cold. Many vegetables are so hardy to cold that they can be planted a month or more before the average date of the last freeze, or about 6 weeks before the frost-free date. Furthermore, most, if not all, cold-tolerant crops actually thrive better in cool weather than in hot weather and should not be planted late in the spring in the southern two-thirds of the country where summers are hot. Thus, the gardener must time his planting not only to escape cold but with certain crops also to escape heat. Some vegetables that will not thrive when planted in late spring in areas having rather hot summers may be sown in late summer, however, so that they will make most of their growth in cooler weather.

A gardener anywhere in the United States can determine his own safe planting dates for different crops by using the maps, together with tables 4 and 5, in this bulletin. The maps show the average dates of the last killing frosts in fall. They are the dates from which planting times can be determined, and such determinations have been so worked out in tables 4 and 5 that any gardener can use them, with only a little trouble, to find out the planting dates for his locality.

Table 4, for use with the first map, shows planting dates between January 1 and June 30, covering chiefly spring and early-summer crops. It shows *how early it is safe to plant;* it also shows the spring and early-summer dates *beyond which planting usually gives poor results.*

Opposite each vegetable in table 4, the first date in any column is the *earliest generally safe* date that the crop can be sown or transplanted by the gardener using that column. (No gardener needs to use more than one of the columns.) The second date is the latest date that is likely to prove satisfactory for the planting. All times in between these two dates may not, however, give equally good results. Most of the crops listed do better when planted not too far from the earlier date shown.

To determine the best time to plant any vegetable in the spring in your locality:

1. Find your location on the first map and then, the solid line on the map that comes nearest to it.

2. Find the date shown on the solid line. This is the average date of the last killing frost. The first number represents the month; the second number, the day. Thus, 3-10 is March 10. Once you know the date you are through with the map.

3. Turn to table 4; find the column that has your date over it; and draw a heavy line around this entire column. It is the only date column in the table that you will need.

4. Find the dates in the column that are on a line with the name of the crop you want to plant. These dates show the period during which the crop can safely be planted. The best time is on, or soon after, the first of the two dates. A time halfway between them is very good; the second date is not so good.

For areas in the Plains region that warm up quickly in the spring and are subject to dry weather, very early planting is essential to escape heat and drought. In fact, most of the cool-season crops do not thrive when spring-planted in the southern part of the Great Plains and southern Texas.

Table 5 is used with the second map in the same way to find the dates for late plantings. The recommendations for late plantings and for those in the South for overwintered crops are less exact and less dependable than those for early planting. Factors other than direct temperature effects—summer, rainfall, for exam-

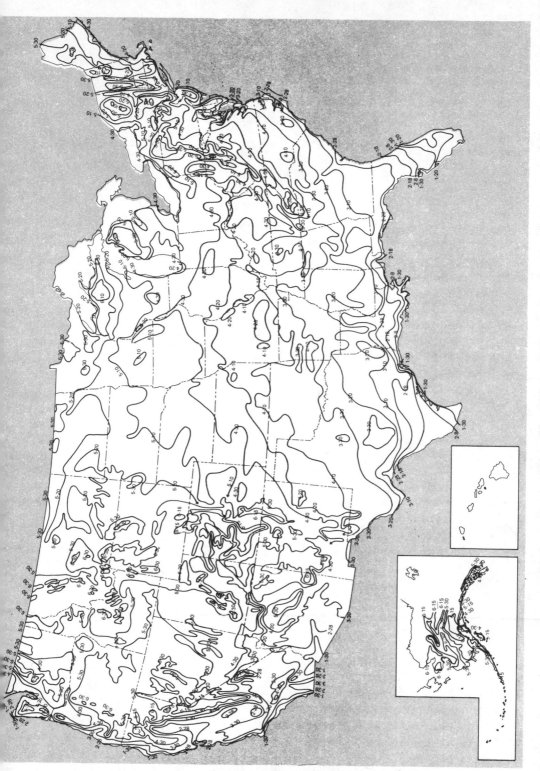

Average dates of the last killing frost in spring.

TABLE 4.—*Earliest dates, and range of dates, for safe spring planting of vegetables in the open*

Crop	Planting dates for localities in which average date of last freeze is—						
	Jan. 30	Feb. 8	Feb. 18	Feb. 28	Mar. 10	Mar. 20	Mar. 30
Asparagus [1]	Feb. 1–Apr. 15	Feb. 10–May 1	Mar. 1–May 1	Mar. 15–June 1	Jan. 1–Mar. 1	Feb. 1–Mar. 10	Feb. 15–Mar. 20.
Beans, lima	Feb. 1–Apr. 1	Feb. 1–May 1	Mar. 1–May 1	Mar. 15–June 1	Mar. 20–June 15	Apr. 1–June 25	Apr. 15–June 20.
Beans, snap	Jan. 1–Apr. 1	Jan. 10–Mar. 15	Jan. 20–Apr. 15	Feb. 1–Mar. 1	Mar. 15–June 15	Mar. 15–May 15	Apr. 1–June 1.
Beet	Jan. 1–Mar. 15	Jan. 10–Mar. 15	Jan. 15–Apr. 15	Feb. 1–Mar. 1	Feb. 15–Mar. 15	Feb. 15–Mar. 15	Mar. 1–20.
Broccoli, sprouting [1]	Jan. 1–30	Jan. 1–30	Jan. 1–30	Jan. 15–Feb. 15	Feb. 15–Mar. 15	Feb. 15–Mar. 15	Mar. 1–20.
Brussels sprouts [1]	Jan. 1–15	Jan. 1–30	Jan. 1–Feb. 25	Jan. 15–Feb. 25	Jan. 25–Mar. 1	Feb. 1–Mar. 1	Feb. 15–Mar. 10.
Cabbage [1]	(2)	(2)	(2)	(2)	(2)	(2)	(2)
Cabbage, Chinese	Jan. 1–Feb. 1	Jan. 1–Feb. 15	Jan. 15–Mar. 1	Feb. 1–Mar. 15	Feb. 10–Mar. 15	Feb. 15–Mar. 20	Mar. 1–Apr. 10.
Carrot	Jan. 1–Feb. 1	Jan. 1–Feb. 10	Jan. 1–Mar. 1	Jan. 10–Mar. 1	Jan. 10–Mar. 1	Feb. 10–Mar. 10	Feb. 20–Mar. 20.
Cauliflower [1]	Jan. 1–Feb. 1	Jan. 1–Feb. 1	Jan. 10–Feb. 10	Jan. 20–Feb. 20	Feb. 1–Mar. 1	Feb. 10–Mar. 10	Mar. 15–Apr. 25.
Celery and celeriac	Jan. 1–Apr. 1	Jan. 10–Feb. 10	Jan. 20–Feb. 20	Feb. 1–Mar. 1	Feb. 20–May 1	Apr. 1–May 1	Mar. 15–Apr. 25.
Chard	Jan. 1–Feb. 1	Jan. 1–Feb. 15	Jan. 15–Mar. 15	Feb. 1–Mar. 15	Feb. 1–Mar. 1	Feb. 1–Apr. 1	Mar. 15–June 15.
Chervil and chives	(2)	(2)	(2)	(2)	June	June 1–July 1	June 1–July 1.
Chicory, witloof	—	—	—	—	Feb. 1–Apr. 1	Feb. 15–May 1	Jan. 1–June 1.
Collards [1]	Jan. 1–Feb. 15	Jan. 1–Feb. 15	Jan. 1–Mar. 15	Jan. 15–Mar. 15	Jan. 1–Apr. 1	Jan. 15–May 1	Mar. 1–June 1.
Cornsalad	Jan. 1–Feb. 15	Jan. 1–Feb. 15	Jan. 1–Mar. 15	Jan. 15–Feb. 1	Jan. 10–Apr. 15	Mar. 15–May 15	Mar. 25–May 15.
Corn, sweet	Feb. 1–Mar. 1	Feb. 10–Apr. 1	Feb. 20–Apr. 15	Mar. 1–Apr. 15	Mar. 10–Apr. 15	Mar. 15–May 15	Apr. 10–May 15.
Cress, upland	Jan. 1–Feb. 15	Jan. 1–Feb. 15	Jan. 15–Feb. 15	Feb. 1–Mar. 15	Feb. 15–Apr. 15	Apr. 1–May 1	Apr. 1–May 1.
Cucumber	Feb. 15–Mar. 15	Feb. 15–Apr. 15	Feb. 15–Apr. 15	Mar. 1–Apr. 15	Mar. 15–Apr. 15	Apr. 1–May 1	Apr. 10–May 15.
Eggplant [1]	Feb. 1–Mar. 1	Feb. 15–Apr. 15	Feb. 20–Apr. 15	Mar. 10–Apr. 15	Mar. 15–Apr. 15	Apr. 1–May 1	Apr. 10–May 15.
Endive	Jan. 1–Mar. 1	Feb. 1–Mar. 1	Jan. 15–Mar. 1	Feb. 1–Mar. 1	Mar. 15–Apr. 15	Mar. 1–Apr. 1	Mar. 10–Apr. 10.
Fennel, Florence	Jan. 1–Mar. 1	Jan. 1–Mar. 1	Jan. 15–Mar. 1	Feb. 1–Mar. 1	Feb. 15–Mar. 15	Mar. 1–Apr. 1	Feb. 10–Mar. 10.
Garlic	(2)	(2)	(2)	(2)	(2)	(2)	(2)
Horseradish [1]	Jan. 1–Feb. 1	Jan. 1–Feb. 1	Jan. 1–Feb. 1	Feb. 1–20	Feb. 10–Mar. 1	Feb. 20–Mar. 10	Mar. 1–20.
Kale	Jan. 1–Feb. 1	Jan. 1–Feb. 1	Jan. 10–Feb. 1	Feb. 1–20	Feb. 10–Mar. 1	Feb. 20–Mar. 10	Feb. 15–Mar. 15.
Kohlrabi	Jan. 1–Feb. 1	Jan. 1–Feb. 1	Jan. 1–Feb. 1	Jan. 15–Feb. 15	Jan. 25–Mar. 1	Feb. 15–Mar. 10	Feb. 15–Mar. 15.
Leek	Jan. 1–Feb. 1	Jan. 1–Feb. 1	Jan. 1–Feb. 1	Jan. 15–Feb. 1	Jan. 1–20	Feb. 1–Mar. 1	Feb. 15–Apr. 1.
Lettuce, head [1]	Feb. 1–Mar. 15	Feb. 15–Mar. 15	Feb. 1–Mar. 15	Feb. 15–Mar. 15	Mar. 15–Apr. 15	Apr. 1–May 1	Apr. 10–May 15.
Lettuce, leaf	Jan. 1–Feb. 1	Jan. 1–Feb. 1	Jan. 1–Feb. 1	Feb. 1–Mar. 1	Feb. 15–Apr. 15	Mar. 20–Apr. 15	Mar. 1–May 15.
Muskmelon	Feb. 15–Apr. 1	Jan. 15–Apr. 1	Feb. 15–Apr. 1	Mar. 10–June 1	Mar. 20–June 1	Apr. 1–June 15	Apr. 10–June 15.
Mustard	Jan. 1–Feb. 1	Jan. 1–Feb. 1	Jan. 1–30	Jan. 1–Feb. 15	Jan. 1–Mar. 1	Feb. 10–Mar. 10	Feb. 15–Mar. 15.
Okra	Feb. 15–Apr. 1	Feb. 15–Apr. 1	Feb. 15–Apr. 1	Mar. 1–Mar. 15	Feb. 15–Mar. 10	Feb. 20–Mar. 20	Mar. 20–Mar. 20.
Onion [1]	Jan. 1–15	Jan. 1–15	Jan. 1–15	Jan. 1–Feb. 15	Jan. 1–Mar. 1	Feb. 10–Mar. 10	Feb. 15–Mar. 15.
Onion, seed	Jan. 1–15	Jan. 1–15	Jan. 1–15	Jan. 1–Feb. 15	Jan. 1–Mar. 1	Feb. 10–Mar. 10	Feb. 20–Mar. 15.
Onion, sets	Jan. 1–15	Jan. 1–15	Jan. 1–30	Jan. 15–Mar. 15	Jan. 15–Mar. 10	Feb. 15–Mar. 20	Feb. 20–Mar. 20.
Parsley	Jan. 1–30	Jan. 1–30	Jan. 1–Mar. 1	Jan. 15–Mar. 1	Jan. 15–Mar. 15	Feb. 15–Mar. 15	Mar. 1–Apr. 1.
Parsnip	—	—	—	—	Mar. 1–Apr. 1	Feb. 15–Mar. 15	Mar. 1–Apr. 1.
Peas, garden	Jan. 1–Feb. 15	Jan. 1–Feb. 15	Jan. 1–Mar. 1	Jan. 15–Mar. 1	Jan. 15–July 1	Apr. 1–July 1	Mar. 10–Mar. 20.
Peas, black-eye	Feb. 15–May 1	Feb. 15–May 15	Mar. 1–June 15	Mar. 10–June 20	Apr. 1–July 1	Apr. 10–June 1	Apr. 15–June 1.
Pepper [1]	Feb. 15–Apr. 1	Feb. 1–Apr. 1	Mar. 1–May 1	Mar. 15–May 1	Mar. 15–May 1	Apr. 10–June 1	Apr. 15–June 1.
Potato	Jan. 1–Feb. 15	Jan. 1–Feb. 15	Jan. 15–Mar. 1	Jan. 15–Mar. 1	Feb. 1–Mar. 1	Feb. 10–Mar. 15	Mar. 10–Apr. 1.
Radish	Jan. 1–Apr. 1	Jan. 1–Apr. 1	Jan. 1–Apr. 1	Jan. 1–Apr. 1	Jan. 1–Apr. 15	Jan. 20–May 1	Feb. 15–May 1.
Rhubarb [1]	—	—	—	—	—	—	—
Rutabaga	Jan. 1–Feb. 1	Jan. 1–Feb. 1	Jan. 15–Feb. 15	Jan. 1–Feb. 1	Jan. 15–Feb. 15	Jan. 15–Mar. 1	Feb. 1–Mar. 1.
Salsify	Jan. 1–Feb. 1	Jan. 1–Feb. 1	Jan. 15–Feb. 20	Jan. 15–Mar. 1	Feb. 1–Mar. 1	Feb. 15–Mar. 1	Mar. 1–15.
Shallot	Jan. 1–Mar. 1	Jan. 1–Mar. 1	Jan. 15–Mar. 15	Jan. 1–Mar. 10	Jan. 1–Mar. 10	Feb. 1–Mar. 15	Feb. 15–Mar. 15.
Sorrel	Jan. 1–Feb. 15	Jan. 1–Feb. 15	Jan. 1–Mar. 1	Jan. 15–Mar. 15	Jan. 15–Apr. 15	Jan. 1–June 30	Feb. 20–June 20.
Soybean	Mar. 1–June 30	Mar. 1–June 30	Mar. 1–June 30	Mar. 1–June 30	Apr. 15–June 30	Apr. 10–June 30	Apr. 20–June 30.
Spinach	Jan. 1–Feb. 15	Jan. 1–Feb. 15	Jan. 1–Mar. 1	Jan. 1–Mar. 1	Jan. 15–Mar. 15	Jan. 15–Mar. 15	Feb. 10–Mar. 15.
Spinach, New Zealand	Feb. 1–Apr. 15	Feb. 1–Apr. 15	Mar. 1–Apr. 15	Mar. 15–May 15	Mar. 20–May 15	Apr. 1–May 15	Apr. 10–June 1.
Squash, summer	Feb. 15–Apr. 15	Feb. 15–Apr. 15	Mar. 1–Apr. 20	Mar. 20–May 1	Apr. 1–May 15	Apr. 10–May 15	Apr. 20–June 1.
Sweetpotato	Feb. 15–May 15	Mar. 20–Apr. 10	Mar. 10–Apr. 15	Mar. 20–May 1	Apr. 1–June 1	Apr. 10–May 20	Apr. 20–June 1.
Tomato	Feb. 1–Apr. 1	Feb. 20–Apr. 10	Mar. 1–Apr. 20	Mar. 20–May 10	Mar. 20–May 10	Apr. 1–May 20	Feb. 20–Mar. 20.
Turnip	Jan. 1–Mar. 1	Jan. 1–Mar. 1	Jan. 10–Mar. 1	Jan. 20–Mar. 1	Feb. 1–Mar. 1	Jan. 1–May 1	Apr. 10–May 15.
Watermelon	Feb. 15–Mar. 15	Feb. 15–Apr. 1	Feb. 15–Apr. 15	Mar. 1–Apr. 15	Mar. 15–Apr. 15	Apr. 1–May 1	Apr. 10–May 15.

[1] Plants.

[2] Generally fall-planted (table 5).

Table 4.—*Earliest dates, and range of dates, for safe spring planting of vegetables in the open*—Continued

Crop	Planting dates for localities in which average date of last freeze is—						
	Apr. 10	Apr. 20	Apr. 30	May 10	May 20	May 30	June 10
Asparagus[1]	Mar. 10–Apr. 10	Mar. 15–Apr. 15	Mar. 20–Apr. 15	Mar. 10–Apr. 30	Apr. 20–May 15	May 1–June 1	May 15–June 1.
Beans, lima	Apr. 10–June 30	Apr. 1–June 20	May 15–June 15	25–June 15			
Beans, snap	Apr. 10–June 30	Apr. 25–June 30	May 10–June 30	May 10–June 30	May–15–June 15		May 15–June 15.
Beet	Mar. 10–June 1	Mar. 20–June 1	Apr. 1–June 15	Apr. 15–June 15	Apr. 25–June 15	May 1–June 15	May 20–June 10.
Broccoli, sprouting[1]	Mar. 15–Apr. 15	Mar. 25–Apr. 20	Apr. 1–May 1	Apr. 15–June 1	May 1–June 15	May 10–June 10	May 20–June 10.
Brussels sprouts[1]	Mar. 15–Apr. 15	Mar. 25–Apr. 20	Apr. 1–May 1	Apr. 15–June 1	May 1–June 15	May 10–June 10	May 20–June 10.
Cabbage[1]	Mar. 1–Apr. 1	Mar. 10–Apr. 1	Mar. 15–Apr. 10	Apr. 1–May 15	May 1–June 15	May 10–June 15	May 20–June 1.
Cabbage, Chinese	(2)	(2)	(2)	(2)	June 1–15	May 1–June 15	May 20–June 15.
Carrot	Mar. 10–Apr. 20	Mar. 15–Apr. 15	Apr. 1–May 1	Apr. 10–June 1	Apr. 20–June 15	May 1–June 1	May 20–June 1.
Cauliflower[1]	Mar. 1–Mar. 20	Mar. 15–Apr. 20	Apr. 10–May 10	Apr. 15–May 15	May 10–July 1	June 1–July 1	June 1–June 15.
Celery and celeriac	Apr. 1–Apr. 20	Apr. 10–May 1	Apr. 15–May 1	Apr. 20–June 15	May 15–May 15	May 20–June 1	June 1–June 15.
Chard	Mar. 15–June 15	Apr. 1–June 15	Apr. 15–June 15	Apr. 20–June 15	May 10–June 15	May 20–June 1	June 1–June 15.
Chervil and chives	Mar. 1–Apr. 1	Mar. 10–Apr. 10	Mar. 15–Apr. 15	Apr. 1–May 1	Apr. 15–May 15	May 1–June 1	May 15–June 1.
Chicory, witloof	June 1–July 1	June 10–July 1	June 15–July 1	June 15–July 1	June 1–20	June 1–15	June 1–15.
Collards[1]	Mar. 1–June 1	Mar. 10–June 1	Apr. 1–June 1	Apr. 15–June 1	May 1–June 1	May 10–June 1	May 20–June 1.
Cornsalad	Feb. 1–Apr. 1	Feb. 15–Apr. 15	Mar. 1–May 1	Apr. 1–June 1	May 15–June 1	May 1–June 15	May 15–June 15.
Corn, sweet	Apr. 1–Apr. 15	Apr. 10–May 15	Apr. 25–June 15	May 10–June 15	May 15–June 1	May 1–June 15	May 20–June 1.
Cress, upland	Feb. 20–Apr. 15	Mar. 10–Apr. 15	Mar. 15–Apr. 15	Apr. 10–May 10	Apr. 20–May 20	May 1–June 1	May 15–June 15.
Cucumber	Apr. 20–June 1	May 1–June 15	May 15–June 15	May 20–June 15			
Eggplant[1]	May 1–June 1	May 10–June 1	May 15–June 10	May 20–June 15	June 1–15	June 1–15	
Endive	Mar. 15–Apr. 15	Mar. 25–Apr. 15	Apr. 1–May 1	Apr. 15–May 15	May 1–30	May 1–30	May 15–June 1.
Fennel, Florence	Mar. 15–Apr. 15	Mar. 25–Apr. 15	Apr. 1–May 1	Apr. 15–May 15	May 1–30	May 1–30	May 15–June 1.
Garlic	Feb. 20–Mar. 20	Mar. 10–Apr. 1	Mar. 15–Apr. 15	Apr. 1–May 1	Apr. 15–May 15	May 1–30	May 15–June 1.
Horseradish[1]	Mar. 10–Apr. 10	Mar. 20–Apr. 20	Apr. 10–Apr. 30	Apr. 15–May 15	Apr. 15–May 15	May 1–30	May 15–June 1.
Kale	Mar. 10–Apr. 1	Mar. 20–Apr. 10	Apr. 1–20	Apr. 10–May 1	Apr. 20–May 20	May 1–30	May 15–June 1.
Kohlrabi	Mar. 10–Apr. 10	Mar. 20–May 1	Apr. 1–May 1	Apr. 10–May 10	Apr. 20–May 20	May 1–30	May 15–June 1.
Leek	Mar. 1–Apr. 1	Mar. 15–Apr. 15	Apr. 1–May 1	Apr. 15–May 15	May 1–May 20	May 1–15	May 1–15.
Lettuce, head[1]	Mar. 10–Apr. 1	Mar. 20–Apr. 10	Apr. 1–May 1	Apr. 15–May 15	May 1–June 30	May 10–June 30	May 20–June 30.
Lettuce, leaf	Mar. 15–May 15	Mar. 20–May 15	Apr. 1–June 1	Apr. 15–June 15	May 1–June 30	May 10–June 30	May 20–June 30.
Muskmelon	Apr. 20–June 1	May 1–June 15	May 15–June 1	June 1–June 15			
Mustard	Mar. 10–Apr. 20	Mar. 20–May 1	Apr. 1–May 10	Apr. 15–June 1	May 1–June 30	May 10–June 30	May 20–June 30.
Okra	Apr. 20–June 15	May 1–June 1	May 10–June 1	May 20–June 10	June 1–20	June 1–20	
Onion[1]	Mar. 1–Apr. 1	Mar. 15–Apr. 10	Apr. 1–May 1	Apr. 10–May 1	Apr. 20–May 15	May 1–30	May 10–June 10.
Onion, seed	Mar. 1–Apr. 1	Mar. 15–Apr. 1	Mar. 15–Apr. 15	Apr. 1–May 1	Apr. 20–May 15	May 1–30	May 10–June 10.
Onion, sets	Mar. 1–Apr. 1	Mar. 10–Apr. 1	Mar. 15–Apr. 15	Apr. 1–May 1	Apr. 20–May 15	May 1–30	May 10–June 10.
Parsley	Mar. 10–Apr. 10	Mar. 20–May 1	Apr. 1–May 15	Apr. 15–May 15	May 1–20	May 10–June 1	May 20–June 10.
Parsnip	Mar. 10–Apr. 10	Mar. 20–Apr. 20	Apr. 1–May 1	Apr. 15–May 15	May 1–20	May 1–June 1	May 10–June 10.
Peas, garden	Feb. 20–Mar. 20	Mar. 10–Apr. 1	Mar. 20–May 1	Apr. 1–May 15	Apr. 15–June 1	May 1–June 15	May 10–June 15.
Peas, black-eye	May 1–July 1	May 10–June 15	May 15–June 1	May 25–June 15			
Pepper[1]	May 1–June 1	May 10–June 1	May 15–June 10	May 20–June 10	June 1–15		
Potato	Mar. 10–Apr. 1	Mar. 15–Apr. 10	Mar. 15–Apr. 15	Apr. 1–May 15	Apr. 20–June 15	May 15–June 1	May 1–June 15.
Radish	Mar. 1–May 1	Mar. 10–May 10	Mar. 20–May 10	Apr. 1–June 1	Apr. 15–June 15	May 1–June 15	May 10–June 10.
Rhubarb[1]	Mar. 1–Apr. 1	Mar. 10–Apr. 10	Mar. 20–Apr. 15	Apr. 1–May 1	Apr. 15–May 15	May 1–June 1	May 15–June 1.
Rutabaga	Mar. 1–Apr. 1	Mar. 10–Apr. 1	Mar. 20–Apr. 15	Apr. 1–May 1	May 1–20	May 1–20	May 10–June 1.
Salsify	Mar. 10–Apr. 15	Mar. 20–May 1	Apr. 1–June 1	Apr. 15–June 1	May 1–20	May 10–June 10	May 20–June 10.
Shallot	Mar. 1–Apr. 1	Mar. 10–Apr. 10	Mar. 20–May 1	Apr. 1–May 1	Apr. 15–May 15	May 1–June 15	May 10–June 10.
Sorrel	Mar. 1–Apr. 15	Mar. 10–Apr. 15	Mar. 20–May 1	Apr. 1–May 15	Apr. 15–May 15	May 1–June 1	May 10–June 10.
Soybean	May 1–June 30	May 15–June 20	May 25–June 10	June 1–25	May 20–May 10	May 1–June 1	May 20–June 10.
Spinach	Feb. 15–Apr. 1	Mar. 1–Apr. 15	Mar. 20–Apr. 20	Apr. 1–June 15	Apr. 10–June 15	Apr. 20–June 15	May 1–June 15.
Spinach, New Zealand	Apr. 20–June 1	May 1–June 15	May 1–June 15	May 15–June 15	May 25–June 15	June 1–15	June 10–20.
Squash, summer	Apr. 20–June 1	May 1–May 15	May 1–May 15	May 15–June 1	May 15–June 15	June 1–15	
Sweetpotato	May 1–June 1	May 10–June 10	May 20–June 10	June 1–15	June 1–15	June 1–15	
Tomato	Apr. 20–June 1	May 5–June 10	May 10–June 15	May 15–June 10	May 25–June 15	May 5–20	June 15–30.
Turnip	Mar. 1–Apr. 1	Mar. 10–May 1	Mar. 20–May 1	Apr. 1–June 1	Apr. 15–June 15	June 1–20	May 15–June 15.
Watermelon	Apr. 20–June 1	May 1–June 15	May 15–June 15	June 1–July 1	June 15–July 1	May 1–June 15	May 15–June 15.

[1] Plants.

[2] Generally fall-planted (table 5).

TABLE 5.—*Latest dates, and range of dates, for safe fall planting of vegetables in the open*

Crop	Planting dates for localities in which average dates of first freeze is—					
	Aug. 30	Sept. 10	Sept. 20	Sept. 30	Oct. 10	Oct. 20
Asparagus [1]					Oct. 20–Nov. 15	Nov. 1–Dec. 15.
Beans, lima				June 1–15	June 1–15	June 15–30.
Beans, snap		May 15–June 15	June 1–July 1	June 1–July 10	June 15–July 20	July 1–Aug. 1.
Beet	May 15–June 15	May 15–June 15	June 1–July 1	June 1–July 10	June 15–July 25	July 1–Aug. 5.
Broccoli, sprouting	May 1–June 1	May 1–June 1	May 1–June 15	June 1–30	June 15–July 15	July 1–Aug. 1.
Brussels sprouts	May 1–June 1	May 1–June 1	May 1–June 15	June 1–30	June 15–July 15	July 1–Aug. 1.
Cabbage [1]	May 1–June 1	May 1–June 1	May 1–June 15	June 1–July 10	June 1–July 15	July 1–20.
Cabbage, Chinese	May 15–June 15	May 15–June 15	June 1–July 1	June 1–July 15	June 15–Aug. 1	July 15–Aug. 15.
Carrot	May 15–June 15	May 15–June 15	June 1–July 1	June 1–July 10	June 1–July 20	June 15–Aug. 1.
Cauliflower [1]	May 1–June 1	May 1–July 1	May 1–July 1	May 10–July 15	June 1–July 25	July 1–Aug. 5.
Celery [1] and celeriac	May 1–June 1	May 15–June 15	May 15–July 1	June 1–July 5	June 1–July 15	June 1–Aug. 1.
Chard	May 15–June 15	May 15–July 1	June 1–July 1	June 1–July 5	June 1–July 20	June 1–Aug. 1.
Chervil and chives	May 10–June 10	May 1–June 15	May 15–June 15	(2)	(2)	(2)
Chicory, witloof	May 15–June 15	May 15–June 15	May 15–June 15	June 1–July 1	June 1–July 1	June 15–July 15.
Collards [1]	May 15–June 15	May 15–June 15	May 15–June 15	June 15–July 15	July 1–Aug. 1	July 15–Aug. 15.
Cornsalad	May 15–June 15	May 15–July 1	June 15–Aug. 1	July 15–Sept. 1	Aug. 15–Sept. 15	Sept. 1–Oct. 15.
Corn, sweet			June 1–July 1	June 1–July 1	June 1–July 10	June 1–July 20.
Cress, upland	May 15–June 15	May 15–July 1	June 15–Aug. 1	July 15–Sept. 1	Aug. 15–Sept. 15	Sept. 1–Oct. 15.
Cucumber			June 1–15	June 1–July 1	June 1–July 1	June 1–July 15.
Eggplant [1]				May 20–June 10	May 15–June 15	June 1–July 1.
Endive	June 1–July 1	June 1–July 1	June 15–July 15	June 15–Aug. 1	July 1–Aug. 15	July 15–Sept. 1.
Fennel, Florence	May 15–June 15	May 15–July 15	June 1–July 1	June 1–July 1	June 15–July 15	June 1–Aug. 1.
Garlic	(2)	(2)	(2)	(2)	(2)	(2)
Horseradish [1]	(2)	(2)	(2)	(2)	(2)	(2)
Kale	May 15–June 15	May 15–June 15	June 1–July 1	June 15–July 15	July 1–Aug. 1	July 15–Aug. 15.
Kohlrabi	May 15–June 15	June 1–July 1	June 1–July 15	June 15–July 15	July 1–Aug. 1	July 15–Aug. 15.
Leek	May 1–June 1	May 1–June 1	(2)	(2)	(2)	(2)
Lettuce, head [1]	May 15–July 1	May 15–July 1	June 1–July 15	June 15–Aug. 1	July 15–Aug. 15	Aug. 1–30.
Lettuce, leaf	May 15–July 15	May 15–July 15	June 1–Aug. 1	June 1–Aug. 1	July 15–Sept. 1	July 15–Sept. 1.
Muskmelon			May 15–June 15	May 15–June 1	June 1–June 15	June 15–July 20.
Mustard	May 15–July 15	May 15–July 15	June 1–Aug. 1	June 15–Aug. 1	July 15–Aug. 15	Aug. 1–Sept. 1.
Okra			June 1–20	June 1–July 1	June 1–July 15	June 1–Aug. 1.
Onion [1]	May 1–June 10	May 1–June 10	(2)	(2)	(2)	(2)
Onion, seed	May 1–June 1	May 1–June 10	(2)	(2)	(2)	(2)
Onion, sets	May 1–June 1	May 1–June 10	(2)	(2)	(2)	(2)
Parsley	May 15–June 15	May 1–June 15	June 1–July 1	June 1–July 15	June 15–Aug. 1	July 15–Aug. 15.
Parsnip	May 15–June 1	May 1–June 15	May 15–June 15	June 1–July 1	June 1–July 10	(2)
Peas, garden	May 10–June 15	May 1–July 1	June 1–July 15	June 1–Aug. 1	(2)	(2)
Peas, black-eye			June 1–June 20	June 1–July 1	June 1–July 1	June 1–July 1.
Pepper [1]					June 1–July 1	June 1–July 10.
Potato	May 15–June 1	May 1–June 15	May 1–June 15	May 1–June 15	May 15–June 15	June 15–July 15
Radish	May 1–July 15	May 1–Aug. 1	June 1–Aug. 15	July 1–Sept. 1	July 15–Sept. 15	Aug. 1–Sept. 1.
Rhubarb [1]	Sept. 1–Oct. 1	Sept. 15–Oct. 15	Sept. 15–Nov. 1	Oct. 1–Nov. 1	Oct. 15–Nov. 15	Oct. 15–Dec. 1.
Rutabaga	May 15–June 15	May 1–June 15	June 1–July 1	June 1–July 1	June 15–July 15	July 10–20.
Salsify	May 15–June 1	May 10–June 10	May 20–June 20	June 1–20	June 1–July 1	June 1–July 1.
Shallot	(2)	(2)	(2)	(2)	(2)	(2)
Sorrel	May 15–June 15	May 1–June 15	June 1–July 1	June 1–July 15	July 1–Aug. 1	July 15–Aug. 15.
Soybean				May 25–June 10	June 1–25	June 1–July 5.
Spinach	May 15–July 1	June 1–July 15	June 1–Aug. 1	July 1–Aug. 15	Aug. 1–Sept. 1	Aug. 20–Sept. 10
Spinach, New Zealand				May 15–July 1	June 1–July 15	June 1–Aug. 1.
Squash, summer	June 10–20	June 1–20	May 15–July 1	June 1–July 1	June 1–July 15	June 1–July 20.
Squash, winter			May 20–June 10	June 1–15	June 1–July 1	June 1–July 1.
Sweetpotato					May 20–June 10	June 1–15.
Tomato	June 20–30	June 10–20	June 1–20	June 1–20	June 1–20	June 1–July 1.
Turnip	May 15–June 15	June 1–July 1	June 1–July 15	June 1–Aug. 1	July 1–Aug. 1	July 15–Aug. 15
Watermelon			May 1–June 15	May 1–June 1	June 1–June 15	June 15–July 20

[1] Plants.
[2] Generally spring-planted (table 4).

TABLE 5.—*Latest dates, and range of dates, for safe fall planting of vegetables in the open*—Continued

Crop	Planting dates for localities in which average date of first freeze is—					
	Oct. 30	Nov. 10	Nov. 20	Nov. 30	Dec. 10	Dec. 20
Asparagus [1]	Nov. 15–Jan. 1	Dec. 1–Jan. 1				
Beans, lima	July 1–Aug. 1	July 1–Aug. 15	July 15–Sept. 1	Aug. 1–Sept. 15	Sept. 1–30	Sept. 1–Oct. 1.
Beans, snap	July 1–Aug. 1	July 1–Aug. 15	July 1–Sept. 10	Aug. 15–Sept. 20	Sept. 1–30	Sept. 1–Nov. 1.
Beet	Aug. 1–Sept. 1	Aug. 1–Oct. 1	Sept. 1–Dec. 1	Sept. 1–Dec. 15	Sept. 1–Dec. 31	Sept. 1–Dec. 31.
Broccoli, sprouting	July 1–Aug. 15	Aug. 1–Sept. 1	Aug. 1–Sept. 15	Aug. 1–Oct. 1	Aug. 1–Nov. 1	Sept. 1–Dec. 31.
Brussels sprouts	July 1–Aug. 15	Aug. 1–Sept. 1	Aug. 1–Sept. 15	Aug. 1–Oct. 1	Aug. 1–Nov. 1	Sept. 1–Dec. 31.
Cabbage [1]	Aug. 1–Sept. 1	Sept. 1–15	Sept. 1–Dec. 1	Sept. 1–Dec. 31	Sept. 1–Dec. 31	Sept. 1–Dec. 31.
Cabbage, Chinese	Aug. 1–Sept. 15	Aug. 15–Oct. 1	Sept. 1–Oct. 15	Sept. 1–Nov. 1	Sept. 1–Nov. 15	Sept. 1–Dec. 1.
Carrot	July 1–Aug. 15	Aug. 1–Sept. 1	Sept. 1–Nov. 1	Sept. 15–Dec. 1	Sept. 15–Dec. 1	Sept. 15–Dec. 1.
Cauliflower [1]	July 15–Aug. 15	Aug. 1–Sept. 1	Aug. 1–Sept. 15	Aug. 15–Oct. 10	Sept. 1–Oct. 20	Sept. 15–Nov. 1.
Celery [1] and celeriac	June 15–Aug. 15	July 1–Aug. 15	July 15–Sept. 1	Aug. 1–Dec. 1	Sept. 1–Dec. 31	Oct. 1–Dec. 31.
Chard	June 1–Sept. 10	June 1–Sept. 15	June 1–Oct. 1	June 1–Nov. 1	June 1–Dec. 1	June 1–Dec. 31.
Chervil and chives	(2)	(2)	Nov. 1–Dec. 31	Nov. 1–Dec. 31	Nov. 1–Dec. 31	Nov. 1–Dec. 31.
Chicory, witloof	July 1–Aug. 10	July 10–Aug. 20	July 20–Sept. 1	Aug. 15–Sept. 30	Aug. 15–Oct. 15	Aug. 15–Oct. 15.
Collards [1]	Aug. 1–Sept. 15	Aug. 15–Oct. 1	Aug. 25–Nov. 1	Sept. 1–Dec. 1	Sept. 1–Dec. 31	Sept. 1–Dec. 31.
Cornsalad	Sept. 15–Nov. 1	Oct. 1–Dec. 1	Oct. 1–Dec. 1	Oct. 1–Dec. 31	Oct. 1–Dec. 31	Oct. 1–Dec. 31.
Corn, sweet	June 1–Aug. 1	June 1–Aug. 15	June 1–Sept. 1			
Cress, upland	Sept. 15–Nov. 1	Oct. 1–Dec. 1	Oct. 1–Dec. 1	Oct. 1–Dec. 31	Oct. 1–Dec. 31	Oct. 1–Dec. 31.
Cucumber	June 1–Aug. 1	June 1–Aug. 15	June 1–Aug. 15	July 15–Sept. 15	Aug. 15–Oct. 1	Aug. 15–Oct. 1.
Eggplant [1]	June 1–July 1	June 1–July 15	June 1–Aug. 1	July 1–Sept. 1	Aug. 1–Sept. 30	Aug. 1–Sept. 30.
Endive	July 15–Aug. 15	Aug. 1–Sept. 1	Sept. 1–Oct. 1	Sept. 1–Nov. 15	Sept. 1–Dec. 31	Sept. 1–Dec. 31.
Fennel, Florence	July 1–Aug. 1	July 15–Aug. 15	Aug. 15–Sept. 15	Sept. 1–Nov. 15	Sept. 1–Dec. 1	Sept. 1–Dec. 1.
Garlic	(2)	Aug. 1–Oct. 1	Aug. 15–Oct. 1	Sept. 1–Nov. 15	Sept. 15–Nov. 15	Sept. 15–Nov. 15.
Horseradish [1]	(2)	(2)	(2)	(2)	(2)	(2)
Kale	July 15–Sept. 1	Aug. 1–Sept. 15	Aug. 15–Oct. 15	Sept. 1–Dec. 1	Sept. 1–Dec. 31	Sept. 1–Dec. 31.
Kohlrabi	Aug. 1–Sept. 1	Aug. 15–Sept. 15	Sept. 1–Oct. 15	Sept. 1–Dec. 1	Sept. 15–Dec. 31	Sept. 1–Dec. 31.
Leek	(2)	(2)	Sept. 1–Nov. 1	Sept. 1–Nov. 1	Sept. 1–Nov. 1	Sept. 15–Nov. 1
Lettuce, head [1]	Aug. 1–Sept. 15	Aug. 15–Oct. 15	Sept. 1–Nov. 1	Sept. 1–Nov. 1	Sept. 1–Dec. 31	Sept. 15–Dec. 31.
Lettuce, leaf	Aug. 15–Oct. 1	Aug. 25–Oct. 1	Sept. 1–Nov. 1	Sept. 1–Nov. 1	Sept. 15–Dec. 31	Sept. 15–Dec. 31.
Muskmelon	July 1–July 15	July 15–July 30				
Mustard	Aug. 15–Oct. 15	Aug. 15–Nov. 1	Sept. 1–Dec. 1	Sept. 1–Dec. 1	Sept. 1–Dec. 1	Sept. 15–Dec. 1.
Okra	June 1–Aug. 10	June 1–Aug. 20	June 1–Sept. 10	June 1–Sept. 20	Aug. 1–Oct. 1	Aug. 1–Oct. 1.
Onion [1]		Sept. 1–Oct. 15	Sept. 1–Nov. 1	Sept. 1–Nov. 1	Oct. 1–Dec. 31	Oct. 1–Dec. 31.
Onion, seed			Sept. 1–Nov. 1	Sept. 1–Nov. 1	Sept. 1–Nov. 1	Sept. 15–Nov. 1.
Onion, sets		Oct. 1–Dec. 1	Nov. 1–Dec. 31	Nov. 1–Dec. 31	Nov. 1–Dec. 31	Nov. 1–Dec. 31.
Parsley	Aug. 1–Sept. 15	Sept. 1–Nov. 15	Sept. 1–Dec. 31	Sept. 1–Dec. 31	Sept. 1–Dec. 31	Sept. 1–Dec. 31.
Parsnip	(2)	(2)	Aug. 1–Sept. 1	Sept. 1–Nov. 15	Sept. 1–Nov. 15	Sept. 1–Dec. 1.
Peas, garden	Aug. 1–Sept. 15	Sept. 1–Nov. 1	Oct. 1–Dec. 1	Oct. 1–Dec. 31	Oct. 1–Dec. 31	Oct. 1–Dec. 31.
Peas, black-eye	June 1–Aug. 1	June 15–Aug. 15	July 1–Sept. 1	July 1–Sept. 10	July 1–Sept. 20	July 1–Sept. 20.
Pepper [1]	June 1–July 20	June 1–Aug. 1	June 1–Aug. 15	June 15–Sept. 1	Aug. 15–Oct. 1	Aug. 15–Oct. 1.
Potato	July 20–Aug. 10	July 25–Aug. 20	Aug. 10–Sept. 15	Aug. 1–Sept. 15	Aug. 1–Sept. 15	Aug. 1–Sept. 15.
Radish	Aug. 15–Oct. 15	Sept. 1–Nov. 15	Sept. 1–Dec. 1	Sept. 1–Dec. 31	Aug. 1–Sept. 15	Oct. 1–Dec. 31.
Rhubarb [1]	Nov. 1–Dec. 1					
Rutabaga	July 15–Aug. 1	July 15–Aug. 1	Aug. 1–Sept. 1	Sept. 1–Nov. 15	Oct. 1–Nov. 15	Oct. 15–Nov. 15.
Salsify	June 1–July 10	June 15–July 20	July 15–Aug. 15	Aug. 15–Sept. 30	Aug. 15–Oct. 15	Sept. 1–Oct. 31.
Shallot	(2)	Aug. 1–Oct. 1	Aug. 15–Oct. 1	Aug. 15–Oct. 15	Sept. 15–Nov. 1	Sept. 15–Nov. 1.
Sorrel	Aug. 1–Sept. 15	Aug. 15–Oct. 1	Aug. 15–Oct. 15	Sept. 1–Nov. 15	Sept. 1–Dec. 15	Sept. 1–Dec. 31.
Soybean	June 1–July 15	June 1–July 25	June 1–July 30	June 1–July 30	June 1–July 30	June 1–July 30.
Spinach	Sept. 1–Oct. 1	Sept. 15–Nov. 1	Oct. 1–Dec. 1	Oct. 1–Dec. 31	Oct. 1–Dec. 31	Oct. 1–Dec. 31.
Spinach, New Zealand	June 1–Aug. 1	June 1–Aug. 15	June 1–Aug. 15			
Squash, summer	June 1–Aug. 1	June 1–Aug. 10	June 1–Aug. 20	June 1–Sept. 1	June 1–Sept. 15	June 1–Oct. 1.
Squash, winter	June 10–July 10	June 20–Aug. 20	July 1–Aug. 1	July 15–Aug. 15	Aug. 1–Sept. 1	Aug. 1–Sept. 1.
Sweetpotato	June 1–15	June 1–July 1	June 1–July 1	June 1–July 1	June 1–July 1	June 1–July 1.
Tomato	June 1–July 1	June 1–July 15	June 1–Aug. 1	Aug. 1–Sept. 1	Aug. 15–Oct. 1	Sept. 1–Nov. 1.
Turnip	Aug. 1–Sept. 15	Sept. 1–Oct. 15	Sept. 1–Nov. 15	Sept. 1–Nov. 15	Oct. 1–Dec. 1	Oct. 1–Dec. 31.
Watermelon	July 1–July 15	July 15–July 30				

[1] Plants.
[2] Generally spring-planted (table 4).

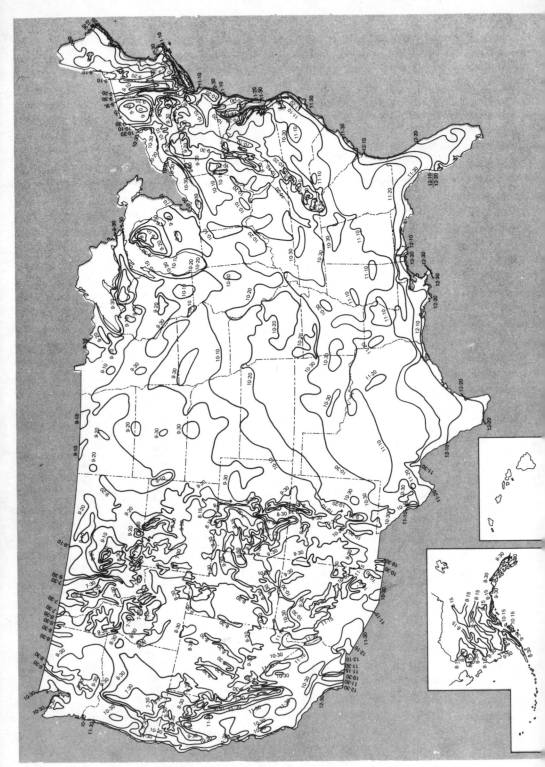

Average dates of the first killing frost in fall.

ple, and the severity of diseases and insects—often make success difficult, especially in the Southeast, although some other areas having the same frost dates are more favorable. A date about halfway between the two shown in table 5 will generally be best, although in most areas fair success can be expected within the entire range of dates shown.

Along the northern half of the Pacific coast, warm-weather crops should not be planted quite so late as the frost date and table would indicate. Although frost comes late, very cool weather prevails for some time before frost, retarding late growth of crops like sweet corn, lima beans, and tomatoes.

Caring for the Garden

Watering

In most areas the garden requires a moisture supply equivalent to about an inch of rain a week during the growing season for best plant growth. It requires roughly that amount of watering a week to maintain good production if the moisture stored in the soil becomes depleted and no rain falls over periods of weeks. An inch of rain is equivalent to about 28,000 gallons on an acre, or 900 gallons on a 30- by 50-foot garden.

It is much better to give the garden a good soaking about once a week than to water it sparingly more often. Light sprinklings at frequent intervals do little, if any, good. The best way to apply water, when the soil and slope are suitable, is to run it the length of furrows between the rows until the soil is well soaked. If the soil is very sandy or the surface too irregular for the furrow method, sprinklers or porous irrigating hose must be used.

Controlling Weeds

Weeds rob cultivated plants of water, nutrients, and light. Some weeds harbor diseases, insects, and nematodes that reinfest garden crops in succeeding years.

As soon as the soil can be properly worked after each rain or irrigation, it should be thoroughly hoed or cultivated to kill weeds that have sprouted and to leave the surface in a loose, friable condition to absorb later rainfall. The primary value of hoeing or cultivating is weed control. This cultivation should be shallow so as to avoid injuring the vegetable plant roots that lie near the surface. Although it is desirable to keep the surface soil loose, there is little to be gained by hoeing or cultivating oftener than necessary to keep weeds out of the garden.

In small gardens, weeds can be controlled with black polyethylene mulch supplemented by hand weeding such as pulling, hoeing, and wheel hoeing. Mulching vegetable crops with organic material also is a common practice in small gardens.

The best organic mulches are partially decomposed hay, straw, or grass clippings. The mulch should be applied 4 to 6 inches deep when the plants are about 6 inches tall. Cabbage, tomato, and other transplants usually are tall enough soon after they are set in the garden. Before applying mulch, hoe out all small weeds. Not only does mulch control weeds, it also conserves moisture, keeps the soil from packing, and increases the humus necessary for vigorous plant growth.

Controlling Diseases and Insects

Garden crops are subject to attack by a number of diseases and insects. Preventive measures are best, but if an attack occurs and the gardener is not familiar with the insect or disease and the proper treatment to protect his crop, he is advised to consult the county agent or write immediately to his experiment station. The United States Department of Agriculture and many of the States have publications containing the necessary information on garden diseases and insects, and these can be procured free upon request. Detailed information can be found in USDA Home and Garden Bulletin 46, Insects and Diseases of Vegetables in the Home Garden.

Among the most important disease-control measures are the use of disease-free seeds and plants, and the use of disease-resistant varieties. Great progress has been made within recent years in the development of varieties that are resistant to certain diseases.

Growing Specific Vegetables

Perennial Vegetables

The larger vegetable gardens need a number of perennials. Asparagus, horseradish, and rhubarb are the most important, but chives, bottom multiplier onions, and some of the flavoring and condiment plants, chiefly sage and mint, are also desirable. Unfortunately, asparagus, horseradish, and rhubarb are not adapted to conditions in the lower South.

All the perennial crops should be grouped together along one side of the garden, where they will not interfere with work on the annual crops.

Asparagus

Asparagus is among the earliest of spring vegetables. An area about 20 feet square, or a row 50 to 75 feet long, will supply plenty of fresh asparagus for a family of five or six persons, provided the soil is well enriched and the plants are given good attention. More must be planted if a supply is to be canned or frozen.

Asparagus does best where winters are cold enough to freeze the ground to a depth of a few inches at least. In many southern areas the plants make a weak growth, producing small shoots. Elevation has some effect, but, in general, the latitude of south-central Georgia is the southern limit of profitable culture.

The crop can be grown on almost any well-drained, fertile soil, and there is little possibility of having the soil too rich, especilly through the use of manure. Loosen the soil far down, either by subsoil plowing or by deep spading before planting. Throw the topsoil aside and spade manure, leafmold, rotten leaves, or peat into the subsoil to a depth of 14 to 16 inches; then mix from 5 to 10 pounds of a complete fertilizer into each 75-foot row or 20-foot bed.

When the soil is ready for planting, the bottom of the trench should be about 6 inches below the natural level of the soil. After the crowns are set and covered to a depth of a inch or two, gradually work the soil into the trench around the plants during the first season. When set in beds, asparagus plants should be at least 1½ feet apart each way; when set in rows, they should be about 1½ feet apart with the rows from 4 to 5 feet apart.

Asparagus plants, or crowns, are grown from seed. The use of 1-year-old

Asparagus shoots ready to be cut.

plants only is recommended. These should have a root spread of at least 15 inches, and larger ones are better. The home gardener will usually find it best to buy his plants from a grower who has a good strain of a recognized variety. Mary Washington and Waltham Washington are good varieties that have the added merit of being rust resistant. Waltham Washington is an improved strain of Mary Washington. It contains very little of the purple over-cast predominant in the Mary Washington, is a high yielder, and has good green color clear into the ground line. In procuring asparagus crowns, it is always well to be sure that they have not been allowed to dry out.

Clean cultivation encourages vigorous growth; it behooves the gardener to keep his asparagus clean from the start. In a large farm garden, with long rows, most of the work can be done with a horse-drawn cultivator or a garden tractor. In a small garden, where the rows are short or the asparagus is planted in beds, however, hand work is necessary.

For a 75-foot row, an application of manure and 6 to 8 pounds of a high-grade complete fertilizer, once each year, is recommended. Manure and fertilizer may be applied either before or after the cutting season.

Remove no shoots the year the plants are set in the permanent bed and keep the cutting period short the year after setting. Remove all shoots during the cutting season in subsequent years. Cease cutting about July 1 to 10 and let the tops grow. In the autumn, remove and burn the dead tops.

Asparagus rust and asparagus beetles are the chief enemies of the crop.

Horseradish

Horseradish is adapted to the north-temperate regions of the United States, but not to the South, except possibly in the high altitudes.

Any good soil, except possibly the lightest sands and heaviest clays, will grow horseradish, but it does best on a deep, rich, moist loam that is well supplied with organic matter. Avoid shallow soil; it produces rough, prongy roots. Mix organic matter with the soil a few months before the plants or cuttings are set. Some fertilizer may be used at the time of planting and more during the subsequent seasons. A top dressing of organic matter each spring is advisable.

Horseradish is propagated either by crowns or by root cuttings. In propagating by crowns a portion of an old plant consisting of a piece of root and crown buds is merely lifted and planted in a new place. Root cuttings are pieces of older roots 6 to 8 inches long and of the thickness of a lead pencil. They may be saved when preparing the larger roots for grating, or they may be purchased from seedsmen. A trench 4 or 5 inches deep is opened with a hoe and the root cuttings are placed at an angle with their tops near the surface of the ground. Plants from these cuttings usually make good roots the first year. As a rule, the plants in the home garden are allowed to grow from year to year, and portions of the roots are removed as needed. Pieces of roots and crowns remaining in the soil are usually sufficient to reestablish the plants.

There is very little choice in the matter of varieties of horseradish. Be sure, however, to obtain good healthy planting stock of a strain that is giving good results in the area where it is being grown. New Bohemian is perhaps the best known sort sold by American seedsmen.

Rhubarb

Rhubarb thrives best in regions having cool moist summers and winters cold enough to freeze the ground to a depth of several inches. It is not adapted to most parts of the South, but in certain areas of higher elevation it does fairly well. A few hills along the garden fence will supply all that a family can use.

Any deep, well-drained, fertile soil is suitable for rhubarb. Spade the soil or plow it to a depth of 12 to 16 inches and mix in rotted manure, leafmold, decayed hardwood leaves, sods, or other form of organic matter. The methods of soil preparation suggested for asparagus are suitable for rhubarb. As rhubarb is planted in hills 3 to 4 feet apart, however, it is usually sufficient to prepare each hill separately.

Rhubarb plants may be started from seed and transplanted, but seedlings vary from the parent plant. The usual method of starting the plants is to obtain pieces of crowns from established hills and set them in prepared hills. Top-dress the planting with a heavy application of organic matter in either early spring or late fall. Organic matter applied over the hills during early spring greatly hastens growth, or forces the plant.

A pound of complete commercial fertilizer high in nitrogen applied around each hill every year insures an abundant supply of plant food. The plants can be mulched with green grass or weeds.

Remove seedstalks as soon as they form. No leaf stems should be harvested before the second year and but few until the third. Moreover, the harvest season must be largely confined to early spring. The hills should be divided and reset every 7 or 8 years. Otherwise, they become too thick and produce only slender stems.

Crimson, Red Valentine, MacDonald, Canada Red, and Victoria are standard varieties. Use only the leafstalk as a food. **Rhubarb leaves contain injurious substances, including oxalic acid. Never use them for food.**

Sorrel

Sorrel is a perennial that is usually started from seeds. It requires a rich, mellow, well-drained soil. Rows may be of any convenient distance apart. Thin the plants to about 8 inches apart in the rows. If the leaves alone are gathered

Swiss chard is especially suitable for hot-weather culture.

and the plants are cultivated to prevent the growth of weeds, a planting should last 3 or 4 years. French Broad Leaf is a well-known variety.

Greens

Greens are usually the leaves and leaf stems of immature plants, which in their green state are boiled for food. Young, tender branches of certain plants, New Zealand spinach, for example, are also used this way. All the plants treated here as greens except New Zealand spinach are hardy vegetables, most of them adapted to fall sowing and winter culture over the entire South and in the more temperate parts of the North. Their culture may be extended more widely in the North by growing them with some protection, such as mulching or frames.

Chard

Chard, or Swiss chard, is a type of beet that has been developed for its tops instead of its roots. Crop after crop of the outer leaves may be harvested without injuring the plant. Only one planting is necessary, and a row 30 to 40 feet long will supply a family for the entire summer. Each seed cluster contains several seeds, and fairly wide spacing of the seeds facilitates thinning. The culture of chard is practically the same as that of beets, but the plants grow larger and need to be thinned to at least 6 inches apart in the row. Chard needs a rich, mellow soil, and it is sensitive to soil acidity.

Witloof Chicory

Witloof chicory, or French endive, is grown for both roots and tops. It is a hardy plant, not especially sensitive to heat or cold. It does, however, need a deep, rich, loamy soil without too much organic matter. The tops are sometimes harvested while young. The roots are lifted in autumn and placed in a box or bed of moist soil in a warm cellar for forcing. They must be covered with a few inches of sand. Under this covering the leaves form in a solid head, known on the market as witloof.

The culture of chicory is simple. Sow the seeds in spring or early summer in drills about 18 inches apart. Later, thin the plants to 6 or 8 inches apart in the rows. If sown too early the plants shoot to seed and are worthless for forcing. The kind known as witloof is most generally used.

Collards

Collards are grown and used about like cabbage. They withstand heat better than other members of the cabbage group, and are well liked in the South for both summer and winter use. Collards do not form a true head, but a large rosette of leaves, which may be blanched by tying together.

Cornsalad

Cornsalad is also known as lamb's-lettuce and fetticus. Sow the seed in early spring in drills and cultivate the plants the same as lettuce or mustard. For an extra early crop, plant the seed in the autumn and cover the plants lightly through the winter. In the Southern States the covering is not necessary, and the plants are ready for use in February and March. The leaves are frequently used in their natural green state, but they may be blanched by covering the rows with anything that will exclude light.

Kale

Kale, or borecole, is hardy and lives over winter in latitudes as far north as northern Maryland and southern Pennsylvania and in other areas where similar winter conditions prevail. It is also resistant to heat and may be grown in summer. Its real merit, however, is a cool-weather greens.

Kale is a member of the cabbage family. The best garden varieties are low-growing, spreading plants, with thick, more or less crinkled leaves. Vates Blue Curled, Dwarf Blue Scotch, and Siberian are well-known garden varieties.

No other plant is so well adapted to fall sowing throughout a wide area of both North and South or in areas characterized by winters of moderate severity. Kale may well follow some such early-season vegetable as green beans, potatoes, or peas.

In the autumn the seed may be broadcast very thinly and then lightly raked into the soil. Except for spring sowings, made when weeds are troublesome, sow kale in rows 18 to 24 inches apart and later thin the plants to about a foot apart.

Kale may be harvested either by cutting the entire plant or by taking the larger leaves while young. Old kale is tough and stringy.

Mustard

Mustard grows well on almost any good soil. As the plants require but a short time to reach the proper stage for use, frequent sowings are recommended. Sow the seeds thickly in drills as early as possible in the spring or, for late use, in September or October. The forms of Indian mustard, the leaves of which are often curled and frilled, are generally used. Southern Curled and Green Wave are common sorts.

Spinach

Spinach is a hardy cool-weather plant that withstands winter conditions in the South. In most of the North, spinach is primarily an early-spring and late-fall crop, but in some areas, where summer temperatures are mild, it may be grown continuously from early spring until late fall. It should be emphasized that summer and winter culture of spinach is possible only where moderate temperatures prevail.

Spinach will grow on almost any well-drained, fertile soil where sufficient moisture is available. It is very sensitive to acid soil. If a soil test shows the need, apply lime to the part of the garden used for spinach, regardless of the treatment given the rest of the area.

The application of 100 pounds of rotted manure and 3 to 4 pounds of commercial fertilizer to each 100 square feet of land is suitable for spinach in the home garden. Broadcast both manure and fertilizer and work them in before sowing the seed.

Long Standing Bloomsdale is perhaps the most popular variety seed in spring. It is attractive, grows quickly, is very productive, and will stand for a moderate length of time before going to seed. Virginia Savoy and Hybrid No. 7 are valuable varieties for fall planting, as they are resistant to yellows, or blight. Hybrid No. 7 is also resistant to downy mildew (blue mold). These two varieties are very cold-hardy but are not suitable for the spring crop, as they produce seedstalks too early. For horse or tractor cultivation, the rows of the garden should be not less than 24 inches apart; when land is plentiful they may be 30 inches apart. For wheel-hoe or hand work, the rows should be 14 to 16 inches apart. Spinach may be drilled by hand in furrows about 1 inch deep and covered with fine earth not more than ½ inch deep, or it may be drlled with a seed drill, which distributes the seed more evenly than is ordinarily possible by hand. Thin the plant to 3 or 4 inches apart before they crowd in the row.

New Zealand Spinach

New Zealand spinach is not related to common spinach. It is a large plant, with thick, succulent leaves and stems, and grows with a branching, spreading habit to a height of 2 or more feet. It thrives in hot weather and is grown as a substitute in seasons when ordinary spinach cannot withstand the heat. New Zealand spinach thrives on soils suitable for common spinach. Because of their larger size, these plants must have more room. The rows should be at least 3 feet apart, with the plants about 1½ feet apart in the rows. As prompt germination may be difficult, the seeds should be soaked for 1 or 2 hours in water at 120° F. before being planted. They may be sown, 1 to 1½ inches deep, as soon as danger of frost is past. Successive harvests of the tips may be made from a single planting, as new leaves and branches are readily produced. Care must be taken not to remove too large a portion of the plant at one time.

Turnip Greens

Varieties of turnips usually grown for the roots are also planted for the greens.

Shogoin is a favorable variety for greens. It is resistant to aphid damage and produces fine-quality white roots if allowed to grow. Seven Top is a leafy sort that produces no edible root. As a rule, sow turnips to be used for greens thickly and then thin them, leaving all but the greens to develop as a root crop. Turnip greens are especially adapted to winter and early-spring culture in the South. The cultural methods employed are the same as those for turnip and rutabaga.

Salad Vegetables

The group known as salad crops includes vegetables that are usually eaten raw with salt, pepper, vinegar, and salad oil, or with mayonnaise or other dressings. This classification is entirely one of convenience; some vegetables not included in this group are used in the same way. Some members of this class may be cooked and used as greens.

Celery

Celery can be grown in home gardens in most parts of the country at some time during the year. It is a cool-weather crop and adapted to winter culture in the lower South. In the upper South and in the North it may be grown either as an early-spring or as a late-fall crop. Farther north in certain favored locations it can be grown throughout the summer.

Rich, moist but well-drained, deeply prepared, mellow soil is essential for celery. Soil varying from sand to clay loam and to peat may be used as long as these requirements are met. Unless the ground is very fertile, plenty of organic material, supplemented by liberal applications of commercial fertilizer, is necessary. For a 100-foot row of celery, 5 pounds of a high-grade complete fertilizer thoroughly mixed with the soil are none too much. Prepare the celery row a week or two before setting the plants.

The most common mistake with celery is failure to allow enough time for growing the plants. About 10 weeks are needed to grow good celery plants. Celery seed is small and germinates slowly. A good method is to place the seeds in a muslin bag and soak them overnight, then mix them with dry sand, distribute them in shallow trenches in the seed flats or seedbed, and cover them with leafmold or similar material to a depth of not more than ½ inch. Keep the bed covered with moist burlap sacks. Celery plants are very delicate and must be kept free from weeds. They are made more stocky by being transplanted once before they are set in the garden, but this practice retards their growth. When they are to be transplanted before being set in the ground, the rows in the seed box or seedbed may be only a few inches apart. When they are to remain in the box until transplanted to the garden, however, the plants should be about 2 inches apart each way. In beds, the rows should be 10 to 12 inches apart, with seedlings 1 to 1½ inches apart in the row.

For hand culture celery plants are set in rows 18 to 24 inches apart; for tractor cultivation 30 to 36 inches apart. The plants are spaced about 6 inches in the row. Double rows are about a foot apart. Set celery on a cool or cloudy day, if possible; and if the soil is at all dry, water the plants thoroughly. If the plants are large, it is best to pinch off the outer leaves 3 or 4 inches from the base before setting. In bright weather it is well also to shade the plants for a day or two after they are set. Small branches bearing green leaves, stuck in the ground, protect the plants from intense sun without excluding air. As soon as the plants attain some size, gradually work the soil around them to keep them upright. Be careful to get no soil into the hearts of the plants. Early celery is blanched, by excluding the light with boards, paper, drain tiles, or other devices. Late celery may be blanched also by banking with earth or by storing in the dark. Banking celery with soil in warm weather causes it to decay.

Late celery may be kept for early-winter use by banking with earth and covering the tops with leaves or straw to keep them from freezing, or it may be dug and stored in a cellar or a coldframe, with the roots well embedded in moist soil. While in storage it must be kept as cool as possible without freezing.

For the home garden Golden Detroit, Summer Pascal (Waltham Improved), and the Golden Plume are adapted for the early crop to be used during late summer, fall, and early winter. For storage and for use after the holiday season, it is desirable to plant some such variety as Green Light or Utah 52-70.

Endive

Endive closely resembles lettuce in its requirements, except that it is less sensitive to heat. It may be substituted for lettuce when the culture of lettuce is impracticable. In the South, it is mainly a winter crop. In the North, it is grown in spring, summer, and autumn and is also forced in winter. Full Heart Batavian and Salad King are good varieties. Broadleaved endive is known on the markets as escarole.

Cultural details are the same as those for head lettuce. When the plants are large and well-formed, draw the leaves together and tie them so that the heart will blanch. For winter use, lift the plants with a ball of earth, place them in a cellar or coldframe where they will not freeze, and tie and blanch them as needed.

Lettuce

Lettuce can be grown in any home garden. It is a cool-weather crop, being as sensitive to heat as any vegetable grown. In the South, lettuce culture is confined to late fall, winter, and spring. In colder parts of the South, lettuce may not live through the winter. In the North, lettuce culture is partially limited to spring and autumn. In some favored locations, such as areas of high altitude or in far-northern latitudes, lettuce grows to perfection in summer. Planting at a wrong season is responsible for most of the failures with this crop.

Any rich soil is adapted to lettuce, although the plant is sensitive to acid soil. A commercial fertilizer with a heavy proportion of phosphorus is recommended.

Start spring lettuce indoors or in a hotbed and transplant it to the garden when the plants have four or five leaves. Gardeners need not wait for the end of light frosts, as lettuce is not usually harmed by a temperature as low as 28° F., if the plants have been properly hardened. Allow about 6 weeks for growing the plants. For the fall crop the seed may be sown directly in the row and thinned; there is no gain in transplanting.

For tractor cultivation, set lettuce plants 12 to 15 inches apart in rows 30 to 36 inches apart; for hand culture, about 14 to 16 inches apart each way. Where gardeners grow leaf lettuce or desire merely the leaves and not well-developed heads, the spacing in the rows may be much closer. In any case it is usually best to cut the entire plant instead of removing the leaves.

There are many excellent varieties of lettuce, all of which do well in the garden

Courtesy W. Atlee Burpee Co.

Butterhead Bibb lettuce has small heads and loosely folded leaves.

when conditions are right. Of the loose-leaf kinds, Black-Seeded Simpson, Grand Rapids, Slobolt, and Saladbowl are among the best. Saladbowl and Slobolt are heat resistant and very desirable for warm-weather culture. Of the heading sorts, Buttercrunch, White Boston, Fulton, and Great Lakes are among the best. The White Boston requires less time than the three others. Where warm weather comes early, it is seldom worthwhile to sow head lettuce seed in the open ground in the spring with the expectation of obtaining firm heads.

Parsley

Parsley is hardy to cold but sensitive to heat. It thrives under much the same temperature conditions as kale, lettuce, and spinach. If given a little protection it may be carried over winter through most of the North.

Parsley thrives on any good soil. As the plant is delicate during its early stages of growth, however, the land should be mellow.

Parsley seeds are small and germinate slowly. Soaking in water overnight hastens the germination. In the North, it is a good plan to sow the seeds indoors and transplant the plants to the garden, thereby getting a crop before hot weather. In the South, it is usually possible to sow the seed directly in drills. For the fall crop in the North, row seeding is also practiced. After seeding, it is well to lay a board over the row for a few days until the first seedlings appear. After its removal day-to-day watering will insure germination of as many seeds as possible. Parsley rows should be 14 to 16 inches apart, with the plants 4 to 6 inches apart in the rows. A few feet will supply the family, and a few plants transplanted to the coldframe in the autumn will give a supply during early spring.

Upland Cress

Upland cress, sometimes erroneously called peppergrass, is a hardy plant. It may be sown in all the milder parts of the country in autumn. In the colder sections it is sown in early spring as soon as the ground can be worked. The seeds are small and must not be covered deeply. After the plants are well established, thin them to 4 to 6 inches apart in the rows. This is a short-season crop that should be planted in quick succession to insure a steady supply.

Root Vegetables

Potatoes in the North and sweet potatoes in the South are grown in almost every garden. Beets, carrots, and turnips are also widely grown in gardens. The vegetables in this group may be used throughout the growing season and also be kept for winter.

Courtesy W. Atlee Burpee Co.

Golden beet is good in salads and pickled.

Beet

The beet is well adapted to all parts of the country. It is fairly tolerant of heat; it is also resistant to cold. However, it will not withstand severe freezing. In the Northern States, where winters are too severe, the beet is grown in spring, summer, and autumn.

Beets are sensitive to strongly acid soils, and it is wise to apply lime if a test shows the need for it. Good beet quality depends on quick growth; for this the land must be fertile, well-drained, and in good physical condition.

Midsummer heat and drought may interfere with seed germination. By covering the seeds with sandy soil, leafmold, or other material that will not bake and by keeping the soil damp until the plants are up, much of this trouble can be avoided. Make successive sowings at intervals of about 3 weeks in order to have a continuous supply of young, tender beets throughout the season.

Where cultivating is by hand, the rows may be about 16 inches apart; where it is by tractor, they must be wider. Beet seed as purchased consists of small balls, each containing several seeds. In most soils the seed should be covered to a depth of about an inch. After the plants are well established, thin them to stand 2 or 3 inches apart in the rows.

Early Wonder, Crosby Egyptian, and Detroit Dark Red are standard varieties suitable for early home-garden planting, while Long Season remains tender and edible over a long season.

Carrot

Carrots are usually grown in the fall, winter, and spring in the South, providing an almost continuous supply. In the North, carrots can be grown and used through the summer and the surplus stored for winter. Carrots will grow on almost any type of soil as long as it is moist, fertile, loose, and free from clods and stones, but sandy loams and peats are best. Use commercial fertilizer.

Because of their hardiness, carrots may be seeded as early in the spring as the ground can be worked. Succession plantings at intervals of 3 weeks will insure a continuous supply of tender carrots. Cover carrot seed about ½ inch on most soils; less, usually about ¼ inch, on heavy soils. With care in seeding, little thinning is necessary; carrots can stand some crowding, especially on loose soils. However, they should be no thicker than 10 to 15 plants per foot of row.

Chantenay, Nantes, and Imperator are standard sorts. Carrots should be stored before hard frosts occur, as the roots may be injured by cold.

Celeriac

Celeriac, or turnip-rooted celery, has been developed for the root instead of the top. Its culture is the same as that of celery, and the enlarged roots can be used at any time after they are big enough. The late-summer crop of celeriac may be stored for winter use. In areas having mild winters the roots may be left in the ground and covered with a mulch of several inches of straw or leaves, or they may be lifted, packed in moist sand, and stored in a cool cellar.

Chervil

Chervil comes in two distinct types, salad chervil and turnip-rooted chervil. Salad chervil is grown about like parsley. The seeds must be bedded in damp sand for a few weeks before being sown; otherwise, their germination is very slow.

Turnip-rooted chervil thrives in practically all parts of the country where the soil is fertile and the moisture sufficient. In the South, the seeds are usually sown in the fall, but they may not germinate until spring. In the North, the seeds may be sown in the autumn to germinate in the spring; or the plants may be started indoors in late winter and transplanted to open ground later on. The spacing and culture of chervil are about the same as for beets and carrots.

Dasheen

The dasheen, a large-growing plant, is related to the ordinary elephant's-ear and looks like it. It is a long-season crop, adapted for culture only in the.South, where there is normally a very warm frostless season of at least 7 months. It needs a rich loamy soil, an abundance of moisture with good drainage, and a fairly moist atmosphere. Small tubers—from 2 to 5 ounces in weight—are used for planting in much the same way as potatoes. Planting may be done 2 or 3 weeks before frosts are over, and the season may be lengthened by starting the plants indoors and setting them out after frost is past. Set the plants in 3½- to 4-foot rows, about 2 feet apart in the rows. Dasheen tubers may be dug and dried on the ground in much the same way as sweetpotatoes, and stored at 50° F. with ventilation.

Parsnip

The parsnip is adapted to culture over a wide portion of the United States. It must have warm soil and weather at planting time, but does not thrive in mid-summer in the South.

In many parts of the South parsnips are grown and used during early summer. They should not reach maturity during midsummer, however. Furthermore, it is difficult to obtain good germination in the summer, which limits their culture during the autumn.

Any deep, fertile soil will grow parsnips, but light, friable soil, with no tendency to bake, is best. Stony or lumpy soils are objectionable; they may cause rough, prongy roots.

Parsnip seed must be fresh—not more than a year old—and it is well to sow rather thickly and thin to about 3 inches apart. Parsnips germinate slowly, but it is possible to hasten germination by covering the seed with leafmold, sand, a mixture of sifted coal ashes and soil, peat, or some similar material that will not bake. Rolling a light soil over the row or trampling it firmly after seeding usually hastens and improves germination. Hollow Crown and All American are suitable varieties.

Parsnips may be dug and stored in a cellar or pit or left in the ground until used. Roots placed in cold storage gain in quality faster than those left in the ground, and freezing in the ground in winter improves the quality.

There is no basis for the belief that parsnips that remain in the ground over winter and start growth in the spring are poisonous. All reported cases of poisoning from eating so-called wild parsnips have been traced to water hemlock (*Cicuta*), which belongs to the same family and resembles the parsnip somewhat. **Be very careful in gathering wild plants that look like the parsnip.**

Potato

Potatoes, when grown under favorable conditions, are one of the most productive of all vegetables in terms of food per unit area of land.

Potatoes are a cool-season crop; they do not thrive in midsummer in the southern half of the country. Any mellow, fertile, well-drained soil is suitable for potato production. Stiff, heavy clay soils often produce misshapen tubers. Potatoes respond to a generous use of commercial fertilizer, but if the soil is too heavily limed, the tubers may be scabby.

Commercial 5-8-5 or 5-8-7 mixtures applied at 1,000 to 2,000 pounds to the acre (approximately 7½ to 15 pounds to each 100-foot row) usually provide enough plant food for a heavy crop. The lower rate of application is sufficient for very fertile soils; the higher rate for less fertile ones. Commercial fertilizer can be applied at the time of planting, but it should be mixed with the soil in such a way that the seed pieces will not come in direct contact with it.

In the North, plant two types of potatoes—one to provide early potatoes for summer use, the other for storage and winter use. Early varieties include Irish Cobbler, Early Gem, Norland, Norgold Russet, and Superior. Best late varieties are Katahdin, Kennebec, Chippewa, Russet Burbank, Sebago, and the golden nemotode resistant Wanseon. Irish Cobbler is the most widely adapted of the early varieties and Katahdin of the late. In the Great Plains States, Pontiac and Red La Soda are preferred for summer use; the Katahdin and Russet Burbank for winter. In the Pacific Northwest, the Russet Burbank, White Rose, Kennebec, and Early Gem are used. In the Southern States, the Irish Cobbler, Red La Soda, Red Pontiac, and Pungo are widely grown. The use of certified seed is always advisable.

In preparing seed potatoes for planting, cut them into blocky rather than wedge-shaped pieces. Each piece should be about 1½ ounces in weight and have at least one eye. Medium-sized tubers weighing 5 to 7 ounces are cut to best advantage.

Plant early potatoes as soon as weather and soil conditions permit. Fall preparation of the soil often makes it possible to plant the early crop without delay in late winter or early spring. Potatoes require 2 to 3 weeks to come up, depending on depth of planting and the temperature of the soil. In some sections the ground may freeze slightly, but this is seldom harmful unless the sprouts have emerged. Prolonged cold and wet weather after planting is likely to cause the seed pieces to rot. Hence, avoid too early planting. Young potato plants are often damaged by frost, but they usually renew their growth quickly from uninjured portions of the stems.

Do not dig potatoes intended for stoage until the tops are mature. Careful handling to avoid skinning is desirable, and protection from long exposure to light is necessary to prevent their becoming green and unfit for table use. Store in a well-ventilated place where the temperature is low, 45° to 50° if possible, but where there is no danger of freezing.

Radish

Radishes are hardy to cold, but they cannot withstand heat. In the South, they do well in autumn, winter, and spring. In the North, they may be grown in spring and autumn, and in sections having mild winters they may be grown in coldframes at that season. In high altitudes and in northern locations with cool summers, radishes thrive from early spring to late autumn.

Radishes are not sensitive to the type of soil so long as it is rich, moist, and friable. Apply additional fertilizer when the seeds are sown; conditions must be favorable for quick growth. Radishes that grow slowly have a pungent flavor and are undesirable.

Radishes mature the quickest of our garden crops. They remain in prime condition only a few days, which makes small plantings at week or 10-day intervals advisable. A few yards of row will supply all the radishes a family will consume during the time the radishes are at their best.

There are two types of radishes—the mild, small, quick-maturing sorts such as Scarlet Globe, French Breakfast, and Cherry Belle, all of which reach edible size in from 20 to 40 days; and the more pungent, large, winter radishes such as Long Black Spanish and China Rose, which require 75 days or more for growth. Plant winter radishes so they will reach a desirable size in the autumn. Gather and store them like other root crops.

Salsify

Salsify, or vegetable oyster, may be grown in practically all parts of the country. It is similar to parsnips in its requirements but needs a slightly longer growing season. For this reason it cannot be grown as far north as parsnips. Salsify, however, is somewhat more hardy and can be sown earlier in the spring.

Thoroughly prepare soil for salsify to a depth of at least a foot. Lighten heavy garden soil by adding sand or comparable material. Salsify must have plenty of plant food.

Sandwich Island is the best-known variety. A half ounce of seed will sow a 50-foot row, enough for most families. Always use fresh seed; salsify seed retains its vitality only 1 year.

Salsify may be left in the ground over winter or lifted and stored like parsnips or other root crops.

Sweetpotato

Sweetpotatoes succeed best in the South, but they are grown in home gardens as far north as southern New York and southern Michigan. They can be grown even farther north, in sections having especially mild climates, such as the Pacific Northwest. In general, sweetpotatoes may be grown wherever there is a frost-free period of about 150 days with relatively high temperature. Jersey Orange, Nugget, and Nemagold are the commonest dry-fleshed varieties; Centennial, Porto Rico, and Goldrush are three of the best of the moist type.

A well-drained, moderately deep sandy loam of medium fertility is best for sweetpotatoes. Heavy clays and very deep loose-textured soils encourage the formation of long stringy roots. For best results the soil should be moderately fertilized throughout. If applied under the rows, the fertilizer should be well mixed with the soil.

In most of the area over which sweetpotatoes are grown it is necessary to start the plants in a hotbed, because the season is too short to produce a good crop after the weather warms enough to start plants outdoors. Bed roots used for seed close together in a hotbed and cover them with about 2 inches of sand or fine soil, such as leafmold. It is not safe to set the plants in the open ground until the soil is warm and the weather settled. Toward the last, ventilate the hotbed freely to harden the plants.

The plants are usually set on top of ridges, 3½ to 4 feet apart, with the plants about 12 inches apart in the row. When the vines have covered the ground, no further cultivation is necessary, but some additional hand weeding may be required.

Dig sweetpotatoes a short time before frost, on a bright, drying day when the soil is not too wet to work easily. On a small scale they may be dug with a spading fork, great care being taken not to bruise or injure the roots. Let the roots lie exposed for 2 or 3 hours to dry thoroughly; then put them in containers and place them in a warm room to cure. The proper curing temperature is 85° F. Curing for about 10 days is followed by storage at 50° to 55°.

Turnip and Rutabaga

Turnips and rutabagas, similar cool-season vegetables, are among the most commonly grown and widely adapted root crops in the United States. They are grown in the South chiefly in the fall, winter, and spring; in the North, largely in the spring and autumn. Rutabagas do best in the more northerly areas; turnips are better for gardens south of the latitude of Indianapolis, Ind., or northern Virginia.

Turnips reach a good size in from 60 to 80 days, but rutabagas need about a month longer. Being susceptible to heat and hardy to cold, these crops should be planted as late as possible for fall use, allowing time for maturity before hard frost. In the South, turnips are very popular in the winter and spring. In the North, however, July to August seeding, following early potatoes, peas, or spinach, is the common practice.

Land that has been in a heavily fertilized crop, such as early potatoes, usually gives a good crop without additional fertilizing. The soil need not be prepared deeply, but the surface should be fine and smooth. For spring culture, row planting similar to that described for beets is the best practice. The importance of planting turnips as early as possible for the spring crop is emphasized. When seeding in rows, cover the seeds lightly; when broadcasting, rake the seeds in lightly with a garden rake. A half ounce of seed will sow a 300-foot row or broadcast 300 square feet. Turnips may be thinned as they grow, and the tops used for greens.

Although there are both white-fleshed and yellow-fleshed varieties of turnips and rutabagas, most turnips are white-fleshed and most rutabagas are yellow-fleshed. Purple Top White Globe and Just Right are the most popular white-fleshed varieties; Golden Ball (Orange Jelly) is the most popular yellow-fleshed variety. American Purple Top is the commonly grown yellow-fleshed rutabaga; Sweet German (White Swede, Sweet Russian) is the most widely used white-fleshed variety. For turnip greens, the Seven Top variety is most suitable. This winter-hardy variety overwinters in a majority of locations in the United States.

Turnip-Rooted Parsley

The root is the edible portion of turnip-rooted parsley. The flesh is whitish and dry, with much the same flavor as celeriac.

Turnip-rooted parsley requires the same climate, soil, and culture as parsley. It can withstand much cold, but is difficult to start in dry, hot weather. This vegetable may remain in the ground until after hard frosts. It may be lifted and stored like other root crops.

Vine Vegetables

The vine crops, including cucumbers, muskmelons, pumpkins, squashes, watermelons, and citrons, are similar in their cultural requirements. In importance to the home gardener they do not compare with some other groups, especially the root crops and the greens, but there is a place in most gardens for at least bush squashes and a few hills of cucumbers. They all make rank growth and require much space. In large gardens, muskmelons and watermelons are often desirable.

Burpee Hybrid cucumbers are highly disease resistant.

Cucumber

Cucumbers are a warm-weather crop. They may be grown during the warmer months over a wide portion of the country, but are not adapted to winter growing in any but a few of the most southerly locations. Moreover, the extreme heat of midsummer in some places is too severe, and there cucumber culture is limited to spring and autumn.

The cucumber demands an exceedingly fertile, mellow soil high in decomposed organic matter from the compost pile. Also, an additional application of organic matter and commercial fertilizer is advisable under the rows or hills. Be sure the organic matter contains no remains of any vine crops; they might carry injurious diseases. Three or four wheelbarrow loads of well-rotted organic matter and 5 pounds of commercial fertilizer to a 50-foot drill or each 10 hills are enough. Mix the organic matter and fertilizer well with the top 8 to 10 inches of soil.

For an early crop, the seed may be started in berry boxes or pots, or on sods in a hotbed, and moved to the garden after danger of late frost is past. During the early growth and in cool periods, cucumbers may be covered with plant protectors made of panes of glass with a top of cheesecloth, parchment paper, or muslin. A few hills will supply the needs of a family.

When the seed is planted in drills, the rows should be 6 or 7 feet apart, with the plants thinned to 2 to 3 feet apart in the rows. In the hill method of planting, the hills should be at least 6 feet apart each way, with the plants thinned to 2 in each hill. It is always wise to plant 8 or 10 seeds in each hill, thinned to the desired stand. Cover the seeds to a depth of about ½ inch. If the soil is inclined to bake, cover them with loose earth, such as a mixture of soil and coarse sand, or other material that will not harden and keep the plants from coming through.

When cucumbers are grown primarily for pickling, plant one of the special small-size pickling varieties, such as Chicago Pickling or National Pickling; if they are grown for slicing, plant such varieties as White Spine or Straight Eight. It is usually desirable to plant a few hills of each type; both types can be used for either purpose.

Cucumbers require almost constant vigilance to prevent destructive attacks by cucumber beetles. These insects not only eat the foliage but also spread cucumber wilt and other serious diseases.

Success in growing cucumbers depends largely on the control of diseases and insect pests that attack the crop.

Removal of the fruits before any hard seeds form materially lengthens the life of the plants and increases the size of the crop.

Gourd

Gourds have the same general habit of growth as pumpkins and squashes and should have the same general cultural treatment, except that most species require some form of support or trellis to climb upon.

Gourds are used in making dippers, spoons, ladles, salt and sugar containers, and many other kinds of household utensils. They are also used for birdhouses and the manufacture of calabash pipes. But they are of interest chiefly because of their ornamental and decorative possibilities. The thin-shelled, or hard-drying, gourds are the most durable and are the ones that most commonly serve as decorations. The thick-fleshed gourds are more in the nature of pumpkins and squashes, and are almost as perishable.

The thin-shelled gourds of the Lagenaria group are gathered and cured at the time the shells begin to harden, the fruits become lighter in weight, and the tendrils on the vines near the gourds begin to shrivel and dry. For best results, give the gourds plenty of time to cure. Some kinds require 6 months or a year to cure.

The thick-shelled gourds of the Cucurbita group are more difficult to cure than the thin-shelled ones. Their beauty is of short duration; they usually begin to fade after 3 or 4 months.

All types of gourds should be handled carefully. Bruises discolor them and cause them to soften and decay.

Muskmelon

The climatic, soil, and cultural requirements of muskmelons are about the same as for cucumbers, except that they are less tolerant of high humidity and rainy weather. They develop most perfectly on light-textured soils. The plants are vigorous growers, and need a somewhat wider spacing than cucumbers.

Hearts of Gold, Hale's Best, and Rocky Ford, the last-named a type not a variety, are usually grown in the home garden. Where powdery mildew is prevalent, resistant varieties such as Gulf Stream, Dulce, and Perlita are better adapted. Osage and Pride of Wisconsin (Queen of Colorado) are desirable home-garden sorts, particularly in the Northern States. Sweet Air (Knight) is a popular sort in the Maryland-Virginia area.

The Casaba and Honey Dew are well adapted only to the West, where they are grown under irrigation.

Pumpkin

Pumpkins are sensitive to both cold and heat. In the North, they cannot be planted until settled weather; in the South they do not thrive during midsummer.

The gardener is seldom justified in devoting any part of a limited garden area to pumpkins, because many other vegetables give greater returns from the same space. However, in gardens where there is plenty of room and where they can follow an early crop like potatoes, pumpkins can be grown to advantage.

The pumpkin is one of the few vegetables that thrives under partial shade. Therefore it may be grown among sweet corn or other tall plants. Small Sugar and Connecticut Field are well-known orange-yellow-skinned varieties. The Kentucky Field has a grayish-orange rind with salmon flesh. All are good-quality, productive varieties.

Hills of pumpkins, containing one to two plants, should be at least 10 feet apart each way. Pumpkin plants among corn, potato, or other plants usually should be spaced 8 to 10 feet apart in every third or fourth row.

Gather and store pumpkins before they are injured by hard frosts. They keep best in a well-ventilated place where the temperature is a little above 50° F.

Courtesy W. Atlee Burpee Co.

Golden Zucchini squash has a glossy yellow color.

Squash

Squashes are among the most commonly grown garden plants. They do well in practically all parts of the United States where the soil is fertile and moisture sufficient. Although sensitive to frost, squashes are more hardy then melons and cucumbers. In the warmest parts of the South they may be grown in winter. The use of well-rotted composted material thoroughly mixed with the soil is recommended.

There are two classes of squash varieties, summer and winter. The summer class includes the Bush Scallop, known in some places as the Cymling, the Summer Crookneck, Straightneck, and Zucchini. It also includes the vegetable marrows, of which the best known sort is Italian Vegetable Marrow (Cocozelle). All the summer squashes and the marrows must be used while young and tender, when the rind can be easily penetrated by the thumbnail. The winter squashes include varieties such as Hubbard, Delicious, Table Queen (Acorn), and Boston Marrow. They have hard rinds and are well adapted for storage.

Summer varieties, like yellow Straightneck, should be gathered before the seeds ripen or the rinds harden, but the winter sorts will not keep unless well-matured. They should be taken in before hard frosts and stored in a dry, moderately warm place, such as on shelves in a basement with a furnace. Under favorable conditions such varieties as Hubbard may be kept until midwinter.

Watermelon

Only gardeners with a great deal of space can afford to grow watermelons. Moreover, they are rather particular in their soil requirements, sand or sandy loam being best. Watermelon hills should be at least 8 feet apart. The plan of mixing a half wheelbarrow load of composted material with the soil in each hill is good, provided the compost is free from the remains of cucurbit plants that might carry diseases. A half pound of commercial fertilizer also should be thoroughly mixed with the soil in the hill. It is a good plan to place several seeds in a ring about 1 foot in diameter in each hill. Later the plants should be thinned to two to each hill.

New Hampshire Midget, Rhode Island Red, and Charleston Gray are suitable varieties for the home garden. New Hampshire Midget and Sugar Baby are small, extra early, widely grown, very productive varieties. The oval fruits are about 5 inches in diameter; they have crisp, red flesh and dark seeds. Rhode Island Red is an early variety. The fruits are medium in size, striped, and oval; they have a firm rind and bright pink-red flesh of choice quality. Charleston Gray is a large, long, high-quality, gray-green watermelon with excellent keeping and shipping qualities. It is resistant to anthracnose and fusarium wilt and requires a long growing season.

The preserving type of watermelon—citron—is not edible when raw. Its culture is the same as that for watermelon.

Legumes

Beans and peas are among our oldest and most important garden plants. The popularity of both is enhanced by their wide climatic and soil adaptation.

Tendercrop is a mosaic-resistant, heavy yielding snap bean with tender, round, green pods and a wide range of adaptability.

Beans

Green beans, both snap and lima, are more important than dry beans to the home gardener. Snap beans cannot be planted until the ground is thoroughly warm, but succession plantings may be made every 2 weeks from that time until 7 or 8 weeks before frost. In the lower South and Southwest, green beans may be grown during the fall, winter, and spring, but they are not well adapted to mid-summer. In the extreme South, beans are grown throughout the winter.

Green beans are adapted to a wide range of soils as long as the soils are well drained, reasonably fertile, and of such physical nature that they do not interfere with germination and emergence of the plants. Soil that has received a general application of manure and fertilizer should need no additional fertilization. When beans follow early crops that have been fertilized, the residue of this fertilizer is often sufficient for the beans.

On very heavy lands it is well to cover the planted row with sand, a mixture of sifted coal ashes and sand, peat, leafmold, or other material that will not bake. Bean seed should be covered not more than 1 inch in heavy soils and 1½ inches in sandy soils. When beans are planted in hills, they may be covered with plant protectors. These covers make it possible to plant somewhat earlier.

Tendercrop, Topcrop, Tenderette, Contender, Harvester, and Kinghorn Wax are good bush varieties of snap beans. Dwarf Horticultural is an outstanding green-shell bean. Brown-seeded or white-seeded Kentucky Wonders are the best pole varieties for snap pods. White Navy, or pea beans, white or red Kidney, and the horticultural types are excellent for dry-shell purposes.

Two types of lima beans, called butter beans in the South, are grown in home gardens. Most of the more northerly parts of the United States, including the northern New England States and the northern parts of other States along the Canadian border, are not adapted to the culture of lima beans. Lima beans need a growing season of about 4 months with relatively high temperature; they cannot be planted safely until somewhat later than snap beans. The small butter beans mature in a shorter period than the large-seeded lima beans. The use of plant protectors over the seeds is an aid in obtaining earliness.

Lima beans may be grown on almost any fertile, well-drained, mellow soil, but it is especially desirable that the soil be light-textured and not subject to baking, as the seedlings cannot force their way through a hard crust. Covering with some material that will not bake, as suggested for other beans, is a wise precaution when using heavy soils. Lima beans need a soil somewhat richer than is necessary for kidney beans, but the excessive use of fertilizer containing a high percentage of nitrogen should be avoided.

Both the small- and large-seeded lima beans are available in pole and bush varieties. In the South, the most commonly grown lima bean varieties are Jackson Wonder, Nemagreen, Henderson Bush, and Sieva pole; in the North, Thorogreen, Dixie Butterpea, and Thaxter are popular small-seeded bush varieties. Fordhook 242 is the most popular midseason large, thick-seeded bush lima bean. King of the Garden and Challenger are the most popular large-seeded pole lima bean varieties.

Pole beans of the kidney and lima types require some form of support, as they normally make vines several feet long. A 5-foot fence makes the best support for pole beans. A more complicated support can be prepared from 8-foot metal fence posts, spaced about 4 feet apart and connected horizontally and diagonally with coarse stout twine to make a trellis. Bean plants usually require some assistance to get started on these supports. Never cultivate or handle bean plants when they are wet; to do so is likely to spread disease.

English Peas

English peas are a cool-weather crop and should be planted early. In the lower South they are grown at all seasons except summer; farther north, in spring and autumn. In the Northern States and at high altitudes, they may be grown from spring until autumn, although in many places summer heat is too severe and the season is practically limited to spring. A few succession plantings may be made at 10-day intervals. The later plantings rarely yield as well as the earlier ones. Planting may be resumed as the cool weather of autumn approaches, but the yield is seldom as satisfactory as that from the spring planting.

Alaska and other smooth-seeded varieties are frequently used for planting in the early spring because of the supposition that they can germinate well in cold, wet soil. Thomas Laxton, Greater Progress, Little Marvel, Freezonia, and Giant Stride are recommended as suitable early varieties with wrinkled seeds. Wando

Fordhook 242 bush lima beans are vigorous, productive, and heat-resistant. Courtesy W. Atlee Burpee Co.

has considerable heat resistance. Alderman and Lincoln are approximately 2 weeks later than Greater Progress, but under favorable conditions yield heavily. Alderman is a desirable variety for growing on brush or a trellis. Peas grown on supports are less liable to destruction by birds.

Sugar Peas

Sugar peas (edible podded peas) possess the tenderness and fleshy podded qualities of snap beans and the flavor and sweetness of fresh English peas. When young, the pods are cooked like snap beans; the peas are not shelled. At this stage, pods are stringless, brittle, succulent, and free of fiber or parchment. However, if the pods develop too fast, they are not good to use like snap beans, but the seeds may be eaten as shelled peas and are of the best flavor before they have reached full size. Dwarf Gray Sugar is the earliest and dwarfest sugar pea. It is ideal for home gardens, especially where space is limited and seasons are short. A larger and later variety, Mammoth Melting Sugar, is resistant to fusarium wilt and requires support to climb upon.

Blackeye Peas

Blackeye peas, also known as cowpeas or Southern table peas, are highly nutritious, tasty, and easily grown. Do not plant until danger of frost has passed because they are very susceptible to cold. Leading varieties are Dixilee, Brown Crowder, Lady, Conch, White Acre, Louisiana Purchase, Texas Purple Hull 49, Knuckle Purple Hull, and Monarch Blackeye. Dixilee is a later variety of southern pea. Quality is excellent and it yields considerably more than such old standbys as blackeyes and crowders. It is also quite resistant, or at least tolerant, to nematodes. This fact alone makes it a desirable variety wherever this pest is present. Monarch Blackeye is a fairly new variety of the blackeye type and much better adapted to southern conditions.

Heavy applications of nitrogen fertilizer should not be used for southern peas. Fertilize moderately with a low-nitrogen analysis such as 4-12-12.

For the effort necessary to grow them, few if any other vegetables will pay higher dividends than Southern table peas.

Soybeans

The soil and cultural requirements and methods of growing soybeans are essentially the same as for bush forms of common beans. Soybeans, however, are slower growing then most garden beans, requiring 3 to 5 months for maturity, and warmer weather. They also are taller growing, the larger, later varieties requiring a greater distance between rows than dwarf snap beans. Small, early varieties may be planted in rows as close as 2 feet, but the larger, later ones require 3 feet between rows. The planting dates given in tables 4 and 5 are for midseason varieties (about 120 days), neither the earliest nor the latest kinds. Differences in time of development among varieties are so great that the gardener must choose the proper variety and know its time of maturity in making plans for planting in any particular locality. Kanrich and Giant Green are the most widely grown vegetables.

In cooler sections the rate of development will be slower. Only the early varieties should be grown in the more northerly States, and the medium or late varieties in the South. Plantings should be made principally when tomatoes and other long-season, warm-weather crops are put in the garden.

For use as a green vegetable, soybean pods should be harvested when the seeds are fully grown but before the pods turn yellow. Most varieties produce beans in usable condition over a period of a week to 10 days. The green beans are difficult to remove from the pods unless the pods are boiled or steamed 4 to 5 minutes, after which they are easily shelled.

The yields per unit area of land are about the same as usually obtained with peas and are thus less than can be obtained with many other vegetables. On this account, they appear of major interest only to gardeners having medium to large gardens.

Cabbage Group

The cabbage, or cole, group of vegetables is noteworthy because of its adaptation to culture in most parts of the country having fertile soil and sufficient moisture and because of its hardiness to cold.

Broccoli

Heading broccoli is difficult to grow, therefore, only sprouting broccoli is discussed here. Sprouting broccoli forms a loose flower head (on a tall, green, fleshy, branching stalk) instead of a compact head or curd found on cauliflower or heading broccoli. It is one of the newer vegetables in American gardens, but has been grown by Europeans for hundreds of years.

Sprouting broccoli with center head and side shoots.

Sprouting broccoli is adapted to winter culture in areas suitable for winter cabbage. It is also tolerant of heat. Spring-set plants in the latitude of Washington, D.C., have yielded good crops of sprouts until midsummer and later under conditions that caused cauliflower to fail. In the latitude of Norfolk, Va., the plant has yielded good crops of sprouts from December until spring.

Sprouting broccoli is grown in the same way as cabbage. Plants grown indoors in the early spring and set in the open about April 1 begin to yield sprouts about 10 weeks later. The fall crop may be handled in the same way as late cabbage, except that the seed is sown later. The sprouts carrying flower buds are cut about 6 inches long, and other sprouts arise in the axils of the leaves, so that a continuous harvest may be obtained. Green Comet, Calabrese, and Waltham 29 are among the best known varieties.

Brussels Sprouts

Brussels sprouts are somewhat more hardy than cabbage and will live outdoors over winter in all the milder sections of the country. They may be grown as a winter crop in the South and as early and late as cabbage in the North. The sprouts, or small heads, are formed in the axils (the angle between the leaf stem and the main stalk) of the leaves. As the heads begin to crowd, break the lower leaves from the stem of the plant to give them more room. Always leave the top leaves; the plant needs them to supply nourishment. For winter use in cold areas, take up the plants that are well laden with heads and set them close together in a pit, a coldframe, or a cellar, with some soil tamped around the roots. Keep the stored plants as cool as possible without freezing. Jade Cross, a true F hybrid, has a wide range of adaptability.

Cabbage

Cabbage ranks as one of the most important home-garden crops. In the lower South, it can be grown in all seasons except summer, and in latitudes as far

Earliana cabbage gives a small, uniform compact head ready in 60 days.

north as Washington, D.C., it is frequently set in the autumn, as its extreme hardiness enables it to live over winter at relatively low temperatures and thus become one of the first spring garden crops. Farther north, it can be grown as an early summer crop and as a late fall crop for storage. Cabbage can be grown throughout practically the entire United States.

Cabbage is adapted to widely different soils as long as they are fertile, of good texture, and moist. It is a heavy feeder; no vegetable responds better to favorable growing conditions. Quality in cabbage is closely associated with quick growth. Both compost and commercial fertilizer should be liberally used. In addition to the applications made at planting time, a side dressing or two of nitrate of soda, sulfate of ammonia, or other quickly available nitrogenous fertilizer is advisable. These may be applied sparingly to the soil around the plants at intervals of 3 weeks, not more than 1 pound being used to each 200 square feet of space, or, in terms of single plants, 1/3 ounce to each plant. For late cabbage the supplemental feeding with nitrates may be omitted. Good seed is especially important. Only a few seed is needed for starting enough plants for the home garden, as 2 or 3 dozen heads of early cabbage are as many as the average family can use. Early Jersey Wakefield and Golden Acre are standard early sorts. Copenhagen Market and Globe are excellent midseason kinds. Flat Dutch and Danish Ballhead are largely used for late planting.

Where cabbage yellows is a serious disease, resistant varieties should be used. The following are a few of the wilt-resistant varieties adapted to different seasons: Wisconsin Hollander, for late storage; Wisconsin All Seasons, a kraut cabbage, somewhat earlier; Marion Market and Globe, round-head cabbages, for midseason; and Stonehead for an early, small, round-head variety.

Cabbage plants for spring setting in the North may be grown in hotbeds or greenhouses from seeding made a month to 6 weeks before planting time, or may be purchased from southern growers who produce them outdoors in winter.

Chinese cabbage is a desirable autumn crop in the Northern States.

The winter-grown, hardened plants, sometimes referred to as frostproof, are hardier than hotbed plants and may be set outdoors in most parts of the North as soon as the ground can be worked in the spring. Northern gardeners can have cabbage from their gardens much earlier by using healthy southern-grown plants or well-hardened, well-grown hotbed or greenhouse plants. Late cabbage, prized by northern gardeners for fall use and for storage, is grown from plants produced in open seedbeds from sowings made about a month ahead of planting. Late cabbage may well follow early potatoes, peas, beets, spinach, or other early crop. Many gardeners set cabbage plants between potato rows before the potatoes are ready to dig, thereby gaining time. In protected places, or when plant protectors are used, it is possible always to advance dates somewhat, especially if the plants are well hardened.

Chinese Cabbage

Chinese cabbage is more closely related to mustard than to cabbage. It is variously called Crispy Choy, Chihili, Michili, and Wong Bok. Also, it is popularly known as celery cabbage, although it is unrelated to celery. The non-heading types deserve greater attention.

Chinese cabbage seems to do best as an autumn crop in the northern tier of States. When fullgrown, it is an attractive vegetable. It is not especially successful as a spring crop, and gardeners are advised not to try to grow it at any season other than fall in the North or in the winter in the South.

The plant demands a very rich, well-drained but moist soil. The seeds may be sown and the plants transplanted to the garden, or the seed may be drilled in the garden rows and the plants thinned to the desired stand.

Cauliflower

Cauliflower is a hardy vegetable but it will not withstand as much frost as cabbage. Too much warm weather keeps cauliflower from heading. In the South, its culture is limited to fall, winter, and spring; in the North, to spring and fall. However, in some areas of high altitude and when conditions are otherwise favorable, cauliflower culture is continuous throughout the summer.

A good head of cauliflower on a plant mulched with hay.

Cauliflower is grown on all types of land from sands to clay and peats. Although the physical character is unimportant, the land must be fertile and well drained. Manure and commercial fertilizer are essential.

The time required for growing cauliflower plants is the same as for cabbage. In the North, the main cause of failure with cauliflower in the spring is delay in sowing the seed and setting the plants. The fall crop must be planted at such a time that it will come to the heading stage in cool weather. Snowball and Purple Head are standard varieties of cauliflower. Snow King is an extremely early variety with fair sized, compact heads of good quality; it has very short stems. Always take care to obtain a good strain of seed; poor cauliflower seed is most objectionable. The Purple Head variety, well adapted for the home garden, turns green when cooked.

A necessary precaution in cauliflower culture with all varieties, except Purple Head, is to tie the leaves together when the heads, or buttons, begin to form. This keeps the heads white. Cauliflower does not keep long after the heads form; 1 or 2 dozen heads are enough for the average garden in the season.

Kohlrabi

Kohlrabi is grown for its swollen stem. In the North, the early crop may be started like cabbage and transplanted to the garden, but usually it is sown in place. In the South, kohlrabi may be grown almost any time except midsummer. The seeds may be started indoors and the plants transplanted in the garden; or the seeds may be drilled in the garden rows and the plants thinned to the desired stand. Kohlrabi has about the same soil and cultural requirements as cabbage, principally a fertile soil and enough moisture. It should be harvested while young and tender. Standard varieties are Purple Vienna and White Vienna.

Onion Group

Practically all members of the onion group are adapted to a wide variety of soils. Some of them can be grown at one time of the year or another in any part of the country that has fertile soil and ample moisture. They require but little garden space to produce enough for a family's needs.

A pot of chives grown in a kitchen window.

Chives

Chives are small onionlike plants that will grow in any place where onions do well. They are frequently planted as a border, but are equally well adapted to culture in rows. Being a perennial, chives should be planted where they can be left for more than one season.

Chives may be started from either seed or clumps of bulbs. Once established, some of the bulbs can be lifted and moved to a new spot. When left in the same place for several years the plants become too thick; occasionally dividing and resetting is desirable.

Garlic

Garlic is more exacting in its cultural requirements than are onions, but it may be grown with a fair degree of success in almost any home garden where good results are obtained with onions.

Garlic is propagated by planting the small cloves, or bulbs, which make up the large bulbs. Each large bulb contains about 10 small ones. Carefully separate the small bulbs and plant them singly.

The culture of garlic is practically the same as that of onions. When mature the bulbs are pulled, dried, and braided into strings or tied in bunches, which are hung in a cool, well-ventilated place.

In the South, where the crop matures early, care must be taken to keep the garlic in a cool, dry place; otherwise it spoils. In the North, where the crop matures later in the season, storage is not so difficult, but care must be taken to prevent freezing.

Leeks are used for almost any purpose that onions are used for.

Leek

The leek resembles the onion in its adaptability and cultural requirements. Instead of forming a bulb it produces a thick, fleshy cylinder like a large green onion. Leeks are started from seeds, like onions. Usually the seeds are sown in a shallow trench, so that the plants can be more easily hilled up as growth proceeds. Leeks are ready for use any time after they reach the right size. Under favorable conditions they grow to 1½ inches or more in diameter, with white parts 6 to 8 inches long. They may be lifted in the autumn and stored like celery in a coldframe or a cellar.

Onion

Onions thrive under a wide variety of climatic and soil conditions, but do best with an abundance of moisture and a temperate climate, without extremes of heat or cold through the growing season. In the South, the onion thrives in the fall, winter, and spring. Farther north, winter temperatures may be too severe for certain types. In the North, onions are primarily a spring, summer, and fall crop.

Any type of soil will grow onions, but is must be fertile, moist, and in the highest state of tilth. Both compost and commercial fertilizer, especially one high in phosphorus and potash, should be applied to the onion plot. A pound of compost to each square foot of ground and 4 or 5 pounds of fertilizer to each 100 square feet are about right. The soil should be very fine and free from clods and foreign matter.

Onions may be started in the home garden by the use of sets, seedlings, or seeds. Sets, or small dry onions grown the previous year—preferably not more than ¾ inch in diameter—are usually employed by home gardeners. Small green plants grown in an outdoor seedbed in the South or in a hotbed or a greenhouse are also in general use. The home-garden culture of onions from seed is satisfactory in the North where the summers are comparatively cool.

Sets and seedlings cost about the same; seeds cost much less. In certainty of results the seedlings are best; practically none form seedstalks. Seed-sown onions are uncertain unless conditions are extremely favorable.

Several distinct types of onions may be grown. The Potato (Multiplier) and Top (Tree) onions are planted in the fall or early spring for use green. Yellow Bermuda, Granex, and White Granex are large, very mild, flat onions for spring harvest in the South; they have short storage life. Sweet Spanish and the hybrids Golden Beauty, Fiesta, Bronze, Perfection, El Capitan are large, mild, globular onions suited for growing in the middle latitudes of the country; they store moderately well. Southport White Globe, Southport Yellow Globe, Ebenezer, Early Yellow Globe, Yellow Globe Danvers, and the hybrid Abundance are all firm-fleshed, long-storage onions for growing as a "main crop" in the Northeast and Midwest. Early Harvest is an early F_1 hybrid adapted to all northern regions of the United States. Varieties that produce bulbs may also be used green.

Shallot

The shallot is a small onion of the Multiplier type. Its bulbs have a more delicate flavor than most onions. Its growth requirements are about the same as those of most other onions. Shallots seldom form seed and are propagated by means of the small cloves or divisions, into which the plant splits during growth. The plant is hardy and may be left in the ground from year to year, but best results are had by lifting the clusters of bulbs at the end of the growing season and replanting the smaller ones at the desired time.

Fleshy-Fruited Vegetables

The fleshy-fruited, warm-season vegetables, of which the tomato is the most important, are closely related and have about the same cultural requirements. All must have warm weather and fertile, well-drained soil for good results.

Courtesy W. Atlee Burpee Co.

Early Beauty hybrid eggplant has a dark purple color.

Eggplant

Eggplant is extremely sensitive to the conditions under which it is grown. A warm-weather plant, it demands a growing season of from 100 to 140 days with high average day and night temperatures. The soil, also, must be well warmed up before eggplant can safely be set outdoors.

In the South, eggplants are grown in spring and autumn; in the North, only in summer. The more northerly areas, where a short growing season and low summer temperatures prevail, are generally unsuitable for eggplants. In very fertile garden soil, which is best for eggplant, a few plants will yield a large number of fruits.

Sow eggplant seeds in a hotbed or greenhouse, or, in warm areas, outdoors about 8 weeks before the plants are to be transplanted. It is important that the plants be kept growing without check from low or drying temperatures or other causes. They may be transplanted like tomatoes. Good plants have stems that are not hard or woody; one with a woody stem rarely develops satisfactorily. Black Beauty, Early Beauty Hybrid, and Jersey King Hybrid are good varieties.

Courtesy W. Atlee Burpee Co.

California Wonder variety of pepper.

Pepper

Peppers are more exacting than tomatoes in their requirements, but may be grown over a wide range in the United States. Being hot-weather plants, peppers cannot be planted in the North until the soil has warmed up and all danger of frost is over. In the South, planting dates vary with the location, fall planting being practiced in some locations. Start pepper plants 6 to 8 weeks before needed. The seeds and plants require a somewhat higher temperature than those of the tomato. Otherwise they are handled in exactly the same way.

Hot peppers are represented by such varieties as Red Chili and Long Red

104 **GROWING AND PRESERVING ...**

The VF hybrid tomato is verticillium and fusarium wilt resistant.

Cayenne; the mild-flavored by Penn Wonder, Ruby King, World-beater, California Wonder, and Yale Wonder, which mature in the order given.

Tomato

Tomatoes grow under a wide variety of conditions and require only a relatively small space for a large production. Of tropical American origin, the tomato does not thrive in very cool weather. It will, however, grow in winter in home gardens in the extreme South. Over most of the upper South and the North, it is suited to spring, summer, and autumn culture. In the more northern areas, the growing season is likely to be too short for heavy yields, and it is often desirable to increase earliness and the length of the growing season by starting the plants indoors. By adopting a few precautions, the home gardener can grow tomatoes practically everywhere, given fertile soil with sufficient moisture.

A liberal application of compost and commercial fertilizer in preparing the soil should be sufficient for tomatoes under most conditions. Heavy applications of fertilizer should be broadcast, not applied in the row; but small quantities may be mixed with the soil in the row in preparing for planting.

Start early tomato plants from 5 to 7 weeks before they are to be transplanted to the garden. Enough plants for the home garden may be started in a window box and transplanted to small pots, paper drinking cups with the bottoms removed, plant bands (round or square), or other soil containers. In boxes, the seedlings are spaced 2 to 3 inches apart. Tomato seeds germinate best at about 70° F., or ordinary house temperature. Growing tomato seedlings, after the first transplanting, at moderate temperatures, with plenty of ventilation, as in a cold-

TABLE 6.—*Tomato varieties for areas other than the Southwest*

Variety	Area
Ace	West
Atkinson	South
C17	East, Midwest
Fireball VF	East, North
Floradel	South
R1350	East, Midwest
Homestead–24	South
Manalucie	South
Marion	South
Morton Hybrid	North, East
Moscow VR	West
Small Fry	All areas
Spring Giant	East, Midwest
Supermarket	South
Supersonic	East, Midwest
Tropi-Gro	South
VFW-8	West

frame, gives stocky, hardy growth. If desired, the plants may be transplanted again to larger containers, such as 4-inch clay pots or quart cans with holes in the bottom.

Tomato plants for all but the early spring crop are usually grown in outdoor seedbeds. Thin seeding and careful weed control will give strong, stocky plants for transplanting. A list of tomato varieties for home garden use in areas other than the Southwest is given in table 6.

In the Southwest, Pearson, Early Pack No. 7, VF 36, California 145, VF 13L, and Ace are grown.

Tomatoes are sensitive to cold. Never plant them until danger of frost is past. By using plant protectors during cool periods the home gardener can set tomato plants somewhat earlier than would otherwise be possible. Hot, dry weather, like mid-summer weather in the South is also unfavorable for planting tomatoes. Planting distances depend on the variety and on whether the plants are to be pruned and staked or not. If pruned to one stem, trained, and tied to stakes or a trellis, they may be set 18 inches apart in 3-foot rows; if not, they may be planted 3 feet apart in rows 4 to 5 feet apart. Pruning and staking have many advantages for the home gardener. Cultivation is easier, and the fruits are always clean and easy to find. Staked and pruned tomatoes are, however, more subject to losses from blossom-end rot than those allowed to grow naturally.

Miscellaneous Vegetables

Florence Fennel

Florence fennel is related to celery and celeriac. Its enlarged, flattened leafstalk is the portion used. For a summer crop, sow the seeds in the rows in spring; for an autumn and winter crop in the South, sow them toward the end of the summer. Thin the plants to stand about 6 inches apart. When the leafstalks have grown to about 2 inches in diameter the plants may be slightly mounded up and partially blanched. They should be harvested and used before they become tough and stringy.

Okra

Okra, or gumbo, has about the same degree of hardiness as cucumbers and tomatoes and may be grown under the same conditions. It thrives on any fertile, well-drained soil. An abundance of quickly available plant food will stimulate growth and insure a good yield of tender, high-quality pods.

As okra is a warm-weather vegetable, the seeds should not be sown until the soil is warm. The rows should be from 3 to 3½ feet apart, depending on whether the variety is dwarf or large growing. Sow the seeds every few inches and thin the plants to stand 18 inches to 2 feet apart in the rows. Clemson Spineless, Emerald, and Dwarf Green are good varieties. The pods should be picked young and tender, and none allowed to ripen. Old pods are unfit for use and soon exhaust the plant.

Physalis

Physalis known also as groundcherry and husk tomato, is closely related to the tomato and can be grown wherever tomatoes do well. The kind ordinarlly grown in gardens produces a yellow fruit about the size of a cherry. The seeds may be started indoors or sown in rows in the garden.

Sweet Corn

Sweet corn requires plenty of space and is adapted only to the larger gardens. Although a warm-weather plant, it may be grown in practically all parts of the United States. It needs a fertile, well-drained, moist soil. With these requirements met, the type of the soil does not seem to be especially important, but a clay loam is almost ideal for sweet corn.

In the South, sweet corn is planted from early spring until autumn, but the corn earworm, drought, and heat make it difficult to obtain worthwhile results in midsummer. The ears pass the edible stage very quickly, and succession plantings are necessary to insure a constant supply. In the North, sweet corn cannot be safely planted until the ground has thoroughly warmed up. Here, too, succession plantings need to be made to insure a steady supply. Sweet corn is frequently planted to good advantage after early potatoes, peas, beets, lettuce, or other early, short-season crops. Sometimes, to gain time, it may be planted before the early crop is removed.

Sweet corn may be grown in either hills or drills, in rows at least 3 feet apart. It is well to plant the seed rather thickly and thin to single stalks 14 to 16 inches apart or three plants to each 3-foot hill. Experiments have shown that in the eastern part of the country there is no advantage in removing suckers from sweet corn. Cultivation sufficient to control weeds is all that is needed.

Hybrid sweet corn varieties, both white and yellow, are usually more productive than the open-pollinated sorts. As a rule, they need a more fertile soil and heavier feeding. They should be fertilized with 5-10-5 fertilizer about every 3 weeks until they start to silk. Many are resistant to disease, particularly bacterial wilt. Never save seed from a hybrid crop for planting. Such seed does not come true to the form of the plants from which it was harvested.

Good yellow-grained hybrids, in the order of the time required to reach edible maturity, are Span-cross, Marcross, Golden Beauty, Golden Cross Bantam, and Ioana. White-grained hybrids are Evergreen and Country Gentleman.

Early Sunglow hybrid corn.

Well-known open-pollinated yellow sorts are Golden Bantam and Golden Midget. Open-pollinated white sorts, in the order of maturity, are Early Evergreen, Country Gentleman, and Stowell Evergreen.

Home Canning of
Fruits and Vegetables

Organisms that cause food spoilage—molds, yeasts, and bacteria—are always present in the air, water, and soil. Enzymes that may cause undesirable changes in flavor, color, and texture are present in raw fruits and vegetables.

When you can fruits and vegetables you heat them hot enough and long enough to destroy spoilage organisms. This heating (or processing) also stops the action of enzymes. Processing is done in either a boiling-water-bath canner or a steam-pressure canner. The kind of canner that should be used depends on the kind of food being canned.

Right Canner for Each Food

For fruits, tomatoes, and pickled vegetables, use a boiling-water-bath canner. You can process these acid foods safely in boiling water.

For all common vegetables except tomatoes, use a steam-pressure canner. To process these low-acid foods safely in a reasonable length of time takes a temperature higher than that of boiling water.

A pressure saucepan equipped with an accurate indicator or gage for controlling pressure at 10 pounds (240° F.) may be used as a steam-pressure canner for vegetables in pint jars or No. 2 tin cans. If you use a pressure saucepan, add 20 minutes to the processing times given in this publication for each vegetable.

Getting Your Equipment Ready

Steam-Pressure Canner

For safe operation of your canner, clean petcock and safety-valve openings by drawing a string or narrow strip of cloth through them. Do this at beginning of canning season and often during the season.

Check pressure gage.—An accurate pressure gage is necessary to get the processing temperatures needed to make food keep.

A weighted gage needs to be thoroughly clean.

A dial gage, old or new, should be checked before the canning season, and also during the season if you use the canner often. Ask your county home demonstration agent, dealer, or manufacturer about checking it.

If your gage is off 5 pounds or more, you'd better get a new one. But if the gage is not more than 4 pounds off, you can correct for it as shown below. As a reminder, tie on the canner a tag stating the reading to use to get the correct pressure.

The food is to be processed at 10 pounds steam pressure; so—

If the gage reads high—	If the gage reads low—
1 pound high—process at 11 pounds.	1 pound low—process at 9 pounds.
2 pounds high—process at 12 pounds.	2 pounds low—process at 8 pounds.
3 pounds high—process at 13 pounds.	3 pounds low—process at 7 pounds.
4 pounds high—process at 14 pounds.	4 pounds low—process at 6 pounds.

Have canner thoroughly clean.—Wash canner kettle well if you have not used it for some time. Don't put cover in water—wipe it with a soapy cloth, then with a damp, clean cloth. Dry well.

Water-Bath Canner

Water-bath canners are available on the market. Any big metal container may be used as a boiling-water-bath canner if it is deep enough so that the water is well over tops of jars and has space to boil freely. Allow 2 to 4 inches above jar tops for brisk boiling (see sketch). The canner must have a tight-fitting cover and a wire or wooden rack. If the rack has dividers, jars will not touch each other or fall against the sides of the canner during processing.

If a steam-pressure canner is deep enough, you can use it for a water bath. Cover, but do not fasten. Leave petcock wide open, so that steam escapes and pressure does not build up inside the canner.

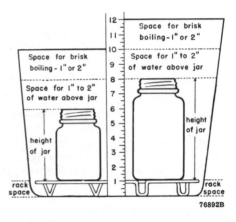

76892B

Glass Jars

Be sure all jars and closures are perfect. Discard any with cracks, chips, dents, or rust; defects prevent airtight seals.

Select the size of closure—widemouth or regular—that fits your jars.

Wash glass jars in hot, soapy water and rinse well. Wash and rinse all lids and bands. Metal lids with sealing compound may need boiling or holding in boiling water for a few minutes—follow the manufacturer's directions.

If you use rubber rings, have clean, new rings of the right size for the jars. Don't test by stretching. Wash rings in hot, soapy water. Rinse well.

Tin Cans

Select desired type and size.—Three types of tin cans are used in home canning—plain tin, C-enamel (corn enamel), and R-enamel (sanitary or standard enamel). For most products plain tin cans are satisfactory. Enameled cans are recommended for certain fruits and vegetables to prevent discoloration of food, but they are not necessary for a wholesome product.

The types of cans and the foods for which they are recommended are:

Type	Recommended for—
C-enamel	Corn, hominy.
R-enamel	Beets, red berries, red or black cherries, plums, pumpkin, rhubarb, winter squash.
Plain	All other fruits and vegetables for which canning directions are given in this bulletin.

In this bulletin, directions are given for canning most fruits and vegetables in No. 2 and No. 2½ tin cans. A No. 2 can holds about 2½ cups, and a No. 2½ can about 3½ cups.

Use only cans in good condition.—See that cans, lids, and gaskets are perfect. Discard badly bent, dented, or rusted cans, and lids with damaged gaskets. Keep lids in paper packing until ready to use. The paper protects the lids from dirt and moisture.

Wash cans.—Just before use, wash cans in clean water; drain upside down. Do not wash lids; washing may damage the gaskets. If lids are dusty or dirty, rinse with clean water or wipe with a damp cloth just before you put them on the cans.

Check the sealer.—Make sure the sealer you use is properly adjusted. To test, put a little water into a can, seal it, then submerge can in boiling water for a few seconds. If air bubbles rise from around the can, the seam is not tight. Adjust sealer, following manufacturer's directions.

76627B

A can sealer is needed if tin cans are used.

General Canning Procedure

Selecting Fruits and Vegetables for Canning

Choose fresh, firm fruits and young, tender vegetables. Can them before they lose their freshness. If you must hold them, keep them in a cool, airy place. If you buy fruits and vegetables to can, try to get them from a nearby garden or orchard.

For best quality in the canned product, use only perfect fruits and vegetables. Sort them for size and ripeness; they cook more evenly that way.

Washing

Wash all fruits and vegetables thoroughly, whether or not they are to be pared. Dirt contains some of the bacteria hardest to kill. Wash small lots at a time, under running water or through several changes of water. Lift the food out of the water each time so dirt that has been washed off won't go back on the food. Rinse pan thoroughly between washings. Don't let fruits or vegetables soak; they may lose flavor and food value. Handle them gently to avoid bruising.

Filling Containers

Raw pack or hot pack.—Fruits and vegetables may be packed raw into glass jars or tin cans or preheated and packed hot. In this publication directions for both raw and hot packs are given for most of the foods.

Most raw fruits and vegetables should be packed tightly into the container because they shrink during processing; a few—like corn, lima beans, and peas—should be packed loosely because they expand.

Hot food should be packed fairly loosely. It should be at or near boiling temperature when it is packed.

There should be enough sirup, water, or juice to fill in around the solid food in the container and to cover the food. Food at the top of the container tends to darken if not covered with liquid. It takes from ½ to 1½ cups of liquid for a quart glass jar or a No. 2½ tin can.

Head space.—With only a few exceptions, some space should be left between the packed food and the closure. The amount of space to allow at the top of the jar or can is given in the detailed directions for canning each food.

Closing Glass Jars

Closures for glass jars are of two main types:

Metal screwband and flat metal lid with sealing compound. To use this type, wipe jar rim clean after produce is packed. Put lid on, with sealing compound next to glass. Screw metal band down tight by hand. When band is tight, this lid has enough give to let air escape during processing. Do not tighten screw band further after taking jar from canner.

Screw bands that are in good condition may be reused. You may remove bands as soon as jars are cool. Metal lids with sealing compound may be used only once.

Porcelain-lined zinc cap with shoulder rubber ring. Fit wet rubber ring down on jar shoulder, but don't stretch unnecessarily. Fill jar; wipe rubber ring and jar rim clean. Then screw cap down firmly and turn it back ¼ inch. As soon as you take jar from canner, screw cap down tight, to complete seal.

Porcelain-lined zinc caps may be reused as long as they are in good condition. Rubber rings should not be reused.

75944B

Exhausting and Sealing Tin Cans

Tin cans are sealed before processing. The temperature of the food in the cans must be 170° F. or higher when the cans are sealed. Food is heated to this temperature to drive out air so that there will be a good vacuum in the can after processing and cooling. Removal of air also helps prevent discoloring of canned food and change in flavor.

Food packed raw must be heated in the cans (exhausted) before the cans are sealed. Food packed hot may be sealed without further heating if you are sure the temperature of the food has not dropped below 170° F. To make sure, test with a thermometer, placing the bulb at the center of the can. If the thermometer registers lower than 170°, or if you do not make this test, exhaust the cans.

To exhaust, place open, filled cans on a rack in a kettle in which there is enough boiling water to come to about 2 inches below the tops of the cans. Cover the kettle. Bring water back to boiling. Boil until a thermometer inserted at the center of the can registers 170° F.—or for the length of time given in the directions for the fruit or vegetable you are canning.

Remove cans from the water one at a time, and add boiling packing liquid or water if necessary to bring head space back to the level specified for each product. Place clean lid on filled can. Seal at once.

Processing

Process fruits, tomatoes, and pickled vegetables in a boiling-water-bath canner according to the directions on page 116. Process vegetables in a steam-pressure canner according to the directions on page 122.

Cooling Canned Food

Glass jars.—As you take jars from the canner, complete seals at once if necessary. If liquid boiled out in processing, do not open jar to add more. Seal the jar just as it is.

Cool jars top side up. Give each jar enough room to let air get at all sides. Never set a hot jar on a cold surface; instead set the jars on a rack or on a folded cloth. Keep hot jars away from drafts, but don't slow cooling by covering them.

BN21476

Cool jars top side up on a rack, leaving space between jars so air can circulate.

76619B

Cool tin cans in cold water; change water frequently to cool cans quickly.

Tin cans.—Put tin cans in cold, clean water to cool them; change water as needed to cool cans quickly. Take cans out of the water while they are still warm so they will dry in the air. If you stack cans, stagger them so that air can get around them.

Day-After-Canning Jobs

Test the seal on glass jars with porcelain-lined caps by turning each jar partly over in your hands. To test a jar that has a flat metal lid, press center of lid; if lid is down and will not move, jar is sealed. Or tap the center of the lid with a spoon. A clear, ringing sound means a good seal. A dull note does not always mean a poor seal; store jars without leaks and check for spoilage before use.

BN21468

Label jars after they have been cooled.

If you find a leaky jar, use unspoiled food right away. Or can it again; empty the jar, and pack and process food as if it were fresh. Before using jar or lid again check for defects.

When jars are thoroughly cool, take off the screw bands carefully. If a band sticks, covering for a moment with a hot, damp cloth may help loosen it.

Before storing canned food, wipe containers clean. Label to show contents, date, and lot number—if you canned more than one lot in a day.

Wash bands; store them in a dry place.

Storing Canned Food

Properly canned food stored in a cool, dry place will retain good eating quality for a year. Canned food stored in a warm place near hot pipes, a range, or a furnace, or in direct sunlight may lose some of its eating quality in a few weeks or months, depending on the temperature.

Dampness may corrode cans or metal lids and cause leakage so the food will spoil.

Freezing does not cause food spoilage unless the seal is damaged or the jar is broken. However, frozen canned food may be less palatable than properly stored canned food. In an unheated storage place it is well to protect canned food by wrapping the jars in paper or covering them with a blanket.

On Guard Against Spoilage

Don't use canned food that shows any sign of spoilage. Look closely at each container before opening it. Bulging can ends, jar lids, or rings, or a leak— these may mean the seal has broken and the food has spoiled. When you open a container look for other signs—spurting liquid, an off odor, or mold.

It's possible for canned vegetables to contain the poison causing botulism— a serious food poisoning—without showing signs of spoilage. To avoid any risk of botulism, it is essential that the pressure canner be in perfect order and that every canning recommendation be followed exactly. Unless you're absolutely sure of your gage and canning methods, boil home-canned vegetables before tasting. Heating usually makes any odor of spoilage more evident.

Bring vegetables to a rolling boil; then cover and boil for at least 10 minutes. Boil spinach and corn 20 minutes. If the food looks spoiled, foams, or has an off odor during heating, destroy it.

Burn spoiled vegetables, or dispose of the food so that it will not be eaten by humans or animals.

How To Can Fruits, Tomatoes, Pickled Vegetables

Fruits, tomatoes, and pickled vegetables are canned according to the general directions on pages 111 to 114, the detailed directions for each food on pages 117-122, and the special directions given below that apply only to acid foods. (page 115.)

Points on Packing

Raw pack.—Put cold, raw fruits into container and cover with boiling-hot sirup, juice, or water. Press tomatoes down in the containers so they are covered with their own juice; add no liquid.

Hot pack.—Heat fruits in sirup, in water or steam, or in extracted juice before packing. Juicy fruits and tomatoes may be preheated without added liquid and packed in the juice that cooks out.

BN21474

To hot pack fruit, pack heated fruit loosely into jars.

BN21469

Cover fruit with boiling liquid before closing jar and processing in boiling-water bath.

Sweetening Fruit

Sugar helps canned fruit hold its shape, color, and flavor. Directions for canning most fruits call for sweetening to be added in the form of sugar sirup. For very juicy fruit packed hot, use sugar without added liquid.

To make sugar sirup.—Mix sugar with water or with juice extracted from some of the fruit. Use a thin, medium, or heavy sirup to suit the sweetness of the fruit and your taste. To make sirup, combine—

4 cups of water or juice.....	2 cups sugar.....	For 5 cups THIN sirup.
	3 cups sugar.....	For 5½ cups MEDIUM sirup.
	4¾ cups sugar...	For 6½ cups HEAVY sirup.

Boil sugar and water or juice together 5 minutes. Skim if necessary.

To extract juice.—Crush thoroughly ripe, sound juicy fruit. Heat to simmering (185° to 210° F.) over low heat. Strain through jelly bag or other cloth.

To add sugar direct to fruit.—For juicy fruit to be packed hot, add about ½ cup sugar to each quart of raw, prepared fruit. Heat to simmering (185° to 210° F.) over low heat. Pack fruit in the juice that cooks out.

To add sweetening other than sugar.—You can use light corn sirup or mild-flavored honey to replace as much as half the sugar called for in canning fruit. Do not use brown sugar, or molasses, sorghum, or other strong-flavored sirups; their flavor overpowers the fruit flavor and they may darken the fruit.

Canning Unsweetened Fruit

You may can fruit without sweetening—in its own juice, in extracted juice, or in water. Sugar is not needed to prevent spoilage; processing is the same for unsweetened fruit as for sweetened.

Processing in Boiling-Water Bath

Directions.—Put filled glass jars or tin cans into canner containing hot or boiling water. For raw pack in glass jars have water in canner hot but not boiling; for all other packs have water boiling.

Add boiling water if needed to bring water an inch or two over tops of containers; don't pour boiling water directly on glass jars. Put cover on canner.

76786B

After jars are covered with boiling water, place lid on water-bath canner and bring water quickly back to boiling.

When water in canner comes to a rolling boil, start to count processing time. Boil gently and steadily for time recommended for the food you are canning. Add boiling water during processing if needed to keep containers covered.

Remove containers from the canner immediately when processing time is up.

Processing times.—Follow times carefully. The times given apply only when a specific food is prepared according to detailed directions.

If you live at an altitude of 1,000 feet or more, you have to add to these processing times in canning directions, as follows:

| Altitude | Increase in processing time if the time called for is— | |
	20 minutes or less	More than 20 minutes
1,000 feet	1 minute	2 minutes.
2,000 feet	2 minutes	4 minutes.
3,000 feet	3 minutes	6 minutes.
4,000 feet	4 minutes	8 minutes.
5,000 feet	5 minutes	10 minutes.
6,000 feet	6 minutes	12 minutes.
7,000 feet	7 minutes	14 minutes.
8,000 feet	8 minutes	16 minutes.
9,000 feet	9 minutes	18 minutes.
10,000 feet	10 minutes	20 minutes.

To Figure Yield of Canned Fruit From Fresh

The number of quarts of canned food you can get from a given quantity of fresh fruit depends upon the quality, variety, maturity, and size of the fruit, whether it is whole, in halves, or in slices, and whether it is packed raw or hot.

Generally, the following amounts of fresh fruit or tomatoes (as purchased or picked) make 1 quart of canned food:

	Pounds
Apples	2½ to 3
Berries, except strawberries	1½ to 3 (1 to 2 quart boxes)
Cherries (canned unpitted)	2 to 2½
Peaches	2 to 3
Pears	2 to 3
Plums	1½ to 2½
Tomatoes	2½ to 3½

In 1 pound there are about 4 medium apples, peaches, or tomatoes; 3 medium pears; 12 medium plums.

Directions for Fruits, Tomatoes, Pickled Vegetables

Apples

Pare and core apples; cut in pieces. To keep fruit from darkening, drop pieces into water containing 2 tablespoons each of salt and vinegar per gallon. Drain, then boil 5 minutes in thin sirup or water.

In glass jars.—Pack hot fruit to ½ inch of top. Cover with hot sirup or water, leaving ½-inch space at top of jar. Adjust jar lids. Process in boiling-water bath (212° F.)—

Pint jars _____ 15 minutes
Quart jars _____ 20 minutes

As soon as you remove jars from canner, complete seals if necessary.

In tin cans.—Pack hot fruit to ¼ inch of top. Fill to top with hot sirup or water. Exhaust to 170° F. (about 10 minutes) and seal cans. Process in boiling-water bath (212° F.)—

No. 2 cans _____ 10 minutes
No. 2½ cans _____ 10 minutes

Applesauce

Make applesauce, sweetened or unsweetened. Heat to simmering (185°–210° F.); stir to keep it from sticking.

In glass jars.—Pack hot applesauce to ¼ inch of top. Adjust lids. Process in boiling-water bath (212° F.)—

    Pint jars_____ 10 minutes
    Quart jars_____ 10 minutes

As soon as you remove jars from canner, complete seals if necessary.

In tin cans.—Pack hot applesauce to top. Exhaust to 170° F. (about 10 minutes) and seal cans. Process in boiling-water bath (212° F.)—

    No. 2 cans_____ 10 minutes
    No. 2½ cans_____ 10 minutes

Apricots

Follow method for peaches. Peeling may be omitted.

Beets, Pickled

Cut off beet tops, leaving 1 inch of stem. Also leave root. Wash beets, cover with boiling water, and cook until tender. Remove skins and slice beets. For pickling sirup, use 2 cups vinegar (or 1½ cups vinegar and ½ cup water) to 2 cups sugar. Heat to boiling.

Pack beets in glass jars to ½ inch of top. Add ½ teaspoon salt to pints, 1 teaspoon to quarts. Cover with boiling sirup, leaving ½-inch space at top of jar. Adjust jar lids. Process in boiling-water bath (212° F.)—

    Pint jars_____ 30 minutes
    Quart jars_____ 30 minutes

As soon as you remove jars from canner, complete seals if necessary.

Berries, Except Strawberries

● **Raw Pack.**—Wash berries; drain.
In glass jars.—Fill jars to ½ inch of top. For a full pack, shake berries down while filling jars. Cover with boiling sirup, leaving ½-inch space at top. Adjust lids. Process in boiling-water bath (212° F.)—

    Pint jars_____ 10 minutes
    Quart jars_____ 15 minutes

As soon as you remove jars from canner, complete seals if necessary.

In tin cans.—Fill cans to ¼ inch of top. For a full pack, shake berries down while filling cans. Fill to top with boiling sirup. Exhaust to 170° F. (10 minutes); seal cans. Process in boiling-water bath (212° F.)—

    No. 2 cans_____ 15 minutes
    No. 2½ cans_____ 20 minutes

● **Hot Pack.**—(For firm berries)—Wash berries and drain well. Add ½ cup sugar to each quart fruit. Cover pan and bring to boil; shake pan to keep berries from sticking.

In glass jars.—Pack hot berries to ½ inch of top. Adjust jar lids. Process in boiling-water bath (212° F.)—

    Pint jars_____ 10 minutes
    Quart jars_____ 15 minutes

As soon as you remove jars from canner, complete seals if necessary.

In tin cans.—Pack hot berries to top. Exhaust to 170° F. (about 10 minutes) and seal cans. Process in boiling-water bath (212° F.)—

    No. 2 cans_____ 15 minutes
    No. 2½ cans_____ 20 minutes

Cherries

● **Raw Pack.**—Wash cherries; remove pits, if desired.
In glass jars.—Fill jars to ½ inch of top. For a full pack, shake cherries down while filling jars. Cover with boiling sirup, leaving ½-inch space at top. Adjust lids. Process in boiling-water bath (212° F.)—

    Pint jars_____ 20 minutes
    Quart jars_____ 25 minutes

As soon as you remove jars from canner, complete seals if necessary.

In tin cans.—Fill cans to ¼ inch of top. For a full pack, shake cherries down while filling cans. Fill to top with boiling sirup. Exhaust to 170° F. (about 10 minutes) and seal cans. Process in boiling-water bath (212° F.)—

No. 2 cans		20 minutes
No. 2½ cans		25 minutes

● **Hot Pack.**—Wash cherries; remove pits, if desired. Add ½ cup sugar to each quart of fruit. Add a little water to unpitted cherries to keep them from sticking while heating. Cover pan and bring to a boil.

In glass jars.—Pack hot to ½ inch of top. Adjust jar lids. Process in boiling-water bath (212° F.)—

Pint jars		10 minutes
Quart jars		15 minutes

As soon as you remove jars from canner, complete seals if necessary.

In tin cans.—Pack hot to top of cans. Exhaust to 170° F. (about 10 minutes) and seal cans. Process in boiling-water bath (212° F.)—

No. 2 cans		15 minutes
No. 2½ cans		20 minutes

Fruit Juices

Wash; remove pits, if desired, and crush fruit. Heat to simmering (185°–210° F.). Strain through cloth bag. Add sugar, if desired—about 1 cup to 1 gallon juice. Reheat to simmering.

In glass jars.—Fill jars to ½ inch of top with hot juice. Adjust lids. Process in boiling-water bath (212° F.)—

Pint jars		5 minutes
Quart jars		5 minutes

As soon as you remove jars from canner, complete seals if necessary.

In tin cans.—Fill cans to top with hot juice. Seal at once. Process in boiling-water bath (212° F.)—

No. 2 cans		5 minutes
No. 2½ cans		5 minutes

Fruit Purees

Use sound, ripe fruit. Wash; remove pits, if desired. Cut large fruit in pieces. Simmer until soft; add a little water if needed to keep fruit from sticking. Put through a strainer or food mill. Add sugar to taste. Heat again to simmering (185°–210° F.).

In glass jars.—Pack hot to ½ inch of top. Adjust lids. Process in boiling-water bath (212° F.)—

Pint jars		10 minutes
Quart jars		10 minutes

As soon as you remove jars from canner, complete seals if necessary.

In tin cans.—Pack hot to top. Exhaust to 170° F. (about 10 minutes), and seal cans. Process in boiling-water bath (212° F.)—

No. 2 cans		10 minutes
No. 2½ cans		10 minutes

Peaches

Wash peaches and remove skins. Dipping the fruit in boiling water, then quickly in cold water makes peeling easier. Cut peaches in halves; remove pits. Slice if desired. To prevent fruit from darkening during preparation, drop it into water containing 2 tablespoons each of salt and vinegar per gallon. Drain just before heating or packing raw.

BN21470

Peaches can be peeled easily if they are dipped in boiling water, then in cold water.

● **Raw Pack.**—Prepare peaches as directed above.

In glass jars.—Pack raw fruit to ½ inch of top. Cover with boiling sirup, leaving ½-inch space at top of jar. Adjust jar lids. Process in boiling-water bath (212° F.)—

Pint jars_____ 25 minutes
Quart jars_____ 30 minutes

As soon as you remove jars from canner, complete seals if necessary.

In tin cans.—Pack raw fruit to ¼ inch of top. Fill to top with boiling sirup. Exhaust to 170° F. (about 10 minutes) and seal cans. Process in boiling-water bath (212° F.)—

No. 2 cans_____ 30 minutes
No. 2 ½ cans_____ 35 minutes

● **Hot Pack.**—Prepare peaches as directed above. Heat peaches through in hot sirup. If fruit is very juicy you may heat it with sugar, adding no liquid.

In glass jars.—Pack hot fruit to ½ inch of top. Cover with boiling liquid, leaving ½-inch space at top of jar. Adjust jar lids. Process in boiling-water bath (212° F.)—

Pint jars_____ 20 minutes
Quart jars_____ 25 minutes

As soon as you remove jars from canner, complete seals if necessary.

In tin cans.—Pack hot fruit to ¼ inch of top. Fill to top with boiling liquid. Exhaust to 170° F. (about 10 minutes) and seal cans. Process in boiling-water bath (212° F.)—

No. 2 cans_____ 25 minutes
No. 2½ cans_____ 30 minutes

Pears

Wash pears. Peel, cut in halves, and core. Continue as with peaches, either raw pack or hot pack.

Plums

Wash plums. To can whole, prick skins. Freestone varieties may be halved and pitted.

● **Raw Pack.**—Prepare plums as directed above.

In glass jars.—Pack raw fruit to ½ inch of top. Cover with boiling sirup, leaving ½-inch space at top of jar. Adjust jar lids. Process in boiling-water bath (212° F.)—

Pint jars_____ 20 minutes
Quart jars_____ 25 minutes

As soon as you remove jars from canner, complete seals if necessary.

In tin cans.—Pack raw fruit to ¼ inch of top. Fill to top with boiling sirup. Exhaust to 170° F. (about 10 minutes) and seal cans. Process in boiling-water bath (212° F.)—

No. 2 cans_____ 15 minutes
No. 2½ cans_____ 20 minutes

● **Hot Pack.**—Prepare plums as directed above. Heat to boiling in sirup or juice. If fruit is very juicy you may heat it with sugar, adding no liquid.

In glass jars.—Pack hot fruit to ½ inch of top. Cover with boiling liquid, leaving ½-inch space at top of jar. Adjust jar lids. Process in boiling-water bath (212° F.)—

Pint jars_____ 20 minutes
Quart jars_____ 25 minutes

As soon as you remove jars from canner, complete seals if necessary.

In tin cans.—Pack hot fruit to ¼ inch of top. Fill to top with boiling liquid. Exhaust to 170° F. (about 10 minutes) and seal cans. Process in boiling-water bath (212° F.)—

No. 2 cans_____ 15 minutes
No. 2½ cans_____ 20 minutes

Rhubarb

Wash rhubarb and cut into ½-inch pieces. Add ½ cup sugar to each quart rhubarb and let stand to draw out juice. Bring to boiling.

In glass jars.—Pack hot to ½ inch of top. Adjust lids. Process in boiling-water bath (212° F.)—

Pint jars_____ 10 minutes
Quart jars_____ 10 minutes

As soon as you remove jars from canner, complete seals if necessary.

In tin cans.—Pack hot to top of cans. Exhaust to 170° F. (about 10 minutes) and seal cans. Process in boiling-water bath (212° F.)—

No. 2 cans_____ 10 minutes
No. 2½ cans_____ 10 minutes

Tomatoes

Use only firm, ripe tomatoes. To loosen skins, dip into boiling water for about ½ minute; then dip quickly into cold water. Cut out stem ends and peel tomatoes.

76787B

To peel tomatoes, dip them in boiling water, then quickly in cold water to loosen skins.

76792B

To raw pack tomatoes, put peeled tomatoes in jars and press down to fill spaces.

● **Raw Pack.**—Leave tomatoes whole or cut in halves or quarters.

In glass jars.—Pack tomatoes to ½ inch of top, pressing gently to fill spaces. Add no water. Add ½ teaspoon salt to pints; 1 teaspoon to quarts. Adjust lids. Process in boiling-water bath (212° F.)—

Pint jars_____ 35 minutes
Quart jars_____ 45 minutes

As soon as you remove jars from canner, complete seals if necessary.

In tin cans.—Pack tomatoes to top of cans, pressing gently to fill spaces. Add no water. Add ½ teaspoon salt to No. 2 cans; 1 teaspoon to No. 2½ cans. Exhaust to 170° F., (about 15 minutes) and seal cans. Process in boiling-water bath (212° F.)—

No. 2 cans_____ 45 minutes
No. 2½ cans_____ 55 minutes

● **Hot Pack.**—Quarter peeled tomatoes. Bring to boil; stir to keep tomatoes from sticking.

In glass jars.—Pack boiling-hot tomatoes to ½ inch of top. Add ½ teaspoon salt to pints; 1 teaspoon to quarts. Adjust jar lids. Process in boiling-water bath (212° F.)—

Pint jars_____ 10 minutes
Quart jars_____ 10 minutes

As soon as you remove jars from canner, complete seals if necessary.

In tin cans.—Pack boiling-hot tomatoes to ¼ inch of top. Add no water. Add ½ teaspoon salt to No. 2 cans; 1 teaspoon to No. 2½ cans. Exhaust to 170° F. (about 10 minutes) and seal cans. Process in boiling-water bath (212° F.)—

No. 2 cans_____ 10 minutes
No. 2½ cans_____ 10 minutes

Tomato Juice

Use ripe, juicy tomatoes. Wash, remove stem ends, cut into pieces. Simmer until softened, stirring often. Put through strainer. Add 1 teaspoon salt to each quart juice. Reheat at once just to boiling.

In glass jars.—Fill jars with boiling-hot juice to ½ inch of top. Adjust jar lids. Process in boiling-water bath (212° F.)—

    Pint jars_____ 10 minutes
    Quart jars_____ 10 minutes

As soon as you remove jars from canner, complete seals if necessary.

In tin cans.—Fill cans to top with boiling-hot juice. Seal cans at once. Process in boiling-water bath (212° F.)—

    No. 2 cans_____ 15 minutes
    No. 2½ cans_____ 15 minutes

How To Can Vegetables

Can vegetables according to general directions on pages 111 to 114, the detailed directions for each vegetable on pages 124 to 134, and special directions below that apply only to vegetables. (p. 122)

Points on Packing

Raw pack.—Pack cold raw vegetables (except corn, lima beans, and peas) tightly into container and cover with boiling water.

Hot pack.—Preheat vegetables in water or steam.   Cover with cooking liquid or boiling water.   Cooking liquid is recommended for packing most vegetables because it may contain minerals and vitamins dissolved out of the food.   Boiling water is recommended when cooking liquid is dark, gritty, or strong-flavored, and when there isn't enough cooking liquid.

Processing in a Pressure Canner

Use a steam-pressure canner for processing all vegetables except tomatoes and pickled vegetables.

Directions.—Follow the manufacturer's directions for the canner you are using.   Here are a few pointers on the use of any steam-pressure canner:

● Put 2 or 3 inches of boiling water in the bottom of the canner; the amount of water to use depends on the size and shape of the canner.

● Set filled glass jars or tin cans on rack in canner so that steam can flow around each container.   If two layers of cans or jars are put in, stagger the second layer.   Use a rack between layers of glass jars.

● Fasten canner cover securely so that no steam can escape except through vent (petcock or weighted-gage opening).

● Watch until steam pours steadily from vent.   Let it escape for 10 minutes or more to drive all air from the canner.   Then close petcock or put on weighted gage.

● Let pressure rise to 10 pounds (240° F.).   The moment this pressure is reached start counting processing time.   Keep pressure constant by regulating heat under the canner.   Do not lower pressure by opening petcock.   Keep drafts from blowing on canner.

● When processing time is up, remove canner from heat immediately.

With glass jars, let canner stand until pressure is zero.   Never try to rush the cooling by pouring cold water over the canner.   When pressure registers zero, wait a minute or two, then slowly open petcock or take off weighted gage. Unfasten cover and tilt the far side up so steam escapes away from you.   Take jars from canner.

BN 22389

To process vegetables, bring pressure in canner up to 10 pounds, then start to count processing time.

With tin cans, release steam in canner as soon as canner is removed from heat by opening petcock or taking off weighted gage. Then take off canner cover and remove cans.

Processing times.—Follow processing times carefully. The times given apply only when a specific food is prepared according to detailed directions.

If you live at an altitude of less than 2,000 feet above sea level, process vegetables at 10 pounds pressure for the times given.

At altitudes above sea level, it takes more than 10 pounds pressure to reach 240° F. If you live at an altitude of 2,000 feet, process vegetables at 11 pounds pressure. At 4,000 feet, use 12 pounds pressure; at 6,000 feet, 13 pounds pressure; at 8,000 feet, 14 pounds pressure; at 10,000 feet, 15 pounds pressure.

A weighted gage may need to be corrected for altitude by the manufacturer.

To Figure Yield of Canned Vegetables From Fresh

The number of quarts of canned food you can get from a given amount of fresh vegetables depends on quality, condition, maturity, and variety of the vegetable, size of pieces, and on the way the vegetable is packed—raw or hot pack.

Generally, the following amounts of fresh vegetables (as purchased or picked) make 1 quart of canned food:

	Pounds		Pounds
Asparagus	2½ to 4½	Okra	1½
Beans, lima, in pods	3 to 5	Peas, green, in pods	3 to 6
Beans, snap	1½ to 2½	Pumpkin or winter squash	1½ to 3
Beets, without tops	2 to 3½	Spinach and other greens	2 to 6
Carrots, without tops	2 to 3	Squash, summer	2 to 4
Corn, sweet, in husks	3 to 6	Sweetpotatoes	2 to 3

Directions for Vegetables

Asparagus

● **Raw Pack.**—Wash asparagus; trim off scales and tough ends and wash again. Cut into 1-inch pieces.

In glass jars.—Pack asparagus as tightly as possible without crushing to ½ inch of top. Add ½ teaspoon salt to pints; 1 teaspoon to quarts. Cover with boiling water, leaving ½-inch space at top of jar. Adjust jar lids. Process in pressure canner at 10 pounds pressure (240° F.)—

Pint jars	25 minutes
Quart jars	30 minutes

As soon as you remove jars from canner, complete seals if necessary.

In tin cans.—Pack asparagus as tightly as possible without crushing to ¼ inch of top. Add ½ teaspoon salt to No. 2 cans; 1 teaspoon to No. 2½ cans. Fill to top with boiling water. Exhaust to 170° F. (about 10 minutes) and seal cans. Process in pressure canner at 10 pounds pressure (240° F.)—

No. 2 cans	20 minutes
No. 2½ cans	20 minutes

● **Hot Pack.**—Wash asparagus; trim off scales and tough ends and wash again. Cut in 1-inch pieces; cover with boiling water. Boil 2 or 3 minutes.

In glass jars.—Pack hot asparagus loosely to ½ inch of top. Add ½ teaspoon salt to pints; 1 teaspoon to quarts. Cover with boiling-hot cooking liquid, or if liquid contains grit use boiling water. Leave ½-inch space at top of jar. Adjust jar lids. Process in pressure canner at 10 pounds pressure (240° F.)—

Pint jars	25 minutes
Quart jars	30 minutes

As soon as you remove jars from canner, complete seals if necessary.

In tin cans.—Pack hot asparagus loosely to ¼ inch of top. Add ½ teaspoon salt to No. 2 cans; 1 teaspoon to No. 2½ cans. Fill to top with boiling-hot cooking liquid, or if liquid contains grit use boiling water. Exhaust to 170° F. (about 10 minutes) and seal cans. Process in pressure canner at 10 pounds pressure (240° F.)—

No. 2 cans	20 minutes
No. 2½ cans	20 minutes

Beans, Dry, With Tomato or Molasses Sauce

Sort and wash dry beans (kidney, navy, or yellow eye). Cover with boiling water; boil 2 minutes, remove from heat and let soak 1 hour. Heat to boiling, drain, and save liquid for making sauce.

In glass jars.—Fill jars three-fourths full with hot beans. Add a small piece of salt pork, ham, or bacon. Fill to 1 inch of top with hot sauce (see recipes below). Adjust jar lids. Process in pressure canner at 10 pounds pressure (240° F.)—

Pint jars	65 minutes
Quart jars	75 minutes

As soon as you remove jars from canner, complete seals if necessary.

In tin cans.—Fill cans three-fourths full with hot beans. Add a small piece of salt pork, ham, or bacon. Fill to ¼ inch of top with hot sauce (see recipes below). Exhaust to 170° F. (about 20 minutes) and seal cans. Process in pressure canner at 10 pounds pressure (240° F.)—

No. 2 cans	65 minutes
No. 2½ cans	75 minutes

Tomato sauce.—Mix 1 quart tomato juice, 3 tablespoons sugar, 2 teaspoons salt, 1 tablespoon chopped onion, and ¼ teaspoon mixture of ground cloves, allspice, mace, and cayenne. Heat to boiling.

Or mix 1 cup tomato catsup with 3 cups of water or soaking liquid from beans and heat to boiling.

Molasses sauce.—Mix 1 quart water or soaking liquid from beans, 3 tablespoons dark molasses, 1 tablespoon vinegar, 2 teaspoons salt, and ¾ teaspoon powdered dry mustard. Heat to boiling.

Beans, Dry, Baked

Soak and boil beans according to directions for beans with sauce.

Place small pieces of salt pork, ham, or bacon in earthenware crock or a pan.

Add beans. Add enough molasses sauce to cover beans. Cover crock and bake 4 to 5 hours at 350° F. (moderate oven). Add water as needed—about every hour.

In glass jars.—Pack hot beans to 1 inch of top. Adjust jar lids. Process in pressure canner at 10 pounds pressure (240° F.)—

Pint jars_____ 80 minutes
Quart jars_____ 100 minutes

As soon as you remove jars from canner, complete seals if necessary.

In tin cans.—Pack hot beans to ¼ inch of top. Exhaust to 170° F. (about 15 minutes) and seal cans. Process in pressure canner at 10 pounds pressure (240° F.)—

No. 2 cans_____ 95 minutes
No. 2½ cans_____ 115 minutes

Beans, Fresh Lima

Can only young, tender beans.

● **Raw Pack.**—Shell and wash beans.

In glass jars.—Pack raw beans into clean jars. For small-type beans, fill to 1 inch of top of jar for pints and 1½ inches for quarts; for large beans, fill to ¾ inch of top for pints and 1¼ inches for quarts. Beans should not be pressed or shaken down. Add ½ teaspoon salt to pints; 1 teaspoon to quarts. Fill jar to ½ inch of top with boiling water. Adjust jar lids. Process in pressure canner at 10 pounds pressure (240° F.)—

Pint jars_____ 40 minutes
Quart jars_____ 50 minutes

As soon as you remove jars from canner, complete seals if necessary.

In tin cans.—Pack raw beans to ¾ inch of top; do not shake or press beans down. Add ½ teaspoon salt to No. 2 cans; 1 teaspoon to No. 2½ cans. Fill cans to top with boiling water. Exhaust to 170° F. (about 10 minutes) and seal cans. Process in pressure canner at 10 pounds pressure (240° F.)—

No. 2 cans_____ 40 minutes
No. 2½ cans_____ 40 minutes

● **Hot Pack.**—Shell the beans, cover with boiling water, and bring to boil.

In glass jars.—Pack hot beans loosely to 1 inch of top. Add ½ teaspoon salt to pints; 1 teaspoon to quarts. Cover with boiling water, leaving 1-inch space at top of jar. Adjust jar lids. Process in pressure canner at 10 pounds pressure (240° F.)—

Pint jars_____ 40 minutes
Quart jars_____ 50 minutes

As soon as you remove jars from canner, complete seals if necessary.

In tin cans.—Pack hot beans loosely to ½ inch of top. Add ½ teaspoon salt to No. 2 cans; 1 teaspoon to No. 2½ cans. Fill to top with boiling water. Exhaust to 170° F. (about 10 minutes) and seal cans. Process in pressure canner at 10 pounds pressure (240° F.)—

No. 2 cans_____ 40 minutes
No. 2½ cans_____ 40 minutes

Beans, Snap

● **Raw Pack.**—Wash beans. Trim ends; cut into 1-inch pieces.

In glass jars.—Pack raw beans tightly to ½ inch of top. Add ½ teaspoon salt to pints; 1 teaspoon to quarts. Cover with boiling water, leaving ½-inch space at top of jar. Adjust jar lids. Process in pressure canner at 10 pounds pressure (240° F.)—

Pint jars_____ 20 minutes
Quart jars_____ 25 minutes

As soon as you remove jars from canner, complete seals if necessary.

In tin cans.—Pack raw beans tightly to ¼ inch of top. Add ½ teaspoon salt to No. 2 cans; 1 teaspoon to No. 2½ cans. Fill to top with boiling water. Exhaust to 170° F. (about 10 minutes) and seal cans. Process in pressure canner at 10 pounds pressure (240° F.)—

> No. 2 cans_____ 25 minutes
> No. 2½ cans_____ 30 minutes

● **Hot Pack.**—Wash beans. Trim ends; cut into 1-inch pieces. Cover with boiling water; boil 5 minutes.

In glass jars.—Pack hot beans loosely to ½ inch of top. Add ½ teaspoon salt to pints; 1 teaspoon to quarts. Cover with boiling-hot cook-

BN21475

To hot pack snap beans, cover cut beans with boiling water and boil 5 minutes.

BN21471

Then pack hot beans loosely in jar and cover with hot cooking liquid before processing in a pressure canner.

ing liquid, leaving ½-inch space at top of jar. Adjust jar lids. Process in pressure canner at 10 pounds pressure (240° F.)—

> Pint jars_____ 20 minutes
> Quart jars_____ 25 minutes

As soon as you remove jars from canner, complete seals if necessary.

In tin cans.—Pack hot beans loosely to ¼ inch of top. Add ½ teaspoon salt to No. 2 cans; 1 teaspoon to No. 2½ cans. Fill to top with boiling-hot cooking liquid. Exhaust to 170° F. (about 10 minutes) and seal cans. Process in pressure canner at 10 pounds pressure (240° F.)—

> No. 2 cans_____ 25 minutes
> No. 2½ cans_____ 30 minutes

Beets

Sort beets for size. Cut off tops, leaving an inch of stem. Also leave root. Wash beets. Cover with boiling water and boil until skins slip easily— 15 to 25 minutes, depending on size. Skin and trim. Leave baby beets whole. Cut medium or large beets in ½-inch cubes or slices; halve or quarter very large slices.

In glass jars.—Pack hot beets to ½ inch of top. Add ½ teaspoon salt to pints; 1 teaspoon to quarts. Cover with boiling water, leaving ½-inch space at top of jar. Adjust jar lids. Process in pressure canner at 10 pounds pressure (240° F.)—

> Pint jars_____ 30 minutes
> Quart jars_____ 35 minutes

As soon as you remove jars from canner, complete seals if necessary.

In tin cans.—Pack hot beets to ¼ inch of top. Add ½ teaspoon salt to No. 2 cans; 1 teaspoon to No. 2½ cans. Fill to top with boiling water. Exhaust to 170° F. (about 10 minutes) and seal cans. Process in pressure canner at 10 pounds pressure (240° F.)—

> No. 2 cans_____ 30 minutes
> No. 2½ cans_____ 30 minutes

Beets, Pickled

See page 12.

Carrots

● **Raw Pack.**—Wash and scrape carrots. Slice or dice.

In glass jars.—Pack raw carrots tightly into clean jars, to 1 inch of top of jar. Add ½ teaspoon salt to pints; 1 teaspoon to quarts. Fill jar to ½ inch of top with boiling water. Adjust jar lids. Process in pressure canner at 10 pounds pressure (240° F.)—

Pint jars	25 minutes
Quart jars	30 minutes

As soon as you remove jars from canner, complete seals if necessary.

In tin cans.—Pack raw carrots tightly into cans to ½ inch of top. Add ½ teaspoon salt to No. 2 cans; 1 teaspoon to No. 2½ cans. Fill cans to top with boiling water. Exhaust to 170° F. (about 10 minutes) and seal cans. Process in pressure canner at 10 pounds pressure (240° F.)—

No. 2 cans	25 minutes
No. 2½ cans	30 minutes

● **Hot Pack.**—Wash and scrape carrots. Slice or dice. Cover with boiling water and bring to boil.

In glass jars.—Pack hot carrots to ½ inch of top. Add ½ teaspoon salt to pints; 1 teaspoon to quarts. Cover with boiling-hot cooking liquid, leaving ½-inch space at top of jar. Adjust jar lids. Process in pressure canner at 10 pounds pressure (240° F.)—

Pint jars	25 minutes
Quart jars	30 minutes

As soon as you remove jars from canner, complete seals if necessary.

In tin cans.—Pack hot carrots to ¼ inch of top. Add ½ teaspoon salt to No. 2 cans; 1 teaspoon to No. 2½ cans. Fill with boiling-hot cooking liquid. Exhaust to 170° F. (about 10 minutes) and seal cans. Process in pressure canner at 10 pounds pressure (240° F.)—

No. 2 cans	20 minutes
No. 2½ cans	25 minutes

Corn, Cream-Style

● **Raw Pack.**—Husk corn and remove silk. Wash. Cut corn from cob at about center of kernel and scrape cobs.

In glass jars.—Use pint jars only. Pack corn to 1½ inches of top; do not shake or press down. Add ½ teaspoon salt to each jar. Fill to ½ inch of top with boiling water. Adjust jar lids. Process in pressure canner at 10 pounds pressure (240° F.)—

Pint jars	95 minutes

As soon as you remove jars from canner, complete seals if necessary.

In tin cans.—Use No. 2 cans only. Pack corn to ½ inch of top; do not shake or press down. Add ½ teaspoon salt to each can. Fill cans to top with boiling water. Exhaust to 170° F. (about 25 minutes) and seal cans. Process in pressure canner at 10 pounds pressure (240° F.)—

No. 2 cans	105 minutes

● **Hot Pack.**—Husk corn and remove silk. Wash. Cut corn from cob at about center of kernel and scrape cob. To each quart of corn add 1 pint boiling water. Heat to boil.

In glass jars.—Use pint jars only. Pack hot corn to 1 inch of top. Add ½ teaspoon salt to each jar. Adjust jar lids. Process in pressure canner at 10 pounds pressure (240° F.)—

Pint jars	85 minutes

As soon as you remove jars from canner, complete seals if necessary.

In tin cans.—Use No. 2 cans only. Pack hot corn to top. Add ½ teaspoon salt to each can. Exhaust to 170° F. (about 10 minutes) and seal cans. Process in pressure canner at 10 pounds pressure (240° F.)—

No. 2 cans	105 minutes

Corn, Whole-Kernel

● **Raw Pack.**—Husk corn and remove silk. Wash. Cut from cob at about two-thirds the depth of kernel.

In glass jars.—Pack corn to 1 inch of top; do not shake or press down.

A nail driven at an angle through the cutting board (see arrow) holds the cob steady and makes it easy to cut corn from the cob.

Add ½ teaspoon salt to pints; 1 teaspoon to quarts. Fill to ½ inch of top with boiling water. Adjust jar lids. Process in pressure canner at 10 pounds pressure (240° F.)—

Pint jars_____ 55 minutes
Quart jars_____ 85 minutes

As soon as you remove jars from canner, complete seals if necessary.

In tin cans.—Pack corn to ½ inch of top; do not shake or press down. Add ½ teaspoon salt to No. 2 cans; 1 teaspoon to No. 2½ cans. Fill to top with boiling water. Exhaust to 170° F. (about 10 minutes) and seal cans. Process in pressure canner at 10 pounds pressure (240° F.)—

No. 2 cans_____ 60 minutes
No. 2½ cans_____ 60 minutes

● **Hot Pack.**—Husk corn and remove silk. Wash. Cut from cob at about two-thirds the depth of kernel. To each quart of corn add 1 pint boiling water. Heat to boiling.

In glass jars.—Pack hot corn to 1 inch of top and cover with boiling-hot cooking liquid, leaving 1-inch space at top of jar. Or fill to 1 inch of top with mixture of corn and liquid. Add ½ teaspoon salt to pints; 1 teaspoon to quarts. Adjust jar lids. Process in pressure canner at 10 pounds pressure (240° F.)—

Pint jars_____ 55 minutes
Quart jars_____ 85 minutes

As soon as you remove jars from canner, complete seals if necessary.

76624B

To hot pack corn, put heated corn loosely in C-enamel cans; fill cans with boiling liquid.

In tin cans.—Pack hot corn to ½ inch of top and fill to top with boiling-hot cooking liquid. Or fill to top with mixture of corn and liquid. Add ½ teaspoon salt to No. 2 cans; 1 teaspoon to No. 2½ cans. Exhaust to 170° F. (about 10 minutes) and seal cans. Process in pressure canner at 10 pounds pressure (240° F.)—

No. 2 cans_____	60 minutes
No. 2½ cans_____	60 minutes

Hominy

Place 2 quarts of dry field corn in an enameled pan; add 8 quarts of water and 2 ounces of lye. Boil vigorously ½ hour, then allow to stand for 20 minutes. Rinse off the lye with several hot water rinses. Follow with cold water rinses to cool for handling.

Work hominy with the hands until dark tips of kernels are removed (about 5 minutes). Separate the tips from the corn by floating them off in water or by placing the corn in a coarse sieve and washing thoroughly. Add sufficient water to cover hominy about 1 inch, and boil 5 minutes; change water. Repeat 4 times. Then cook until kernels are soft (½ to ¾ hour) and drain. This will make about 6 quarts of hominy.

In glass jars.—Pack hot hominy to ½ inch of top. Add ½ teaspoon salt to pints; 1 teaspoon to quarts. Cover with boiling water, leaving ½-inch space at top of jar. Adjust jar lids. Process in pressure canner at 10 pounds pressure (240° F.)—

Pint jars_____	60 minutes
Quart jars_____	70 minutes

As soon as you remove jars from canner, complete seals if necessary.

In tin cans.—Pack hot hominy to ¼ inch of top. Add ½ teaspoon salt to No. 2 cans; 1 teaspoon to No. 2½ cans. Fill to top with boiling water. Exhaust to 170° F. (about 10 minutes) and seal cans. Process in pressure canner at 10 pounds pressure (240° F.)—

No. 2 cans_____	60 minutes
No. 2½ cans_____	70 minutes

Mushrooms

Trim stems and discolored parts of mushrooms. Soak mushrooms in cold water for 10 minutes to remove adhering soil. Wash in clean water. Leave small mushrooms whole; cut larger ones in halves or quarters. Steam 4 minutes or heat gently for 15 minutes without added liquid in a covered saucepan.

In glass jars.—Pack hot mushrooms to ½ inch of top. Add ¼ teaspoon salt to half pints; ½ teaspoon to pints. For better color, add crystalline ascorbic acid—$\frac{1}{16}$ teaspoon to half-pints; ⅛ teaspoon to pints. Add boiling-hot cooking liquid or boiling water to cover mushrooms, leaving ½-inch space at top of jar. Adjust jar lids. Process in pressure canner at 10 pounds pressure (240° F.)—

Half-pint jars_____	30 minutes
Pint jars_____	30 minutes

As soon as you remove jars from canner, complete seals if necessary.

In tin cans.—Pack hot mushrooms to ¼ inch of top of cans. Add ½ teaspoon salt to No. 2 cans. For better color, add ⅛ teaspoon of crystalline ascorbic acid to No. 2 cans. Then fill to top with boiling-hot cooking liquid or boiling water. Exhaust to 170° F. (about 10 minutes) and seal cans. Process in pressure canner at 10 pounds pressure (240° F.)—

No. 2 cans_____	30 minutes

Okra

Can only tender pods. Wash; trim. Cook for 1 minute in boiling water. Cut into 1-inch lengths or leave pods whole.

In glass jars.—Pack hot okra to ½ inch of top. Add ½ teaspoon salt to pints; 1 teaspoon to quarts. Cover with boiling water, leaving ½-inch space at top of jar. Adjust jar lids. Process in pressure canner at 10 pounds pressure (240° F.)—

    Pint jars_____ 25 minutes
    Quart jars_____ 40 minutes

As soon as you remove jars from canner, complete seals if necessary.

In tin cans.—Pack hot okra to ¼ inch of top. Add ½ teaspoon salt to No. 2 cans; 1 teaspoon to No. 2½ cans. Fill to top with boiling water. Exhaust to 170° F. (about 10 minutes) and seal cans. Process in pressure canner at 10 pounds pressure (240° F.)—

    No. 2 cans_____ 25 minutes
    No. 2½ cans_____ 35 minutes

Peas, Fresh Blackeye (Cowpeas, Blackeye Beans)

● **Raw Pack.**—Shell and wash blackeye peas.

In glass jars.—Pack raw blackeye peas to 1½ inches of top of pint jars and 2 inches of top of quart jars; do not shake or press peas down. Add ½ teaspoon salt to pints; 1 teaspoon to quarts. Cover with boiling water, leaving ½-inch space at top of jars. Adjust jar lids. Process in pressure canner at 10 pounds pressure (240° F.)—

    Pint jars_____ 35 minutes
    Quart jars_____ 40 minutes

As soon as you remove jars from canner, complete seals if necessary.

In tin cans.—Pack raw blackeye peas to ¾ inch of top; do not shake or press down. Add ½ teaspoon salt to No. 2 cans; 1 teaspoon to No. 2½ cans. Cover with boiling water, leaving ¼-inch space at top of cans. Exhaust to 170° F. (about 10 minutes)

and seal cans. Process in pressure canner at 10 pounds pressure (240° F.)—

    No. 2 cans_____ 35 minutes
    No. 2½ cans_____ 40 minutes

● **Hot Pack.**—Shell and wash blackeye peas, cover with boiling water, and bring to a rolling boil. Drain.

In glass jars.—Pack hot blackeye peas to 1¼ inches of top of pint jars and 1½ inches of top of quart jars; do not shake or press peas down. Add ½ teaspoon salt to pints; 1 teaspoon to quarts. Cover with boiling water, leaving ½-inch space at top of jar. Adjust jar lids. Process in pressure canner at 10 pounds pressure (240° F.)—

    Pint jars_____ 35 minutes
    Quart jars_____ 40 minutes

As soon as you remove jars from canner, complete seals if necessary.

In tin cans.—Pack hot blackeye peas to ½ inch of top; do not shake or press peas down. Add ½ teaspoon salt to No. 2 cans; 1 teaspoon to No. 2½ cans. Cover with boiling water, leaving ¼-inch space at top of cans. Exhaust to 170° F. (about 10 minutes) and seal cans. Process in pressure canner at 10 pounds pressure (240° F.)—

    No. 2 cans_____ 30 minutes
    No. 2½ cans_____ 35 minutes

Peas, Fresh Green

● **Raw Pack.**—Shell and wash peas.

In glass jars.—Pack peas to 1 inch of top; do not shake or press down. Add ½ teaspoon salt to pints; 1 teaspoon to quarts. Cover with boiling water, leaving 1½ inches of space at top of jar. Adjust jar lids. Process in pressure canner at 10 pounds pressure (240° F.)—

    Pint jars_____ 40 minutes
    Quart jars_____ 40 minutes

As soon as you remove jars from canner, complete seals if necessary.

In tin cans.—Pack peas to ¼ inch of top; do not shake or press down. Add ½ teaspoon salt to No. 2 cans; 1 teaspoon to No. 2½ cans. Fill to top with boiling water. Exhaust to 170° F. (about 10 minutes) and seal cans. Process at 10 pounds pressure (240° F.)—

  No. 2 cans_____ 30 minutes
  No. 2½ cans_____ 35 minutes

● **Hot Pack.**—Shell and wash peas. Cover with boiling water. Bring to boil.

In glass jars.—Pack hot peas loosely to 1 inch of top. Add ½ teaspoon salt to pints; 1 teaspoon to quarts. Cover with boiling water, leaving 1-inch space at top of jar. Adjust jar lids. Process in pressure canner at 10 pounds pressure (240° F.)—

  Pint jars_____ 40 minutes
  Quart jars_____ 40 minutes

As soon as you remove jars from canner, complete seals if necessary.

In tin cans.—Pack hot peas loosely to ¼ inch of top. Add ½ teaspoon salt to No. 2 cans; 1 teaspoon to No. 2½ cans. Fill to top with boiling water. Exhaust to 170° F. (about 10 minutes) and seal cans. Process at 10 pounds pressure (240° F.)—

  No. 2 cans_____ 30 minutes
  No. 2½ cans_____ 35 minutes

Potatoes, Cubed

Wash, pare, and cut potatoes into ½-inch cubes. Dip cubes in brine (1 teaspoon salt to 1 quart water) to prevent darkening. Drain. Cook for 2 minutes in boiling water, drain.

In glass jars.—Pack hot potatoes to ½ inch of top. Add ½ teaspoon salt to pints; 1 teaspoon to quarts. Cover with boiling water, leaving ½-inch space at top of jar. Adjust jar lids. Process in pressure canner at 10 pounds pressure (240° F.)—

  Pint jars_____ 35 minutes
  Quart jars_____ 40 minutes

As soon as you remove jars from canner, complete seals if necessary.

In tin cans.—Pack hot potatoes to ¼ inch of top. Add ½ teaspoon salt to No. 2 cans; 1 teaspoon to No. 2½ cans. Fill to top with boiling water. Exhaust to 170° F. (about 10 minutes) and seal cans. Process in pressure canner at 10 pounds pressure (240° F.)—

  No. 2 cans_____ 35 minutes
  No. 2½ cans_____ 40 minutes

Potatoes, Whole

Use potatoes 1 to 2½ inches in diameter. Wash, pare, and cook in boiling water for 10 minutes. Drain.

In glass jars.—Pack hot potatoes to ½ inch of top. Add ½ teaspoon salt to pints; 1 teaspoon to quarts. Cover with boiling water, leaving ½-inch space at top of jar. Adjust jar lids. Process in pressure canner at 10 pounds pressure (240° F.)—

  Pint jars_____ 30 minutes
  Quart jars_____ 40 minutes

As soon as you remove jars from canner, complete seals if necessary.

In tin cans.—Pack hot potatoes to ¼ inch of top. Add ½ teaspoon salt to No. 2 cans; 1 teaspoon to No. 2½ cans. Fill to top with boiling water. Exhaust to 170° F. (about 10 minutes) and seal cans. Process in pressure canner at 10 pounds pressure (240° F.)—

  No. 2 cans_____ 35 minutes
  No. 2½ cans_____ 40 minutes

Pumpkin, Cubed

Wash pumpkin, remove seeds, and pare. Cut into 1-inch cubes. Add just enough water to cover; bring to boil.

In glass jars.—Pack hot cubes to ½ inch of top. Add ½ teaspoon salt to pints; 1 teaspoon to quarts. Cover with hot cooking liquid, leaving ½-inch space at top of jar. Adjust jar lids. Process in pressure canner at 10 pounds pressure (240° F.)—

  Pint jars_____ 55 minutes
  Quart jars_____ 90 minutes

As soon as you remove jars from canner, complete seals if necessary.

In tin cans.—Pack hot cubes to ¼ inch of top. Add ½ teaspoon salt to No. 2 cans; 1 teaspoon to No. 2½ cans. Fill to top with hot cooking liquid. Exhaust to 170° F. (about 10 minutes) and seal cans. Process in pressure canner at 10 pounds pressure (240° F.)—

No. 2 cans_____ 50 minutes
No. 2½ cans_____ 75 minutes

Pumpkin, Strained

Wash pumpkin, remove seeds, and pare. Cut into 1-inch cubes. Steam until tender, about 25 minutes. Put through food mill or strainer. Simmer until heated through; stir to keep pumpkin from sticking to pan.

In glass jars.—Pack hot to ½ inch of top. Add no liquid or salt. Adjust jar lids. Process at 10 pounds pressure (240° F.)—

Pint jars_____ 65 minutes
Quart jars_____ 80 minutes

As soon as you remove jars from canner, complete seals if necessary.

In tin cans.—Pack hot to ⅛ inch of top. Add no liquid or salt. Exhaust to 170° F. (about 10 minutes) and seal cans. Process in pressure canner at 10 pounds pressure (240° F.)—

No. 2 cans_____ 75 minutes
No. 2½ cans_____ 90 minutes

Spinach (and Other Greens)

Can only freshly picked, tender spinach. Pick over and wash thoroughly. Cut out tough stems and midribs. Place about 2½ pounds of spinach in a cheesecloth bag and steam about 10 minutes or until well wilted.

In glass jars.—Pack hot spinach loosely to ½ inch of top. Add ¼ teaspoon salt to pints; ½ teaspoon to quarts. Cover with boiling water, leaving ½-inch space at top of jar. Adjust jar lids. Process in pressure canner at 10 pounds pressure (240° F.)—

Pint jars_____ 70 minutes
Quart jars_____ 90 minutes

As soon as you remove jars from canner, complete seals if necessary.

In tin cans.—Pack hot spinach loosely to ¼ inch of top. Add ¼ teaspoon salt to No. 2 cans; ½ teaspoon to No. 2½ cans. Fill to top with boiling water. Exhaust to 170° F. (about 10 minutes) and seal cans. Process in pressure canner at 10 pounds pressure (240° F.)—

No. 2 cans_____ 65 minutes
No. 2½ cans_____ 75 minutes

78351B

To raw pack squash, pack uniform pieces of squash tightly into jars.

78352B

Cover squash with boiling water just before closing jars and putting in pressure canner.

Squash, Summer

● **Raw Pack.**—Wash but do not pare squash. Trim ends. Cut squash into ½-inch slices; halve or quarter to make pieces of uniform size.

In glass jars.—Pack raw squash tightly into clean jars to 1 inch of top of jar. Add ½ teaspoon salt to pints; 1 teaspoon to quarts. Fill jar to ½

BN21467

When processing time is up, let pressure in canner drop to zero. Slowly open petcock or take off weighted gage. Unfasten cover, tilting far side up so steam escapes away from you.

inch of top with boiling water. Adjust jar lids. Process in pressure canner at 10 pounds pressure (240° F.) —

Pint jars_____ 25 minutes
Quart jars_____ 30 minutes

As soon as you remove jars from canner, complete seals if necessary.

In tin cans.—Pack raw squash tightly into cans to ½ inch of top. Add ½ teaspoon salt to No. 2 cans; 1 teaspoon to No. 2½ cans. Fill cans to top with boiling water. Exhaust to 170° F. (about 10 minutes) and seal cans. Process in pressure canner at 10 pounds pressure (240° F.)—

No. 2 cans_____ 20 minutes
No. 2½ cans_____ 20 minutes

● **Hot Pack.**—Wash squash and trim ends; do not pare. Cut squash into ½-inch slices; halve or quarter to make pieces of uniform size. Add just enough water to cover. Bring to boil.

In glass jars.—Pack hot squash loosely to ½ inch of top. Add ½ teaspoon salt to pints; 1 teaspoon to quarts. Cover with boiling-hot cooking liquid, leaving ½-inch space at top of jar. Adjust jar lids. Process in pressure canner at 10 pounds pressure (240° F.)—

Pint jars_____ 30 minutes
Quart jars_____ 40 minutes

As soon as you remove jars from canner, complete seals if necessary.

In tin cans.—Pack hot squash loosely to ¼ inch of top. Add ½ teaspoon salt to No. 2 cans; 1 teaspoon to No. 2½ cans. Fill to top with boiling-hot cooking liquid. Exhaust to 170° F. (about 10 minutes) and seal cans. Process in pressure canner at 10 pounds pressure (240° F.)—

> No. 2 cans_____ 20 minutes
> No. 2½ cans_____ 20 minutes

Squash, Winter

Follow method for pumpkin.

Sweetpotatoes, Dry Pack

Wash sweetpotatoes. Sort for size. Boil or steam until partially soft (20 to 30 minutes). Skin. Cut in pieces if large.

In glass jars.—Pack hot sweetpotatoes tightly to 1 inch of top, pressing gently to fill spaces. Add no salt or liquid. Adjust jar lids. Process in pressure canner at 10 pounds pressure (240° F.)—

> Pint jars_____ 65 minutes
> Quart jars_____ 95 minutes

As soon as you remove jars from canner, complete seals if necessary.

In tin cans.—Pack hot sweetpotatoes tightly to top of can, pressing gently to fill spaces. Add no salt or liquid. Exhaust to 170° F. (about 10 minutes) and seal cans. Process in pressure canner at 10 pounds pressure (240° F.)—

> No. 2 cans_____ 80 minutes
> No. 2½ cans_____ 95 minutes

Sweetpotatoes, Wet Pack

Wash sweetpotatoes. Sort for size. Boil or steam just until skins slip easily. Skin and cut in pieces.

In glass jars.—Pack hot sweetpotatoes to 1 inch of top. Add ½ teaspoon salt to pints; 1 teaspoon to quarts. Cover with boiling water or medium sirup, leaving 1-inch space at top of jar. Adjust jar lids. Process in pressure canner at 10 pounds pressure (240° F.)—

> Pint jars_____ 55 minutes
> Quart jars_____ 90 minutes

As soon as you remove jars from canner, complete seals if necessary.

In tin cans.—Pack hot sweetpotatoes to ¼ inch of top. Add ½ teaspoon salt to No. 2 cans; 1 teaspoon to No. 2½ cans. Fill to top with boiling water or medium sirup. Exhaust to 170° F. (about 10 minutes) and seal cans. Process in pressure canner at 10 pounds pressure (240° F.)—

> No. 2 cans_____ 70 minutes
> No. 2½ cans_____ 90 minutes

Questions and Answers

Q. *Is it safe to process foods in the oven?*

A. No, oven canning is dangerous. Jars may explode. The temperature of the food in jars during oven processing does not get high enough to insure destruction of spoilage bacteria in vegetables.

Q. *Why is open-kettle canning not recommended for fruits and vegetables?*

A. In open-kettle canning, food is cooked in an ordinary kettle, then packed into hot jars and sealed without processing. For vegetables, the temperatures obtained in open-kettle canning are not high enough to destroy all the spoilage organisms that may be in the food. Spoilage bacteria may get in when the food is transferred from kettle to jar.

Q. *May a pressure canner be used for processing fruits and tomatoes?*

A. Yes. If it is deep enough it may be used as a water-bath canner. Or you may use a pressure canner to process fruits and tomatoes at 0 to 1 pound pressure without having the containers of food completely covered with water. Put water in the canner to the shoulders of the jars; fasten cover. When live steam pours steadily from the open vent, start counting time. Leave vent open and process for the same times given for the boiling-water bath.

Q. *Must glass jars and lids be sterilized by boiling before canning?*

A. No, not when boiling-water bath or pressure-canner method is used. The containers as well as the food are sterilized during processing. But be sure jars and lids are clean.

Q. *Why is liquid sometimes lost from glass jars during processing?*

A. Loss of liquid may be due to packing jars too full, fluctuating pressure in a pressure canner, or lowering pressure too suddenly.

Q. *Should liquid lost during processing be replaced?*

A. No, never open a jar and refill with liquid—this would let in bacteria and you would need to process again. Loss of liquid does not cause food to spoil, though the food above the liquid may darken.

Q. *Is it safe to use home canned food if liquid is cloudy?*

A. Cloudy liquid may be a sign of spoilage. But it may be caused by the minerals in hard water, or by starch from overripe vegetables. If liquid is cloudy, boil the food. Do not taste or use any food that foams during heating or has an off odor.

Q. *Why does canned fruit sometimes float in jars?*

A. Fruit may float because pack is too loose or sirup too heavy; or because some air remains in tissues of the fruit after heating and processing.

Q. *Is it safe to can foods without salt?*

A. Yes. Salt is used for flavor only and is not necessary for safe processing.

Q. What makes canned foods change color?

A. Darkening of foods at the tops of jars may be caused by oxidation due to air in the jars or by too little heating or processing to destroy enzymes. Overprocessing may cause discoloration of foods throughout the containers.

Pink and blue colors sometimes seen in canned pears, apples, and peaches are caused by chemical changes in the coloring matter of the fruit.

Iron and copper from cooking utensils or from water in some localities may cause brown, black, and gray colors in some foods.

When canned corn turns brown, the discoloring may be due to the variety of corn, to stage of ripeness, to overprocessing, or to copper or iron pans.

Packing liquid may cause fading of highly colored foods. The use of plain tin cans will cause some foods to lose color

Q. Is it safe to eat discolored canned foods?

A. The color changes noted above do not mean the food is unsafe to eat. However, spoilage may also cause color changes. Any canned food that has an unusual color should be examined carefully before use.

Q. Does ascorbic acid help keep fruits and vegetables from darkening?

A. Yes. The addition of ¼ teaspoon of crystalline ascorbic acid (vitamin C) to a quart of fruit or vegetable before it is processed retards oxidation, which is one cause of darkening of canned foods. One teaspoon of crystalline ascorbic acid weighs about 3 grams (or 3,000 milligrams).

Q. Is it all right to use preservatives in home canning?

A. No. Some canning powders or other chemical preservatives may be harmful.

Q. Why do the undersides of metal lids sometimes discolor?

A. Natural compounds in some foods corrode the metal and make a brown or black deposit on the underside of the lid. This deposit is harmless.

Q. When canned or frozen fruits are bought in large containers, is it possible to can them in smaller containers?

A. Any canned or frozen fruit may be heated through, packed, and processed the same length of time as recommended for hot packs. This canned food may be of lower quality than if fruit had been canned when fresh.

Q. Is it safe to leave food in tin cans after opening?

A. Yes. Food in tin cans needs only to be covered and refrigerated.

Q. Is the processing time the same no matter what kind of range is used?

A. Processing times and temperatures in this bulletin are for canning in a pressure canner or boiling-water bath with any type of range.

Q. Can fruits and vegetables be canned without heating if aspirin is used?

A. No. Aspirin cannot be relied on to prevent spoilage or to give satisfactory products. Adequate heat treatment is the only safe procedure.

Home Freezing of Fruits and Vegetables

There is no "out of season" for products of your garden and orchard—if you have a home freezer or space in a neighborhood locker plant.

Freezing is one of the simplest and least time-consuming ways to preserve foods at home. It keeps well the natural color, fresh flavor, and nutritive values of most fruits and vegetables. Frozen fruits and vegetables are ready to serve on short notice because most of the preparation they need for the table is done before freezing.

Directions are given in this bulletin for freezing many fruits and vegetables that give satisfactory products when frozen at home or in the locker plant. It is important that the directions be followed carefully, because the quality of product can vary with freshness of produce used, method of preparation and packaging, and conditions of freezing.

General freezing procedures

What to freeze

Freezing is not necessarily recommended as the preferred way for preserving all products listed in this bulletin. What to freeze must be decided on the basis of family needs and desires, on freezer space and cost of freezer storage, and on other storage facilities available.

It may be more economical, for instance, to store some fruits and vegetables in a vegetable cellar than to freeze them. But to you freezing may be worth the extra cost because of the convenience of having the products prepared so they can be readied quickly for serving.

Costs of owning and operating a home freezer vary with the rate of turnover of foods, electricity used, costs of packaging materials, repairs, and the original price of the freezer.

Some varieties of all fruits and vegetables freeze better than others. Because growing conditions differ widely throughout the country and different varieties of fruits and vegetables are available in different localities, it is not practical to specify in this publication the varieties suitable for freezing. Write to your State extension service, experiment station, or college of agriculture for information on local varieties that give highest quality when frozen.

If you have doubts as to how well a fruit or vegetable will freeze, it would be well to test it before freezing large quantities. To test, freeze three or four packages and sample the food after freezing. This shows the effect of freezing only, not the effect of storage.

Some fruits and vegetables do not make satisfactory products when frozen. They include green onions, lettuce and other salad greens, radishes, tomatoes (except as juice or cooked). Research may provide directions later for preparing good frozen products from some of these foods.

Containers for freezing

The prime purpose of packaging is to keep food from drying out and to preserve food value, flavor, color, and pleasing texture.

All containers should be easy to seal and waterproof so they will not leak. Packaging materials must be durable and must not become so brittle at low temperatures that they crack.

To retain highest quality in frozen food, packaging materials should be moisture-vapor-proof, to prevent evaporation. Many of the packaging materials on the market for frozen food are not moisture-vapor-*proof*, but are sufficiently moisture-vapor-*resistant* to retain satisfactory quality of fruits and vegetables during storage. Glass, metal, and rigid plastic are examples of moisture-vapor-proof packaging materials. Most bags, wrapping materials, and waxed cartons made especially for freezing are moisture-vapor-resistant. Not sufficiently moisture-vapor-resistant to be suitable for packaging foods to be frozen are ordinary waxed papers, household aluminum foil, and cartons for cottage cheese, ice cream, and milk.

Rigid containers. Rigid containers made of aluminum, glass, plastic, tin, or heavily waxed cardboard are suitable for all packs, and especially good for liquid packs. Glass canning jars may be used for freezing most fruits and vegetables except those packed in water. Plain tin or R-enamel cans may be used for all foods, but some foods may be better packed in cans with special enamel linings: C-enamel for foods containing considerable sulfur—corn, lima beans, carrots; R-enamel for highly colored foods—beets, berries, red cherries, fruit juices, plums, pumpkin, rhubarb, squash, sweetpotatoes.

Nonrigid containers. Bags and sheets of moisture-vapor-resistant cellophane, heavy aluminum foil, pliofilm, polyethylene, or laminated papers and duplex bags consisting of various combinations of paper, metal foil, glassine, cellophane, and rubber latex are suitable for dry-packed vegetables and fruits. Bags also can be used for liquid packs.

Bags and sheets are used with or without outer cardboard cartons to protect against tearing. Bags without a protective carton are difficult to stack. The sheets may be used for wrapping such foods as corn-on-the-cob or asparagus. Some of the sheets may be heat-sealed to make a bag of the size you need. Sheets that are heat-sealing on both sides may be used as outer wraps for folding paperboard cartons.

Size. Select a size that will hold only enough of a fruit or vegetable for one meal for your family.

Shape. Rigid containers that are flat on both top and bottom stack well in a freezer. Round containers and those with flared sides or raised bottoms waste freezer space. Nonrigid containers that bulge waste freezer space.

Food can be removed easily before it is thawed from containers with sides that are straight from bottom to top, or that flare out. Food must be partially thawed before it can be removed from containers with openings narrower than the body of the container.

Bags, sheets, and folding paperboard cartons take up little room when not in use. Rigid containers with flared sides will stack one inside the other and save space in your cupboard when not in use. Those with straight sides or narrow top openings cannot be nested.

Sealing. Care in sealing is as important as using the right container. Rigid containers usually are sealed either by pressing on or screwing on the lid. Tin cans such as are used in home canning require a sealing machine or special lids. Some rigid cardboard cartons need to have freezer tape or special wax applied after sealing to make them airtight and leakproof. Glass jars must be sealed with a lid containing composition rubber or with a lid and a rubber ring.

Most bags used for packaging can be heat-sealed or sealed by twisting and folding back the top of the bag and securing with a string, a good quality rubber or plastic band, or other sealing device available on the market. Some duplex bags are sealed by folding over a metal strip attached to the top of the bag.

Special equipment for heat-sealing bags or sheets for freezing is available on the market, or a household iron may be used. To heat-seal polyethylene or pliofilm bags or sheets used as overwraps, first place a piece of paper or heat-resistant material made especially for the purpose over the edges to be sealed. Then press with a warm iron. Regulate heat of the iron carefully—too much heat melts or crinkles the materials and prevents sealing.

As manufacturers are constantly making improvements and developing new containers it is a good idea to note when you buy how containers are to be sealed.

Reuse. Tin cans with slip-top closures, glass and rigid plastic and aluminum containers can be reused indefinitely. It is difficult to reuse aluminum foil boxes, because edges of lids and containers are folded over in sealing. Tin cans that require a sealer must be reflanged with a special attachment to a sealer before they are reused. A tin can or lid that is dented should not be used if it cannot be sealed.

Reuse of rigid cardboard cartons, unless plastic-lined, is not generally advisable because cleaning is difficult. Folding paperboard cartons used to protect an inner bag can be reused.

Cost. When you compare prices of the containers that are available in your locality, consider whether they will be reusable or not. If containers are reusable, a higher initial cost may be a saving in the long run.

Care of packaging materials. Protect packaging materials from dust and insects. Keep bags and rolls of wrapping materials that may become brittle, such as cellophane, in a place that is cool and not too dry.

Freezing accessories. Check on other items that help make packaging easier. Some containers are easier to fill if you use a stand and funnel. Special sealing irons available on the market or a regular household iron may be used for heat-sealing bags, wrappers, and some types of paper cartons. With some sealing irons, a small wooden block or box makes sealing of bags easier and quicker.

Packing

● Pack food and sirup cold into containers. Having materials cold speeds up freezing and helps retain natural color, flavor, and texture of food.

● Pack foods tightly to cut down on the amount of air in the package.

● When food is packed in bags, press air out of unfilled part of bag. Press firmly to prevent air from getting back in. Seal immediately, allowing the head space recommended for the product.

● Allow ample head space. With only a few exceptions, allowance for head space is needed between packed food and closure because food expands as it freezes. A guide to the amount of head space to allow is given in the table on the following page.

Head space to allow between packed food and closure

TYPE OF PACK	Container with wide top opening [1]		Container with narrow top opening [2]	
	Pint	Quart	Pint	Quart
Liquid pack.......... (Fruit packed in juice, sugar, sirup, or water; crushed or puree; juice.)	½ inch	1 inch	¾ inch [3]	1½ inches
Dry pack [4]........... (Fruit or vegetable packed without added sugar or liquid.)	½ inch	½ inch	½ inch	½ inch

[1] This is head space for tall containers—either straight or slightly flared.
[2] Glass canning jars may be used for freezing most fruits and vegetables except those packed in water.
[3] Head space for juice should be 1½ inches.
[4] Vegetables that pack loosely, such as broccoli and asparagus, require no head space.

● Keep sealing edges free from moisture or food so that a good closure can be made.   Seal carefully.

● Label packages plainly.   Include name of food, date it was packed, and type of pack if food is packed in more than one form.   Gummed labels, colored tape, crayons, pens, and stamps are made especially for labeling frozen food packages.

Loading the freezer

Freeze fruits and vegetables soon after they are packed.   Put them in the freezer a few packages at a time as you have them ready, or keep packages in the refrigerator until all you are doing at one time are ready.   Then transfer them to the home freezer or carry them in an insulated box or bag to the locker plant.   Freeze at 0° F. or below.

Put no more unfrozen food into a home freezer than will freeze within 24 hours.   Usually this will be about 2 or 3 pounds of food to each cubic foot of its capacity.   Overloading slows down the rate of freezing, and foods that freeze too slowly may lose quality or spoil.   For quickest freezing, place packages against freezing plates or coils and leave a little space between packages so air can circulate freely.

After freezing, packages may be stored close together. Store them at 0° F. or below. At higher temperatures foods lose quality much faster. Most fruits and vegetables maintain high quality for 8 to 12 months at 0° or below; citrus fruits and citrus juices, for 4 to 6 months. Unsweetened fruits lose quality faster than those packed in sugar or sirup. Longer storage will not make foods unfit for use, but may impair quality.

It's a good idea to post a list of frozen foods near the freezer and keep it up to date by listing the foods and date of freezing as you put them in and checking them off as you take them out. This helps to keep packages from being forgotten.

In case of emergency

If power is interrupted or the freezer fails to refrigerate properly, do not open the cabinet unnecessarily. Food in a loaded cabinet usually will stay frozen for 2 days, even in summer. In a cabinet with less than half a load, food may not stay frozen more than a day.

Dry ice to prevent thawing. If the power is not to be resumed within 1 or 2 days, or if the freezer may not be back to normal operation in that time, use dry ice to keep the temperature below freezing and to prevent deterioration or spoilage of frozen food.

Twenty-five pounds of dry ice in a 10-cubic-foot cabinet should hold the temperature below freezing for 2 to 3 days in a cabinet with less than half a load and 3 to 4 days in a loaded cabinet, if dry ice is obtained quickly following interruption of power. Move any food stored in a freezing compartment of a freezer to the storage compartment. Place dry ice on boards or heavy cardboard on top of the packages and do not open freezer oftener than necessary. Don't handle dry ice with bare hands; it can cause burns. When using dry ice, room should be ventilated. If you can't get dry ice, try to locate a locker plant and move the food there in insulated boxes.

Points on freezing fruits

Most fruits can be frozen satisfactorily, but the quality of the frozen product will vary with the kind of fruit, stage of maturity, and type of pack. Pointers on selecting fruit properly are given in the directions and must be followed carefully to be sure of a good frozen product.

Generally, flavor is well retained by freezing preservation. Texture may be somewhat softer than that of fresh fruit. Some fruits require special treatment when packed to make them more pleasing in color, texture, or flavor after thawing. Most fruits are best frozen soon after harvesting. Some, such as peaches and pears, may need to be held a short time to ripen.

Before packing

All fruits need to be washed in cold water. Wash a small quantity at a time to save undue handling, which may bruise delicate fruits such as berries. A perforated or wire basket is useful. Lift washed fruits out of the water and drain thoroughly. Don't let the fruit stand in the water—some lose food value and flavor that way and some get water-soaked.

In general, fruit is prepared for freezing in about the same way as for serving. Large fruits generally make a better product if cut in pieces or crushed before freezing. Many fruits can be frozen successfully in several forms. Good parts of less perfect fruit are suitable for crushed or pureed packs.

Peel, trim, pit, and slice fruit following the directions on pages 152 to 162. It is best to prepare enough fruit for only a few containers at one time, especially those fruits that darken rapidly. Two or three quarts is a good quantity to work with.

If directions call for fruit to be crushed, suit the method of crushing to the fruit. For soft fruits, a wire potato masher, pastry fork, or slotted spoon may be used; if fruits are firm they may be crushed more easily with a food chopper. For making purees a colander, food press, or strainer is useful.

Use equipment of aluminum, earthenware, enameled ware, glass, nickel, stainless steel, or good-quality tinware. Do not use galvanized ware in direct contact with fruit or fruit juices because the acid in fruit dissolves zinc, which is poisonous.

Metallic off-flavors may result from the use of iron utensils, chipped enameled ware, or tinware that is not well tinned.

Ways to pack

Most fruits have better texture and flavor if packed in sugar or sirup. Some may be packed without sweetening.

In the directions for freezing, three ways of packing are given for fruits whole or in pieces—sirup pack, sugar pack, and unsweetened pack. Directions are also given for packing crushed fruits, purees, and fruit juices.

Your selection of the way to pack the fruit will depend on the intended use. Fruits packed in a sirup are generally best for dessert use; those packed in dry sugar or unsweetened are best for most cooking purposes because there is less liquid in the product.

Even though unsweetened packs generally yield a lower quality product than packs with sugar, directions in this publication include unsweetened packs whenever they are satisfactory, because they are often needed for special diets. Some fruits, such as gooseberries, currants, cranberries, rhubarb, and figs, give as good quality packs without as with sugar.

Sirup pack. A 40-percent sirup is recommended for most fruits. For some mild-flavored fruits lighter sirups are desirable to prevent masking of flavor. Heavier sirups may be needed for very sour fruits.

In the directions for each fruit, sirups are called for according to the percentage of sugar in the sirup. Below is a master recipe from which any of the sirups can be made. It takes one-half to two-thirds cup of sirup for each pint package of fruit.

Sirups for use in freezing fruits

Type of sirup	Sugar [1]	Water	Yield of sirup
	Cups	Cups	Cups
30-percent sirup	2	4	5
35-percent sirup	2½	4	5⅓
40-percent sirup	3	4	5½
50-percent sirup	4¾	4	6½
60-percent sirup	7	4	7¾
65-percent sirup	8¾	4	8⅔

[1] In general, up to one-fourth of the sugar may be replaced by corn sirup. A larger proportion of corn sirup may be used if a very bland, light-colored type is selected.

Dissolve sugar in cold or hot water. If hot water is used, cool sirup before using. Sirup may be made up the day before and kept cold in the refrigerator.

When packing fruit into containers be sure the sirup covers the fruit, so that the top pieces will not change in color and flavor. To keep the fruit under the sirup, place a small piece of crumpled parchment paper or other water-resistant wrapping material on top and press fruit down into sirup before closing and sealing the container.

Sugar pack. Cut fruit into a bowl or shallow pan. Sprinkle the sugar (quantity needed given in the directions for each fruit) over the fruit. To mix, use a large spoon or pancake turner. Mix gently until juice is drawn out and sugar is dissolved.

Put fruit and juice into containers. Place a small piece of crumpled parchment paper or other water-resistant wrapping material on top to hold fruit down in juice. Close and seal the container.

Unsweetened pack. Pack prepared fruit into containers, without added liquid or sweetening, or cover with water containing ascorbic acid. Or pack crushed or sliced fruit in its own juice without sweetening. Press fruit down into juice or water with a small piece of crumpled parchment paper as for sirup and sugar pack. Close and seal containers.

To keep fruit from darkening

Some fruits darken during freezing if not treated to retard darkening. Directions for such fruits list antidarkening treatment as part of the freezing preparation. Several types of antidarkening treatments are used because all fruits are not protected equally well by all treatments.

Ascorbic acid. For most of the fruits that need antidarkening treatment, ascorbic acid (vitamin C) may be used. This is very effective in preserving color and flavor of fruit and adds nutritive value.

Ascorbic acid in crystalline form is available at drug stores and at some locker plants, in various sized containers from 25 to 1,000 grams. (Crystalline ascorbic acid may be obtained also in powdered form.) One teaspoon weighs about 3 grams; thus there are approximately 8 teaspoons of ascorbic acid in a 25-gram container. In the recipes, amounts of crystalline ascorbic acid are given in teaspoons.

Ascorbic acid tablets can be used but are more expensive and more difficult to dissolve than the crystalline form. Also filler in the tablets may make the sirup cloudy. The amount of ascorbic acid in tablets is usually expressed in milligrams. Below are amounts needed in milligrams if tablets are used in place of crystalline ascorbic acid:

Crystalline	Tablets
1/8 teaspoon	375 milligrams
1/4 teaspoon	750 milligrams
1/2 teaspoon	1,500 milligrams
3/4 teaspoon	2,250 milligrams
1 teaspoon	3,000 milligrams

To use, dissolve ascorbic acid in a little cold water. If using tablets, crush them so they will dissolve more easily.

● *In sirup pack.* Add the dissolved ascorbic acid to the cold sirup shortly before using. Stir it in gently so you won't stir in air. Solutions of ascorbic acid should be made up as needed. Keep sirup in refrigerator until used.

● *In sugar pack.* Sprinkle the dissolved ascorbic acid over the fruit just before adding sugar.

● *In unsweetened pack.* Sprinkle the dissolved ascorbic acid over the fruit and mix thoroughly just before packing. If fruit is packed in water, dissolve the ascorbic acid in the water.

● *In fruit juices.* Add ascorbic acid directly to the juice. Stir only enough to dissolve ascorbic acid.

● *In crushed fruits and fruit purees.* Add dissolved ascorbic acid to the fruit preparation and mix.

Ascorbic acid mixtures. There are on the market special anti-darkening preparations—usually made of ascorbic acid mixed with sugar or with sugar and citric acid. If you use one of these, follow the manufacturer's directions. In these mixtures ascorbic acid is usually the important active ingredient. Because of its dilution with other materials, ascorbic acid purchased in these forms may be more expensive than the pure ascorbic acid.

Citric acid, lemon juice. For a few fruits citric acid or lemon juice (which contains both citric acid and ascorbic acid) makes a suitable antidarkening agent. However, neither is as effective as ascorbic acid. Citric acid or lemon juice in the large quantities needed in some cases would mask the natural fruit flavors or make the fruits too sour.

Citric acid in crystalline or powdered form is available at drugstores and some locker plants. When using citric acid, dissolve it in a little cold water before adding to the fruit according to directions for that fruit.

Steam. For some fruits steaming for a few minutes before packing is enough to control darkening.

Table of fruit yields

The following table will help you figure how much frozen fruit you can get from a given quantity of fresh fruit and will help in making cost comparisons.

The number of pints of frozen food you can get depends upon the quality, variety, maturity, and size of the fruit—and whether it is frozen whole or in halves, in slices, in cubes, or in balls.

Approximate yield of frozen fruits from fresh

FRUIT	FRESH, AS PURCHASED OR PICKED	FROZEN
Apples	1 bu. (48 lb.)	32 to 40 pt.
	1 box (44 lb.)	29 to 35 pt.
	1 ¼ to 1½ lb.	1 pt.
Apricots	1 bu. (48 lb.)	60 to 72 pt.
	1 crate (22 lb.)	28 to 33 pt.
	⅔ to ⅘ lb.	1 pt.
Berries [1]	1 crate (24 qt.)	32 to 36 pt.
	1⅓ to 1½ pt.	1 pt.
Cantaloups	1 dozen (28 lb.)	22 pt.
	1 to 1¼ lb.	1 pt.
Cherries, sweet or sour	1 bu. (56 lb.)	36 to 44 pt.
	1¼ to 1½ lb.	1 pt.
Cranberries	1 box (25 lb.)	50 pt.
	1 peck (8 lb.)	16 pt.
	½ lb.	1 pt.
Currants	2 qt. (3 lb.)	4 pt.
	¾ lb.	1 pt.
Peaches	1 bu. (48 lb.)	32 to 48 pt.
	1 lug box (20 lb.)	13 to 20 pt.
	1 to 1½ lb.	1 pt.
Pears	1 bu. (50 lb.)	40 to 50 pt.
	1 western box (46 lb.)	37 to 46 pt.
	1 to 1¼ lb.	1 pt.
Pineapple	5 lb.	4 pt.
Plums and prunes	1 bu. (56 lb.)	38 to 56 pt.
	1 crate (20 lb.)	13 to 20 pt.
	1 to 1½ lb.	1 pt.
Raspberries	1 crate (24 pt.)	24 pt.
	1 pt.	1 pt.
Rhubarb	15 lb.	15 to 22 pt.
	⅔ to 1 lb.	1 pt.
Strawberries	1 crate (24 qt.)	38 pt.
	⅔ qt.	1 pt.

[1] Includes blackberries, blueberries, boysenberries, dewberries, elderberries, gooseberries, huckleberries, loganberries, and youngberries.

Strawberries . . . packed in sugar

Pride of the freezer are strawberries—sliced, sweetened with dry sugar, and frozen. For other fruits packed in sugar, follow the general steps shown here. A pint plastic box is the container illustrated, but other types of containers may also be used.

● Select firm, ripe strawberries —about ⅔ quart fresh berries are needed for each pint frozen.

9116D

● Wash berries a few at a time in cold water. Lift berries gently out of water and drain.

9117D

● Remove hulls; then slice berries into a bowl or shallow pan.

9119D

● Sprinkle sugar over berries— ¾ cup to each quart (1⅓ pounds) berries. Turn berries over and over until sugar is dissolved and juice is formed.

9120D

● Pack berries in container, leaving ½-inch head space in the wide-mouth pint box. Place a small piece of crumpled parchment paper on top of berries. Press berries down into juice.

BN23631

● Press lid on firmly to seal. Be sure the seal is watertight.

BN23630

● Label package with name of fruit and date frozen. Freeze; then store at 0° F. or below.

BN23632

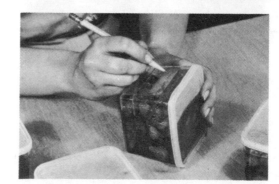

Peaches . . . packed in sirup

Peaches packed in either sirup or sugar make an excellent frozen product. Sliced peaches are shown being packed in sirup. A pint glass freezer jar is used here, but other sizes and types of containers are suitable.

Follow these general directions for packing other fruits in sirup. Vary the sirup as called for in the directions for each fruit.

Make up sirup ahead of time so it will be ready and cold when you need it. Peaches are best packed in a 40-percent sirup—3 cups of sugar to 4 cups of water. This amount makes about 5½ cups of sirup. You need about ⅔ cup of sirup for each pint container of peaches. For details of sirup making, see page 144.

For frozen peaches with better color and flavor, add ascorbic acid to the cold sirup as described on pages 11 and 12. For peaches, use ½ teaspoon crystalline ascorbic acid to each quart of sirup.

● Select mature peaches that are firm-ripe, with no green color in the skins. Allow 1 to 1½ pounds fresh peaches for each pint to be frozen. Wash them carefully and drain.

286A

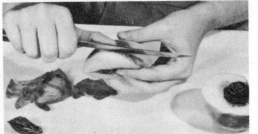

● Pit peaches, and peel them by hand for the best-looking product. Peaches peel more quickly if they are dipped first in boiling water, then cold—but have ragged edges after thawing.

287A

● Pour about ½ cup cold sirup into each pint container. Slice peaches directly into container.

288A

● Add sirup to cover peaches. Leave ½-inch head space at top of wide-mouth pint containers such as these, to allow for the expansion of the fruit during freezing.

289A

● Put a small piece of crumpled parchment paper on top of fruit to keep peaches down in the sirup. Sirup should always cover fruit to keep top pieces from changing color and flavor.

291A

● Wipe all sealing edges clean for a good seal. Screw lid on tight. Label with name of fruit and date of freezing.

292A

● Put sealed containers in the coldest part of freezer or locker. Leave a little space between containers so air can circulate freely. After fruit is frozen, store at 0° F. or below.

293A

Directions for fruits

Apples, slices

Sirup pack is preferred for apples to be used for fruit cocktail or uncooked dessert. Apples packed in sugar or frozen unsweetened are good for pie making. For better quality, apple slices need to be treated to prevent darkening.

Select full-flavored apples that are crisp and firm, not mealy in texture.[1] Wash, peel, and core. Slice medium apples into twelfths, large ones into sixteenths.

Pack in one of the following ways:

Sirup pack. Use 40-percent sirup (p. 144). For a better quality frozen product add ½ teaspoon crystalline ascorbic acid to each quart of sirup.

Slice apples directly into cold sirup in container, starting with ½ cup sirup to a pint container. Press fruit down in containers and add enough sirup to cover.

Leave head space (p. 141). Seal and freeze.

Sugar pack. To prevent darkening of apples during preparation, slice them into a solution of 2 tablespoons salt to a gallon of water. Hold in this solution no more than 15 to 20 minutes. Drain.

To retard darkening, place slices in a single layer in steamer; steam 1½ to 2 minutes, depending on thickness of slice. Cool in cold water; drain.

Over each quart (1¼ pounds) of apple slices sprinkle evenly ½ cup sugar and stir.

Pack apples into containers and press fruit down, leaving head space (p. 141). Seal and freeze.

Unsweetened pack. Follow directions for sugar pack, omitting sugar.

Applesauce

Select full-flavored apples. Wash apples, peel if desired, core, and slice. To each quart of apple slices add ⅓ cup water; cook until tender. Cool and strain if necessary. Sweeten to taste with ¼ to ¾ cup sugar for each quart (2 pounds) of sauce.

Pack into containers, leaving head space. Seal and freeze.

Apricots

● **Halves and slices.** The sirup pack is preferred for fruit to be served uncooked; the sugar pack for apricots to be used for pies or other cooked dishes.

Treatment to prevent darkening is necessary for a satisfactory product if apricots are packed in sugar. Such treatment also improves the quality of apricots packed in sirup.

Select firm, ripe, uniformly yellow apricots. Sort, wash, halve, and pit. Peel and slice if desired.

[1] To firm soft apples that are to be used in cooking or baking after freezing:
Hold sliced apples for 5 to 20 minutes in a solution made from 1 teaspoon calcium chloride (U.S.P. grade) or 2 tablespoons calcium lactate (U.S.P. grade) to each quart of water. The softer the apples the longer the time they should be held in the solution.
Apples differ with variety, stage of ripeness, and the region in which they are grown. Make a trial with a few packages. After freezing, boil apple slices a few minutes to test firmness.

If apricots are not peeled, heat them in boiling water ½ minute to keep skins from toughening during freezing. Then cool in cold water and drain.

Pack into containers in one of the following ways:

Sirup pack. Use 40-percent sirup (p. 144). For a better quality frozen product, add ¾ teaspoon crystalline ascorbic acid to each quart of sirup.

Pack apricots directly into containers. Cover with sirup, leaving head space (p. 141). Seal and freeze.

Sugar pack. Before combining apricots with sugar give the fruit the following treatment to prevent darkening:

Dissolve ¼ teaspoon crystalline ascorbic acid in ¼ cup cold water and sprinkle over 1 quart (⅞ pound) of fruit.

Mix ½ cup sugar with each quart of fruit. Stir until sugar is dissolved. Pack apricots into containers and press down until fruit is covered with juice, leaving head space (p. 141). Seal and freeze.

● **Crushed or puree.** Select fully ripe fruit. For crushed apricots, dip in boiling water for ½ minute and cool in cold water. Peel the apricots. Pit and crush them coarsely.

For puree, pit and quarter the apricots. Press through a sieve; or heat to boiling point in just enough water to prevent scorching and then press through a sieve.

With each quart (2 pounds) of prepared apricots mix 1 cup sugar. For a better product, add ¼ teaspoon

crystalline ascorbic acid dissolved in ¼ cup of water to the fruit just before adding the sugar.

Pack into containers, leaving head space. Seal and freeze.

Avocados

● **Puree.** Avocados are best frozen as puree—unsweetened for salads and sandwiches, sweetened for ice cream and milk shakes. Avocados are not satisfactorily frozen whole or sliced.

Select avocados that are soft ripe—not hard or mushy—with rinds free from dark blemishes. Peel the fruit, cut in half, and remove the pit. Mash the pulp.

Pack in one of the following ways:

Unsweetened pack. For a better quality product add ⅛ teaspoon crystalline ascorbic acid to each quart of puree.

Pack into containers, leaving head space. Seal and freeze.

Sugar pack. Mix 1 cup sugar with 1 quart (2 pounds) of puree. Pack into containers, leaving head space (p. 141). Seal and freeze.

Blackberries, boysenberries, dewberries, loganberries, youngberries

● **Whole.** The sirup pack is preferred for berries to be served uncooked. The sugar pack or the unsweetened pack is satisfactory for berries to be used for cooked products such as pie or jam.

Blackberries—continued

Select firm, plump, fully ripe berries with glossy skins. Green berries may cause off-flavor.

Sort and remove any leaves and stems. Wash and drain.

Use one of the three following packs:

Sirup pack. Pack berries into containers and cover with cold 40- or 50-percent sirup (P. 144), depending on the sweetness of the fruit. Leave head space (P. 141). Seal and freeze.

Sugar pack. To 1 quart (1⅓ pounds) berries, add ¾ cup sugar. Turn berries over and over until most of the sugar is dissolved. Fill containers, leaving head space (P. 141) Seal and freeze.

Unsweetened pack. Pack berries into containers, leaving head space (P. 141). Seal and freeze.

● **Crushed or puree.** Prepare for packing in same way as for whole berries. Then crush. Or press through a sieve for puree.

To each quart (2 pounds) of crushed berries or puree add 1 cup sugar. Stir until sugar is dissolved. Pack into containers, leaving head space (P. 141). Seal and freeze.

Blueberries, elderberries, huckleberries

● **Whole.** The sirup pack is preferred for berries to be served uncooked. Berries frozen unsweetened are satisfactory for cooking.

Select full-flavored, ripe berries all about the same size, preferably with tender skins. Sort, wash, and drain.

If desired, steam for 1 minute and cool immediately. Preheating in steam tenderizes skin and makes a better flavored product.

Use one of the following packs:

Sirup pack. Pack berries into containers and cover with cold 40-percent sirup (P. 144). Leave head space (P. 141). Seal and freeze.

Unsweetened pack. Pack berries into containers, leaving head space (P. 141). Seal and freeze.

● **Crushed or puree.** Select fully ripened berries. Sort, wash, and drain. Crush, or press berries through a fine sieve for puree.

To 1 quart (2 pounds) crushed berries or puree, add 1 to 1⅛ cups sugar, depending on tartness of fruit. Stir until sugar is dissolved. Pack into containers, leaving head space (P. 141). Seal and freeze.

Cherries, sour

● **Whole.** Sirup pack is best for cherries to be served uncooked. Sugar pack is preferable for cherries to be used for pies or other cooked products.

Select bright-red, tree-ripened cherries. Stem, sort, and wash thoroughly. Drain and pit.

Use one of the following packs:

Sirup pack. Pack cherries into containers and cover with cold 60- or 65-percent sirup (P. 144), depending on tartness of the cherries. Leave head space (P. 141). Seal and freeze.

Sugar pack. To 1 quart (1⅓ pounds) cherries add ¾ cup sugar. Mix until sugar is dissolved. Pack into containers, leaving head space (P. 141) Seal and freeze.

● **Crushed.** Prepare for packing as for whole sour cherries. Crush coarsely.

To 1 quart (2 pounds) fruit add 1 to 1½ cups sugar, depending on sweetness desired. Mix thoroughly until sugar is dissolved. Pack into containers, leaving head space(P.141). Seal and freeze.

● **Puree.** Select and prepare for packing same as for whole cherries. Then crush cherries, heat to boiling point, cool, and press through a sieve.

To 1 quart (2 pounds) fruit puree add ¾ cup sugar. Pack puree into containers, leaving head space(P.141). Seal and freeze.

● **Juice.** Select and prepare as for whole sour cherries. Then crush cherries, heat slightly to start flow of juice, and strain juice through a jelly bag. Cool, let stand overnight, and pour off clear juice for freezing. Or juice may be packed as soon as it cools, then strained when it is thawed for serving.

Sweeten with 1½ to 2 cups sugar to each quart of juice or pack without added sugar. Pour into containers, leaving head space (P. 141). Seal and freeze.

Cherries, sweet

● **Whole.** Sweet cherries should be prepared quickly to avoid color and flavor changes. Red varieties are best for freezing.

Select well-colored, tree-ripened fruit with a sweet flavor. Sort, stem, wash, and drain. Remove pits if desired; they tend to give an almond-like flavor to the fruit.

Pack cherries into containers. Cover with cold 40-percent sirup (P. 144) to which has been added ½ teaspoon crystalline ascorbic acid to the quart. Leave head space(P.141). Seal and freeze.

With sour cherries. Use half sweet cherries, half sour. Pack as above using 50-percent sirup (P. 144). Ascorbic acid may be added, but is not essential as it is for sweet cherries alone.

● **Crushed.** Prepare cherries as for freezing whole. Remove pits and crush cherries coarsely.

To each quart (2 pounds) of crushed fruit add 1½ cups sugar and ¼ teaspoon crystalline ascorbic acid. Mix well. Pack into containers, leaving head space (P. 141). Seal and freeze.

● **Juice.** Frozen sweet cherry juice may lack flavor and tartness. For a tastier product, add some sour cherry juice—either before freezing or after thawing.

Select well-colored, tree-ripened fruit. Sort, stem, wash, and drain. Remove pits and crush.

For red cherries, heat slightly (to 165° F.) to start flow of juice. Do not boil. Extract juice in a jelly bag.

For white cherries, extract juice without heating. Then warm juice (to 165° F.) in a double boiler or over low heat.

Cherries, sweet—continued

Juice—continued. For either red or white cherry juice, cool the juice, let stand overnight, and pour off clear juice for freezing. Or pack the juice as soon as it cools; then strain after thawing for serving.

Sweeten with 1 cup sugar to each quart of juice, or pack without adding sugar. Pour into container, leaving head space (P. 141). Seal and freeze.

Coconut, fresh

Shred coconut meat or put it through a food chopper. Pack into containers and cover with the coconut milk. Leave head space (P. 141). Seal and freeze.

Cranberries

● **Whole.** Choose firm, deep-red berries with glossy skins. Stem and sort. Wash and drain.

Unsweetened pack. Pack into containers without sugar. Leave head space (P. 141). Seal and freeze.

Sirup pack. Pack into containers. Cover with cold 50-percent sirup (p. 144). Leave head space (P. 141). Seal and freeze.

● **Puree.** Prepare cranberries as for freezing whole. Add 2 cups water to each quart (1 pound) of berries. Cook until skins have popped. Press through a sieve.

Add sugar to taste, about 2 cups for each quart (2 pounds) of puree. Pack into containers, leaving head space (P. 141). Seal and freeze.

Currants

● **Whole.** Select plump, fully ripe bright-red currants. Wash in cold water and remove stems.

Pack in any of the following ways:

Unsweetened pack. Pack into containers, leaving head space (P. 141). Seal and freeze.

Sirup pack. Pack into containers and cover currants with cold 50-percent sirup (P. 144), leaving head space (P. 141). Seal and freeze.

Sugar pack. To each quart (1⅓ pounds) of fruit add ¾ cup sugar. Stir until most of the sugar is dissolved. Pack currants into containers, leaving head space (P. 141). Seal and freeze.

● **Crushed.** Prepare as directed for whole currants. Crush.

To 1 quart (2 pounds) crushed currants add 1⅛ cups sugar. Mix until sugar is dissolved. Pack into containers, leaving head space (P.141). Seal and freeze.

● **Juice.** For use in beverages, select as directed for whole currants. For use in jelly making, mix slightly underripe and ripe fruit. Wash in cold water and remove stems. Crush currants and warm (to 165° F.) over low heat to start flow of juice. Do not boil. Press hot fruit in jelly bag to extract juice. Cool.

Sweeten with ¾ to 1 cup sugar to each quart of juice, or pack without adding sugar. Pour into containers, leaving head space (P. 141). Seal and freeze.

Dates

Select dates with good flavor and tender texture. Wash and slit to remove pits. Leave whole, or press through a sieve for puree.

Pack into containers, leaving head space (P. 141). Seal and freeze.

Figs

● **Whole or sliced.** Select tree-ripened soft-ripe fruit. Make sure figs have not become sour in the center. Sort, wash, and cut off stems. Peel if desired. Slice or leave whole.

Use one of the following packs:

Sirup pack. Use 35-percent sirup (P. 144). For a better product add ¾ teaspoon crystalline ascorbic acid or ½ cup lemon juice to each quart of sirup. Pack figs into containers and cover with cold sirup, leaving head space (P. 141). Seal and freeze.

Unsweetened pack. Pack into containers, leaving head space (P. 141). Cover with water or not as desired. If water is used, crystalline ascorbic acid may be added to retard darkening of light-colored figs—¾ teaspoon to each quart of water. Leave head space (P. 141). Seal and freeze.

● **Crushed.** Prepare figs as directed for freezing whole or sliced. Crush them coarsely.

With 1 quart (1½ pounds) fruit, mix ⅔ cup sugar. For a product of better quality add ¼ teaspoon crystalline ascorbic acid to each quart of fruit. Pack figs into containers, leaving head space (P. 141). Seal and freeze.

Fruit cocktail

Use any combination of fruits desired . . . sliced or cubed peaches or apricots, melon balls, orange or grapefruit sections, whole seedless grapes, Bing cherries, or pineapple wedges.

Pack into containers; cover with cold 30- or 40-percent sirup (P. 144), depending on fruits used. Leave head space (P. 141). Seal and freeze.

Gooseberries

Whole gooseberries may be frozen with sirup or without sweetening. For use in pie or preserves, the unsweetened pack is better.

Choose fully ripe berries if freezing for pie—berries a little underripe for jelly making. Sort, remove stems and blossom ends, and wash.

Unsweetened pack. Pack into containers without sugar. Leave head space (P. 141). Seal and freeze.

Sirup pack. Pack into containers. Cover with 50-percent sirup (P. 144). Leave head space (P. 141). Seal and freeze.

Grapefruit, oranges

● **Sections or slices.** Select firm tree-ripened fruit heavy for its size and free from soft spots. Wash and peel. Divide fruit into sections, removing all membranes and seeds. Slice oranges if desired. For grapefruit with many seeds, cut fruit in half, remove seeds; cut or scoop out sections.

Grapefruit—continued

Sections or slices—continued.
Pack fruit into containers. Cover
with cold 40-percent sirup (P. 144)
made with excess fruit juice and
water if needed. For better quality,
add ½ teaspoon crystalline ascorbic
acid to a quart of sirup. Leave head
space (P. 141). Seal and freeze.

● **Juice.**   Select fruit as directed for
sections.   Squeeze juice from fruit,
using squeezer that does not press oil
from rind.

Sweeten with 2 tablespoons sugar
for each quart of juice, or pack without sugar. For better quality, add
¾ teaspoon crystalline ascorbic acid
for each gallon of juice. Pour juice
into containers immediately. To
avoid development of off-flavors, pack
juice in glass jars or citrus-enamel tin
cans, if available. Leave head space
(P. 141). Seal and freeze.

Grapes

● **Whole or halves.**   Grapes are best
frozen with sirup, but grapes to be
used for juice or jelly can be frozen
without sweetening.

Select firm-ripe grapes with tender
skins and full color and flavor. Wash
and stem. Leave seedless grapes
whole; cut table grapes with seeds in
half and remove seeds.

Unsweetened pack.   Pack into containers without sweetening. Leave
head space (P. 141). Seal and freeze.

Sirup pack.   Pack into containers
and cover with cold 40-percent sirup
(P. 144).   Leave head space (P. 141).
Seal and freeze.

● **Puree.**   Grapes may be frozen as
puree with sugar added. The puree
may develop a gritty texture because
of tartrate crystals. The crystals
disappear when puree is heated.

Wash, stem, and crush the grapes.
Heat to boiling. Drain off free juice
and freeze or can it separately. Cool
the crushed grapes and press them
through a sieve.

To 1 quart (2 pounds) puree add ½
cup sugar. Pack into containers,
leaving head space (P. 141). Seal and
freeze.

● **Juice.**   For beverages, select as for
whole grapes. For jelly making,
select as recommended in specific
jelly recipe.

Wash, stem, and crush grapes.
Strain them through a jelly bag.
Let juice stand overnight in refrigerator or other cool place while sedi-
ment sinks to bottom. Pour off
clear juice for freezing.

Pour juice into containers, leaving
head space (P. 141). Seal and freeze.

If tartrate crystals form in frozen
juice, they may be removed by
straining the juice after it thaws.

Melons—cantaloup, cren-shaw, honeydew, Persian, watermelon

● **Slices, cubes, or balls.**   Select
firm-fleshed, well-colored, ripe melons.
Cut in half, remove seeds, and peel.
Cut melons into slices, cubes, or
balls. Pack into containers and
cover with cold 30-percent sirup
(P. 144). Leave head space (P. 141).
Seal and freeze.

● **Crushed.** Prepare melons, except watermelon, as for freezing in slices, cubes, or balls. Then crush them. If a food chopper is used for crushing, use the coarse knife.

Add 1 tablespoon sugar to each quart of crushed fruit if desired. Stir until sugar is dissolved. Pack melon into containers, leaving head space (P. 141). Seal and freeze.

Nectarines

● **Halves, quarters, or slices.** Choose fully ripe, well-colored, firm nectarines. Overripe fruit may take on a disagreeable flavor in frozen storage.

Sort, wash, and pit the fruit. Peel if desired. Cut in halves, quarters, or slices.

Cut fruit directly into cold 40-percent sirup (p.144), starting with ½ cup for each pint container. For a better product add ½ teaspoon crystalline ascorbic acid to each quart of sirup. Press fruit down and add sirup to cover, leaving head space (P. 141). Seal and freeze.

● **Puree.** Prepare same as peach puree (see below).

Peaches

● **Halves and slices.** Peaches in halves and slices have better quality when packed in sirup or with sugar, but a water pack will serve if sweetening is not desired.

Select firm, ripe peaches with no green color in the skins.

Sort, wash, pit, and peel. For a better product, peel peaches without a boiling-water dip. Slice if desired.

Sirup pack. Use 40-percent sirup (P. 144). For a better quality product, add ½ teaspoon crystalline ascorbic acid for each quart of sirup.

Put peaches directly into cold sirup in container—starting with ½ cup sirup to a pint container. Press fruit down and add sirup to cover, leaving head space (P. 141). Seal and freeze.

Sugar pack. To each quart (1⅓ pounds) of prepared fruit add ⅔ cup sugar and mix well. To retard darkening, sprinkle ascorbic acid dissolved in water over the peaches before adding sugar. Use ¼ teaspoon crystalline ascorbic acid in ¼ cup cold water to each quart of fruit.

Pack into containers, leaving head space (P. 141). Seal and freeze.

Water pack. Pack peaches into containers and cover with cold water containing 1 teaspoon crystalline ascorbic acid to each quart of water. Leave head space (P. 141). Seal and freeze.

● **Crushed or puree.** To loosen skins, dip peaches in boiling water ½ to 1 minute. The riper the fruit the less scalding needed. Cool in cold water, remove skins, and pit.

Crush peaches coarsely. Or, for puree, press through a sieve, or heat pitted peaches 4 minutes in just enough water to prevent scorching and then press through a sieve.

With each quart (2 pounds) of crushed or pureed peaches mix 1 cup sugar. For better quality, add ⅛ teaspoon crystalline ascorbic acid to each quart of fruit.

Pack into containers, leaving head space (P. 141). Seal and freeze.

Pears

● **Halves or quarters.** Select pears that are well ripened and firm but not hard. Wash fruit in cold water. Peel, cut in halves or quarters, and remove cores.

Heat pears in boiling 40-percent sirup (p. 144) for 1 to 2 minutes, depending on size of pieces. Drain and cool.

Pack pears into containers and cover with cold 40-percent sirup (p. 144). For a better product, add ¾ teaspoon crystalline ascorbic acid to a quart of cold sirup. Leave head space (P. 141). Seal and freeze.

● **Puree.** Select well-ripened pears, firm but not hard or gritty. Peel or not as desired, but do not dip in boiling water to remove skins. Prepare and pack as for peach puree (see directions on p.159).

Persimmons

● **Puree (cultivated and native varieties).** Select orange-colored, soft-ripe persimmons. Sort, wash, peel, and cut into sections. Press the fruit through a sieve.

To each quart of persimmon puree add ⅛ teaspoon crystalline ascorbic acid or 1½ teaspoons crystalline citric acid to help prevent darkening and flavor loss.

Persimmon puree made from native varieties needs no sugar. Puree made from cultivated varieties may be packed with or without sugar.

Unsweetened pack. Pack unsweetened puree into containers. Leave head space (P. 141). Seal and freeze.

Sugar pack. Mix 1 cup sugar with 1 quart (2 pounds) puree and pack into containers. Leave head space (P. 141). Seal and freeze.

Pineapple

Select firm, ripe pineapple with full flavor and aroma. Pare and remove core and eyes. Slice, dice, crush, or cut the pineapple into wedges or sticks.

Unsweetened pack. Pack fruit tightly into containers without sugar. Leave head space (P. 141). Seal and freeze.

Sirup pack. Pack fruit tightly into containers. Cover with 30-percent sirup made with pineapple juice, if available, or with water (p. 144). Leave head space (P. 141). Seal and freeze.

Plums and prunes

● **Whole, halves, or quarters.** Frozen plums and prunes are very good for use in pies and jams, or in salads and desserts. The unsweetened pack is preferred for plums to be used for jams.

Choose firm tree-ripened fruit of deep color. Sort and wash. Leave whole or cut in halves or quarters. Pack in one of the following ways:

Unsweetened pack. Pack whole fruit into containers, leaving head space (P. 141). Seal and freeze.

To serve uncooked, dip frozen fruit in cold water for 5 to 10 seconds, remove skins, and cover with 40-percent sirup to thaw.

Sirup pack. Pack cut fruit into containers. Cover fruit with cold 40- or 50-percent sirup, depending on tartness of fruit (P. 144). For improved quality, add ½ teaspoon crystalline ascorbic acid to a quart of sirup. Leave head space (P. 141). Seal and freeze.

● **Puree.** Select fully ripe fruit. Wash, cut in halves, and remove pits. Puree may be prepared from unheated or heated fruit, depending on softness of fruit.

To prepare puree from unheated fruit, press raw fruit through a sieve. For better quality, add either ¼ teaspoon crystalline ascorbic acid or ½ tablespoon crystalline citric acid to each quart (2 pounds) of puree.

To prepare puree from heated fruit, add 1 cup water for each 4 quarts (4 pounds) of fruit. Bring to a boil, cook 2 minutes, cool, and press through a sieve.

With each quart (2 pounds) of puree, mix ½ to 1 cup sugar, depending on tartness of fruit. Pack into containers, leaving head space (P.141). Seal and freeze.

● **Juice.** For juice to be served in beverages, select plums as for puree. For juice to be used for jelly making, select as recommended in specific jelly recipe. Wash plums, then simmer until soft in enough water to barely cover. Strain through a jelly bag. Cool.

If desired, sweeten with 1 to 2 cups sugar for each quart of juice, depending on tartness of fruit. Pour into containers, leaving head space (P.141). Seal and freeze.

Raspberries

● **Whole.** Raspberries may be frozen in sugar or sirup or unsweetened. Seedy berries are best for use in making purees or juice.

Select fully ripe, juicy berries. Sort, wash carefully in cold water, and drain thoroughly.

Sugar pack. To 1 quart (1⅓ pounds) berries add ¾ cup sugar and mix carefully to avoid crushing. Put into containers, leaving head space (P.141). Seal and freeze.

Sirup pack. Put berries into containers and cover with cold 40-percent sirup (p.144), leaving head space (P.141). Seal and freeze.

Unsweetened pack. Put berries into containers, leaving head space (P.141). Seal and freeze.

● **Crushed or puree.** Prepare as for whole raspberries; then crush or press through a sieve for puree.

To 1 quart (2 pounds) crushed berries or puree add ¾ to 1 cup sugar, depending on sweetness of fruit. Mix until sugar is dissolved. Put into containers, leaving head space (P. 141). Seal and freeze.

● **Juice.** For beverage use, select as for whole raspberries. For jelly making, select as recommended in specific jelly recipe. Crush and heat berries slightly to start flow of juice. Strain in a jelly bag to extract juice.

Sweeten with ½ to 1 cup sugar for each quart of juice if desired. Pour into containers, leaving head space (P. 141). Seal and freeze.

Rhubarb

● **Stalks or pieces.** Choose firm, tender, well-colored stalks with good flavor and few fibers. Wash, trim, and cut into 1- or 2-inch pieces or in lengths to fit the package. Heating rhubarb in boiling water for 1 minute and cooling promptly in cold water helps retain color and flavor.

Unsweetened pack. Pack either raw or preheated rhubarb tightly into containers without sugar. Leave head space (P. 141). Seal and freeze.

Sirup pack. Pack either raw or preheated rhubarb tightly into containers, cover with cold 40-percent sirup (P. 144). Leave head space (P. 141). Seal and freeze.

● **Puree.** Prepare rhubarb as for rhubarb stalks or pieces. Add 1 cup water to 1½ quarts (2 pounds) rhubarb and boil 2 minutes. Cool and press through a sieve. With 1 quart (2 pounds) puree mix ⅔ cup sugar. Pack into containers, leaving head space (P. 141). Seal and freeze.

● **Juice.** Select as for rhubarb stalks or pieces. Wash, trim, and cut into pieces 4 to 6 inches long. Add 1 quart water to 4 quarts (5 pounds) rhubarb and bring just to a boil. Press hot fruit in jelly bag to extract juice. Cool. Sweeten, if desired, using ½ cup sugar to a quart of juice. Pour into containers, leaving head space (P. 141). Seal and freeze.

Strawberries

● **Whole.** Choose firm, ripe, red berries preferably with a slightly tart flavor. Large berries are better sliced or crushed. Sort berries, wash them in cold water, drain well, and remove hulls.

Sugar and sirup packs make better quality frozen strawberries than berries packed without sweetening.

Sirup pack. Put berries into containers and cover with cold 50-percent sirup (P. 144), leaving head space (P. 141). Seal and freeze.

Sugar pack. Add ¾ cup sugar to 1 quart (1⅓ pounds) strawberries and mix thoroughly. Put into containers, leaving head space (P. 141). Seal and freeze.

Unsweetened pack. Pack into containers, leaving head space (P. 141). For better color, cover with water containing 1 teaspoon crystalline ascorbic acid to each quart of water. Seal and freeze.

● **Sliced or crushed.** Prepare for packing as for whole strawberries; then slice, or crush partially or completely.

To 1 quart (1½ pounds) berries add ¾ cup sugar; mix thoroughly. Pack into containers, leaving head space (P. 141). Seal and freeze.

● **Puree.** Prepare strawberries as for freezing whole. Then press berries through a sieve. To 1 quart (2 pounds) puree add ⅔ cup sugar and mix well. Put into containers, leaving head space (P. 141). Seal and freeze.

● **Juice.** Choose fully ripe berries. Sort and wash them in cold water. Drain well and remove hulls. Crush berries and strain juice through a jelly bag. Sweeten with ⅔ to 1 cup sugar to each quart of juice, or leave unsweetened. Pour into containers, leaving head space (P. 141). Seal and freeze.

Points on freezing vegetables

Best for freezing are fresh, tender vegetables right from the garden. The fresher the vegetables when frozen the more satisfactory will be your product.

First steps

Washing is the first step in the preparation of most vegetables for freezing. However, lima beans, green peas, and other vegetables that are protected by pods may not need to be washed.

Wash vegetables thoroughly in cold water. Lift them out of the water as grit settles to the bottom of the pan.

Sort vegetables according to size for heating and packing unless they are to be cut into pieces of uniform size.

Peel, trim, and cut into pieces, as directed for each vegetable on pages 170 to 175.

Heating before packing

An important step in preparing vegetables for freezing is heating or "blanching" before packing. Practically every vegetable, except green pepper, maintains better quality in frozen storage if heated before packing.

The reason for heating vegetables before freezing is that it slows or stops the action of enzymes. Up until the time vegetables are ready to pick, enzymes help them grow and mature. After that they cause loss of flavor and color. If vegetables are not heated enough the enzymes continue to be active during frozen storage. Then the vegetables may develop off-flavors, discolor, or toughen so that they may be unappetizing in a few weeks.

Heating also wilts or softens vegetables and makes them easier to pack. Heating time varies with the vegetable and size of pieces.

To heat in boiling water. For home freezing, the most satisfactory way to heat practically all vegetables is in boiling water. Use a blancher, which has a blanching basket and cover. Or fit a wire basket into a large kettle, and add the cover.

For each pound of prepared vegetable use at least 1 gallon of boiling water in the blancher or kettle. Put vegetables in blanching basket or wire basket and lower into the boiling water. A wire cover for the basket can be used to keep the vegetables down in the boiling water.

Put lid on blancher or kettle and start counting time immediately. Keep heat high for time given in directions for vegetable you are freezing. Heat 1 minute longer than the time specified if you live 5,000 feet or more above sea level.

To heat in steam. In this publication, heating in steam is recommended for a few vegetables. For broccoli, pumpkin, sweetpotatoes, and winter squash both steaming and boiling are satisfactory methods.

To steam, use a kettle with a tight lid and a rack that holds a steaming basket at least 3 inches above the bottom of the kettle. Put an inch or two of water in the kettle and bring the water to a boil.

Put vegetables in the basket in a single layer so that steam reaches all parts quickly. Cover the kettle and keep heat high. Start counting steaming time as soon as the lid is on. Steam 1 minute longer than the time specified in directions if you live 5,000 feet or more above sea level.

Other ways to heat. Pumpkin, sweetpotatoes, and winter squash may be heated in a pressure cooker or in the oven before freezing. Mushrooms may be heated in fat in a fry pan. Tomatoes for juice may be simmered.

Cooling

After vegetables are heated they should be cooled quickly and thoroughly to stop the cooking.

To cool vegetables heated in boiling water or steam, plunge the basket of vegetables immediately into a large quantity of cold water—60° F. or below. Change water frequently or use cold running water or iced water. If ice is used, you'll need about 1 pound of ice for each pound of vegetable. It will take about as long to cool the food as it does to heat it. When the vegetable is cool, remove it from the water and drain thoroughly.

To cool vegetables heated in the oven, a pressure cooker, or a fry pan— set pan of food in water and change water to speed cooling.

Dry pack more practical

Either dry or brine pack may be used for most vegetables to be frozen. However, in this publication the dry pack is recommended for all vegetables, because preparation for freezing and serving is easier.

Table of vegetable yields

The table on page 165 will help you figure the amount of frozen food you can get from a given amount of a fresh vegetable. The number of pints of frozen vegetables you get depends on the quality, condition, maturity, and variety—and on the way the vegetable is trimmed and cut.

Approximate yield of frozen vegetables from fresh

VEGETABLE	FRESH, AS PURCHASED OR PICKED	FROZEN
Asparagus	1 crate (12 2-lb. bunches) 1 to 1½ lb.	15 to 22 pt. 1 pt.
Beans, lima (in pods)	1 bu. (32 lb.) 2 to 2½ lb.	12 to 16 pt. 1 pt.
Beans, snap, green, and wax	1 bu. (30 lb.) ⅔ to 1 lb.	30 to 45 pt. 1 pt.
Beet greens	15 lb. 1 to 1½ lb.	10 to 15 pt. 1 pt.
Beets (without tops)	1 bu. (52 lb.) 1¼ to 1½ lb.	35 to 42 pt. 1 pt.
Broccoli	1 crate (25 lb.) 1 lb.	24 pt. 1 pt.
Brussels sprouts	4 quart boxes 1 lb.	6 pt. 1 pt.
Carrots (without tops)	1 bu. (50 lb.) 1¼ to 1½ lb.	32 to 40 pt. 1 pt.
Cauliflower	2 medium heads 1⅓ lb.	3 pt. 1 pt.
Chard	1 bu. (12 lb.) 1 to 1½ lb.	8 to 12 pt. 1 pt.
Collards	1 bu. (12 lb.) 1 to 1½ lb.	8 to 12 pt. 1 pt.
Corn, sweet (in husks)	1 bu. (35 lb.) 2 to 2½ lb.	14 to 17 pt. 1 pt.
Kale	1 bu. (18 lb.) 1 to 1½ lb.	12 to 18 pt. 1 pt.
Mustard greens	1 bu. (12 lb.) 1 to 1½ lb.	8 to 12 pt. 1 pt.
Peas	1 bu. (30 lb.) 2 to 2½ lb.	12 to 15 pt. 1 pt.
Peppers, green	⅔ lb. (3 peppers)	1 pt.
Pumpkin	3 lb.	2 pt.
Spinach	1 bu. (18 lb.) 1 to 1½ lb.	12 to 18 pt. 1 pt.
Squash, summer	1 bu. (40 lb.) 1 to 1¼ lb.	32 to 40 pt. 1 pt.
Squash, winter	3 lb.	2 pt.
Sweetpotatoes	⅔ lb.	1 pt.

Freezing snap beans

Other vegetables may be frozen in much the same way as snap beans. Beans are heated in boiling water before they are frozen—the most satisfactory home method for nearly all vegetables.

● Select young, tender, stringless beans that snap when broken. Allow ⅔ to 1 pound of fresh beans for 1 pint frozen. Wash thoroughly.

278A

● Cut beans into 1- or 2-inch pieces or slice them lengthwise.

280A

● Put beans in blanching basket, lower basket into boiling water, and cover. Heat for 3 minutes. Keep heat high under the water.

281A

● Plunge basket of heated beans into cold water to stop the cooking. It takes about as long to cool vegetables as to heat them. When beans are cool, remove them from water and drain.

282A

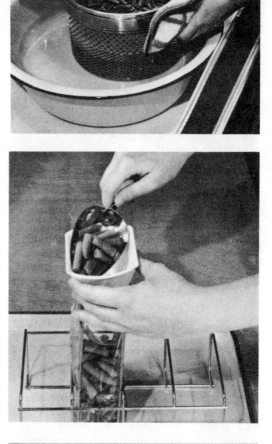

● Pack the beans into bags or other containers. A stand to hold the bags makes filling easier. A funnel helps keep the sealing edges clean.

283A

● Leave ½-inch head space and seal by twisting and folding back top of bag and tying with a string. Freeze beans at once. Store at 0° F. or below. If the bags used are of materials that become brittle at low temperatures, they need an outside carton for protection.

284A

Freezing broccoli

Broccoli, like all vegetables, is best frozen as soon as possible after it is picked. Allow about 1 pound fresh broccoli for each pint frozen. Because broccoli packs loosely, no head space need be allowed. Containers other than those shown here also may be used for packing.

● Select tight, compact, dark-green heads with tender stalks free from woodiness. Trim off large leaves and tough parts of stems and wash thoroughly.

If necessary, soak stalks for ½ hour in salt water (made of 4 teaspoons salt to each gallon of water) to remove insects.

BN23605

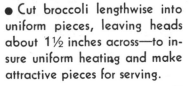

● Cut broccoli lengthwise into uniform pieces, leaving heads about 1½ inches across—to insure uniform heating and make attractive pieces for serving.

BN23603

● Steam pieces by placing them in blanching basket over rapidly boiling water. Cover kettle, keep heat high, and steam for 5 minutes. Or heat pieces in boiling water 3 minutes, as is shown for snap beans (p. 32).

BN23602

● Remove basket from boiling water. Cool broccoli by plunging basket into cold water.

BN23607

● Lift basket from cold water as soon as broccoli is cool and let drain a few minutes.

BN23606

● Pack broccoli so some heads are at each end of the container—to get more broccoli in the package. No head space is needed. Press lid on firmly to seal. Freeze at once. Store at 0° F. or below.

BN23604

Directions for vegetables

Asparagus

Select young, tender stalks with compact tips. Sort according to thickness of stalk.

Wash asparagus thoroughly and cut or break off and discard tough parts of stalks. Leave spears in lengths to fit the package or cut in 2-inch lengths.

Heat stalks in boiling water according to thickness of stalk:

Small stalks............ 2 minutes
Medium stalks......... 3 minutes
Large stalks........... 4 minutes

Cool promptly in cold water and drain.

Pack into containers, leaving no head space. When packing spears, alternate tips and stem ends. In containers that are wider at the top than bottom, pack asparagus with tips down. Seal and freeze.

Beans, lima

Select well-filled pods. Beans should be green but not starchy or mealy. Shell and sort according to size, or leave beans in pods to be shelled after heating and cooling. Heat in boiling water:

Small beans or pods...... 2 minutes
Medium beans or pods... 3 minutes
Large beans or pods...... 4 minutes

Cool promptly in cold water and drain.

Pack into containers, leaving ½-inch head space. Seal and freeze.

Beans, shell, green

Select pods that are plump, not dry or wrinkled. Shell the beans. Heat in boiling water 1 minute. Cool promptly in cold water and drain.

Pack into containers, leaving ½-inch head space. Seal and freeze.

Beans, snap, green, or wax

Select young, tender, stringless beans that snap when broken. Wash thoroughly; then remove ends.

Cut in 1- or 2-inch pieces, or slice lengthwise into strips for frenched (julienne-style) snap beans.

Heat in boiling water for 3 minutes. Chill promptly in cold water and drain.

Pack into containers, leaving ½-inch head space. Seal and freeze.

Beans, soybeans, green

Select firm, well-filled, bright-green pods. Wash. Heat beans in pods 5 minutes in boiling water, and cool promptly in cold water. Squeeze soybeans out of pods.

Pack soybeans into containers, leaving ½-inch head space. Seal and freeze.

Beets

Select young or mature beets not more than 3 inches across.

Wash and sort according to size. Trim tops, leaving ½ inch of stems.

Cook in boiling water until tender—for small beets, 25 to 30 minutes; for medium-size beets, 45 to 50 minutes. Cool promptly in cold water. Peel and cut into slices or cubes.

Pack beets into containers, leaving ½-inch head space. Seal and freeze.

Broccoli

Select tight, compact, dark-green heads with tender stalks free from woodiness. Wash, peel stalks, and trim. If necessary to remove insects, soak for ½ hour in a solution made of 4 teaspoons salt to 1 gallon cold water. Split lengthwise into pieces so that flowerets are not more than 1½ inches across.

Heat in steam 5 minutes or in boiling water 3 minutes. Cool promptly in cold water and drain.

Pack broccoli into containers, leaving no head space. Seal and freeze.

Brussels sprouts

Select green, firm, and compact heads. Examine heads carefully to make sure they are free from insects. Trim, removing coarse outer leaves. Wash thoroughly. Sort into small, medium, and large sizes.

Heat in boiling water:

Small heads . . . . 3 minutes
Medium heads . . . . 4 minutes
Large heads . . . . 5 minutes

Cool promptly in cold water and drain.

Pack brussels sprouts into containers, leaving no head space. Seal and freeze.

Cabbage or chinese cabbage

Frozen cabbage or chinese cabbage is suitable for use only as a cooked vegetable.

Select freshly picked, solid heads. Trim coarse outer leaves from head. Cut into medium to coarse shreds or thin wedges, or separate head into leaves. Heat in boiling water 1½ minutes.

Cool promptly in cold water and drain.

Pack cabbage into containers, leaving ½-inch head space. Seal and freeze.

Carrots

Select tender, mild-flavored carrots. Remove tops, wash, and peel. Leave small carrots whole. Cut others into ¼-inch cubes, thin slices, or lengthwise strips.

Heat in boiling water:

Whole carrots, small . . . . . 5 minutes
Diced or sliced . . . . 2 minutes
Lengthwise strips . . . . 2 minutes

Cool promptly in cold water and drain.

Pack carrots into containers, leaving ½-inch head space. Seal and freeze.

Cauliflower

Choose firm, tender, snow white heads. Break or cut into pieces about 1 inch across. Wash well. If necessary to remove insects, soak for 30 minutes in a solution of salt and water—4 teaspoons salt to each gallon of water. Drain.

Cauliflower—continued

Heat in boiling water containing 4 teaspoons salt to a gallon for 3 minutes. Cool promptly in cold water and drain.

Pack cauliflower into containers, leaving no head space. Seal and freeze.

Celery

Select crisp, tender stalks, free from coarse strings and pithiness.

Wash thoroughly, trim, and cut stalks into 1-inch lengths.

Heat for 3 minutes in boiling water. Cool promptly in cold water and drain.

Pack celery into containers, leaving ½-inch head space. Seal and freeze.

Corn, sweet

● Whole-kernel and cream-style.

Select ears with plump, tender kernels and thin, sweet milk. If the milk is thick and starchy it is better to freeze corn as cream-style.

Husk ears, remove silk, and wash the corn. Heat ears in boiling water for 4 minutes. Cool promptly in cold water and drain.

For whole-kernel corn, cut kernels from cob at about two-thirds the depth of the kernels.

For cream-style corn, cut corn from the cob at about the center of the kernels. Scrape the cobs with the back of the knife to remove the juice and the heart of the kernel.

Pack corn into containers, leaving ½-inch head space. Seal and freeze.

● On-the-cob.
Select same as for whole-kernel sweet corn.

Husk, remove silk, wash, and sort ears according to size.

Heat in boiling water:

Small ears............. 7 minutes
(1¼ inches or less in diameter)
Medium ears.......... 9 minutes
(1¼ to 1½ inches in diameter)
Large ears............ 11 minutes
(over 1½ inches in diameter)

Cool promptly in cold water and drain.

Pack ears into containers or wrap in moisture-vapor-resistant material. Seal and freeze.

Greens—beet greens, chard, collards, kale, mustard greens, spinach, turnip greens

Select young, tender leaves. Wash well. Remove tough stems and imperfect leaves. Cut leaves of chard into pieces as desired.

Heat in boiling water for the following periods:

Beet greens, kale, chard, 2 minutes
mustard greens, turnip greens.
Collards.............. 3 minutes
Spinach and New Zealand spinach. 2 minutes
Very tender leaves....1½ minutes

Cool promptly in cold water and drain.

Pack greens into containers, leaving ½-inch head space. Seal and freeze.

Kohlrabi

Select young, tender, mild-flavored kohlrabi, small to medium in size. Cut off tops and roots. Wash, peel, and leave whole or dice in ½-inch cubes.

Heat in boiling water:

Whole kohlrabi......... 3 minutes
Cubes.................. 1 minute

Cool promptly in cold water and drain.

Pack whole kohlrabi into containers or wrap in moisture-vapor-resistant material. Seal and freeze.

Pack cubes into containers, leaving ½-inch head space. Seal and freeze.

Mushrooms

Choose mushrooms free from spots and decay. Sort according to size. Wash thoroughly in cold water. Trim off ends of stems. If mushrooms are larger than 1 inch across, slice them or cut them into quarters.

Mushrooms may be steamed or heated in fat in a fry pan.

● **To steam.** Mushrooms to be steamed have better color if given antidarkening treatment first.

Dip for 5 minutes in a solution containing 1 teaspoon lemon juice or 1½ teaspoons citric acid to a pint of water. Then steam:

Whole mushrooms....... 5 minutes
　　(not larger than 1 inch
　　across)
Buttons or quarters.... 3½ minutes
Slices................. 3 minutes

Cool promptly in cold water and drain.

● **To heat in fry pan.** Heat small quantities of mushrooms in table fat in an open fry pan until almost done.

Cool in air or set pan in which mushrooms were cooked in cold water.

Pack into containers, leaving ½-inch head space. Seal and freeze.

Okra

Select young, tender, green pods. Wash thoroughly. Cut off stems in such a way as not to cut open seed cells.

Heat in boiling water:

Small pods............. 3 minutes
Large pods............. 4 minutes

Cool promptly in cold water and drain.

Leave whole or slice crosswise.

Pack into containers, leaving ½-inch head space. Seal and freeze.

Parsnips

Choose small to medium-size parsnips that are tender and free from woodiness. Remove tops, wash, peel, and cut in ½-inch cubes or slices.

Heat in boiling water 2 minutes. Cool promptly in cold water; drain.

Pack into containers, leaving ½-inch head space. Seal and freeze.

Peas, field (blackeye)

Select well-filled flexible pods with tender seeds. Shell peas, discarding those that are hard.

Heat in boiling water for 2 minutes. Cool promptly in cold water and drain.

Pack into containers, leaving ½-inch head space. Seal and freeze.

Peas, green

Choose bright-green, plump, firm pods with sweet, tender peas. Do not use immature or tough peas.

Shell peas. Heat in boiling water 1½ minutes. Cool promptly in cold water and drain.

Pack peas into containers, leaving ½-inch head space. Seal and freeze.

Peppers, green and hot

● **Green.** Peppers frozen without heating are best for use in uncooked foods. Heated peppers are easier to pack and good for use in cooking.

Select firm, crisp, thick-walled peppers. Wash, cut out stems, cut in half, and remove seeds. If desired, cut into ½-inch strips or rings.

Heat in boiling water if desired:

Halves . . . . 3 minutes
Slices . . . . 2 minutes

Cool promptly in cold water and drain.

If peppers have not been heated, pack into containers, leaving no head space. Seal and freeze. If peppers have been heated, leave ½-inch head space.

● **Hot.** Wash and stem peppers Pack into small containers, leaving no head space. Seal and freeze.

Pimientos

Select firm, crisp, thick-walled pimientos.

To peel, first roast pimientos in an oven at 400° F. (hot oven) for 3 to 4 minutes. Remove charred skins by rinsing pimientos in cold water. Drain.

Pack pimientos into containers leaving ½-inch head space. Seal and freeze.

Pumpkin

Select full-colored, mature pumpkin with texture that is fine rather than coarse and stringy.

Wash, cut into quarters or smaller pieces, and remove seeds. Cook pumpkin pieces until soft in boiling water, in steam, in a pressure cooker, or in the oven.

Remove pulp from rind and mash it or press it through a sieve.

To cool, place pan containing pumpkin in cold water. Stir pumpkin occasionally.

Pack into containers, leaving ½-inch head space. Seal and freeze.

Rutabagas

Select young, tender, medium-size rutabagas with no tough fibers. Cut off tops, wash, and peel.

● **Cubed.** Cut into ½-inch cubes. Heat in boiling water for 2 minutes. Cool promptly in cold water; drain. Pack into containers, leaving ½-inch head space. Seal and freeze.

● **Mashed.** Cut rutabagas in pieces. Cook until tender in boiling water and drain. Mash or press through a sieve.

To cool, place pan containing rutabagas in cold water. Stir rutabagas occasionally. Pack into containers, leaving ½-inch head space. Seal and freeze.

Squash, summer and winter

● **Summer.** Select young squash with small seeds and tender rind. Wash, cut in ½-inch slices. Heat in boiling water for 3 minutes. Cool squash promptly in cold water and drain.

Pack into containers, leaving ½-inch head space. Seal and freeze.

● **Winter.** Select firm, mature squash. Wash, cut into pieces, and remove seeds. Cook pieces until soft in boiling water, in steam, in a pressure cooker, or in the oven. Remove pulp from rind and mash or press through a sieve.

To cool, place pan containing squash in cold water and stir squash occasionally.

Pack into containers, leaving ½-inch head space. Seal and freeze.

Sweetpotatoes

Sweetpotatoes may be packed whole, sliced, or mashed.

Choose medium to large mature sweetpotatoes that have been cured. Sort according to size, and wash.

Cook until almost tender in water, in steam, in a pressure cooker, or in the oven. Let stand at room temperature until cool. Peel sweetpotatoes; cut in halves, slice, or mash.

If desired, to prevent darkening, dip whole sweetpotatoes or slices for 5 seconds in a solution of 1 tablespoon citric acid or ½ cup lemon juice to 1 quart water.

To keep mashed sweetpotatoes from darkening, mix 2 tablespoons orange or lemon juice with each quart of mashed sweetpotatoes.

Pack into containers, leaving ½-inch head space. Seal and freeze.

● **For variety.** Roll cooked sweetpotato slices in sugar. Pack into containers, leaving ½-inch head space. Seal and freeze.

Or pack whole or sliced cooked sweetpotatoes in containers, cover with cold sirup (made of equal parts by measure of sugar and water). Leave head space (see p.141,for liquid pack). Seal and freeze.

Tomatoes

● **Juice.** Wash, sort, and trim firm, vine-ripened tomatoes. Cut in quarters or eighths. Simmer 5 to 10 minutes. Press through a sieve. If desired, season with 1 teaspoon salt to each quart of juice. Pour into containers, leaving head space (see p.141,for juices). Seal and freeze.

● **Stewed.** Remove stem ends, peel, and quarter ripe tomatoes. Cover and cook until tender (10 to 20 minutes). Place pan containing tomatoes in cold water to cool. Pack into containers, leaving head space (see p.141,for liquid pack). Seal and freeze.

Turnips

Select small to medium, firm turnips that are tender and have a mild flavor. Wash, peel, and cut into ½-inch cubes. Heat in boiling water for 2 minutes. Cool promptly in cold water and drain.

Pack into containers, leaving ½-inch head space. Seal and freeze.

How to use frozen fruits and vegetables

Fruits

Serving uncooked. Frozen fruits need only to be thawed, if they are to be served raw.

For best color and flavor, leave fruit in the sealed container to thaw. Serve as soon as thawed; a few ice crystals in the fruit improve the texture for eating raw.

Frozen fruit in the package may be thawed in the refrigerator, at room temperature, or in a pan of cool water. Turn package several times for more even thawing.

Allow 6 to 8 hours on a refrigerator shelf for thawing a 1-pound package of fruit packed in sirup. Allow 2 to 4 hours for thawing a package of the same size at room temperature—$\frac{1}{2}$ to 1 hour for thawing in a pan of cool water.

Fruit packed with dry sugar thaws slightly faster than that packed in sirup. Both sugar and sirup packs thaw faster than unsweetened packs.

Thaw only as much as you need at one time. If you have leftover thawed fruit it will keep better if you cook it. Cooked fruit will keep in the refrigerator for a few days.

Cooking. First thaw fruits until pieces can be loosened. Then cook as you would cook fresh fruit. If there is not enough juice to prevent scorching, add water as needed. If the recipe calls for sugar, allow for any sweetening that was added before freezing.

Frozen fruits often have more juice than called for in recipes for baked products using fresh fruits. In that case use only part of the juice, or add more thickening for the extra juice.

9125D

Using crushed fruit and purees.   Serve crushed fruit as raw fruit—after it is partially or completely thawed.   Or use it after thawing as a topping for ice cream or cakes, as a filling for sweet rolls, or for jam.

Use thawed purees in puddings, ice cream, sherbets, jams, pies, ripple cakes, fruit-filled coffee cake, and rolls.

Serving juice.   Serve frozen fruit juice as a beverage—after it is thawed but while it is still cold.   Some juices, such as sour cherry, plum, grape, and berry juices, may be diluted ⅓ to ½ with water or a bland juice.

Vegetables

The secret of cooking frozen vegetables successfully is to cook the vegetable until just tender.   That way you save vitamins, bright color, and fresh flavor.

Frozen vegetables may be cooked in a small amount of water or in a pressure saucepan, or by baking or panfrying.

Cooking in a small amount of water.   You should cook most frozen vegetables without thawing them first.   Leafy vegetables, such as spinach, cook more evenly if thawed just enough to separate the leaves before cooking.   Corn-on-the-cob should be partially thawed before cooking, so that the cob will be heated through by the time the corn is cooked.   Holding corn after thawing or cooking causes sogginess.

Bring water to a boil in a covered saucepan.   The amount of water to use depends on the vegetable and the size of the package.   For most vegetables one-half cup of water is enough for a pint package.   The frost in the packages furnishes some additional moisture.

Put the frozen vegetable in the boiling water, cover the pan, and bring the water quickly back to a boil.   To insure uniform cooking, it may be necessary to separate pieces carefully with a fork.   When the water is boiling throughout the pan, reduce the heat and start counting time. Be sure pan is covered to keep in the steam, which aids in cooking. Cook gently until vegetables are just tender.

Add seasonings as desired and serve immediately.

The following timetable shows about how long it takes to cook tender one pint of various frozen vegetables—and how much water to use. Use the table only as a general guide.   Cooking times vary among varieties and with the maturity of the vegetable when it is frozen.

The time required for cooking vegetables is slightly longer at high than at low altitudes because the temperature of boiling water decreases about 2° F. with each 1,000 feet above sea level.

Timetable for cooking frozen vegetables in a small amount of water [1]

VEGETABLE	Time to allow after water returns to boil [2] *Minutes*	VEGETABLE	Time to allow after water returns to boil [2] *Minutes*
Asparagus	5–10	Chard	8–10
Beans, lima:		Corn:	
Large type	6–10	Whole-kernel	3–5
Baby type	15–20	On-the-cob	3–4
Beans, snap, green, or wax:		Kale	8–12
1-inch pieces	12–18	Kohlrabi	8–10
Julienne	5–10	Mustard greens	8–15
Beans, soybeans, green	10–20	Peas, green	5–10
Beet greens	6–12	Spinach	4–6
Broccoli	5–8	Squash, summer	10–12
Brussels sprouts	4–9	Turnip greens	15–20
Carrots	5–10	Turnips	8–12
Cauliflower	5–8		

[1] Use ½ cup of lightly salted water for each pint of vegetable with these exceptions: Lima beans, 1 cup; corn-on-the-cob, water to cover.

[2] Time required at sea level; slightly longer time is required at higher altitudes.

Cooking in a pressure saucepan. Follow directions and cooking times specified by the manufacturer of your saucepan.

Baking. Many frozen vegetables may be baked in a covered casserole. Partially defrost vegetable to separate pieces.

Put vegetable in a greased casserole; add seasonings as desired. Cover and bake until just tender.

The time it takes to bake a vegetable varies with size of pieces and how much you thaw them before baking.

Approximate time for baking most thawed vegetables is 45 minutes at 350° F. (moderate oven). Slightly more time may be required if other foods are being baked at the same time.

To bake corn-on-the-cob, partially thaw the ears first. Brush with melted butter or margarine, salt, and roast at 400° F. (hot oven) about 20 minutes.

Pan frying. Use a heavy fry pan with cover. Place about 1 tablespoon fat in pan. Add 1 pint frozen vegetable, which has been thawed enough to separate pieces. Cook covered over moderate heat. Stir occasionally. Cook until just tender. Season to taste, and serve immediately.

Peas, asparagus, and broccoli will cook tender in a fry pan in about 10 minutes.   Mushrooms will be done in 10 to 15 minutes and snap beans in 15 to 20 minutes.

Other ways to prepare frozen vegetables.   Vegetables that are cooked until tender before freezing need only to be seasoned and heated before serving.   Cooked frozen vegetables can be used in many dishes in the same ways as cooked fresh vegetables.   They may be creamed or scalloped, served au gratin, or added to souffles, cream soups, or salads.

Pumpkin, winter squash, and sweetpotatoes may be thawed and used as the main ingredient in pie fillings.

How to Make Jellies, Jams and Preserves at Home

Jelly, jam, conserve, marmalade, preserves—any of these fruit products can add zest to meals. Most of them also provide a good way to use fruit not at its best for canning or freezing—the largest or smallest fruits and berries and those that are irregularly shaped.

Basically these products are much alike; all of them are fruit preserved by means of sugar, and usually all are jellied to some extent. Their individual characteristics depend on the kind of fruit used and the way it is prepared, the proportions of different ingredients in the mixture, and the method of cooking.

Jelly is made from fruit juice; the product is clear and firm enough to hold its shape when turned out of the container. Jam, made from crushed or ground fruit, tends to hold its shape but generally is less firm than jelly. Conserves are jams made from a mixture of fruits, usually including citrus fruit; often raisins and nuts are added. Marmalade is a tender jelly with small pieces of fruit distributed evenly throughout; a marmalade commonly contains citrus fruit. Preserves are whole fruits or large pieces of fruit in a thick sirup, often slightly jellied.

Not all fruits have the properties needed for making satisfactory jellied products, but with the commercial pectins now on the market, the homemaker need not depend on the jellying quality of the fruit for successful results.

This publication tells how to make various kinds of jellies, jams, and conserves, with and without added pectin. It also includes recipes for marmalades and preserves made with no added pectin.

Four essential ingredients

Proper amounts of fruit, pectin, acid, and sugar are needed to make a jellied fruit product.

Fruit

Fruit gives each product its characteristic flavor and furnishes at least part of the pectin and acid required for successful gels.

Flavorful varieties of fruits are best for jellied products because the fruit flavor is diluted by the large proportion of sugar necessary for proper consistency and good keeping quality.

Pectin

Some kinds of fruit have enough natural pectin to make high-quality products. Others require added pectin, particularly when they are used for making jellies, which should be firm enough to hold their shape. All fruits have more pectin when they are underripe.

Commercial fruit pectins, which are made from apples or citrus fruits, are on the market in two forms—liquid and powdered. Either form is satisfactory when used in a recipe developed especially for that form.

These pectins may be used with any fruit. Many homemakers prefer the added-pectin method for making jellied fruit products because fully ripe fruit can be used, cooking time is shorter and is standardized so that there is no question when the product is done, and the yield from a given amount of fruit is greater.

Fruit pectins should be stored in a cool, dry place so they will keep their gel strength. They should not be held over from one year to the next.

Acid

Acid is needed for flavor and for gel formation. The acid content varies in different fruits and is higher in underripe fruits.

With fruits that are low in acid, lemon juice or citric acid is commonly added in making jellied products. Also, commercial fruit pectins contain some acid.

In the recipes in this publication, lemon juice is included to supply additional acid when necessary. If you wish, use ⅛ teaspoon of crystalline citric acid for each tablespoon of lemon juice called for.

Sugar

Sugar helps in gel formation, serves as a preserving agent, and contributes to the flavor of the jellied product. It also has a firming effect on fruit, a property that is useful in the making of preserves.

Beet and cane sugar can be used with equal success. Although they come from different sources, they have the same composition.

Equipment and containers

Equipment

A large kettle is essential. To bring mixture to a full boil without boiling over, use an 8– or 10–quart kettle with a broad flat bottom.

A jelly bag or a fruit press may be used for extracting fruit juice for jellies. The bag may be made of several thicknesses of closely woven cheesecloth, of firm unbleached muslin, or canton flannel with napped side in. Use a jelly bag or cheesecloth to strain pressed juice. A special stand or collander will hold the jelly bag.

A jelly, candy, or deep-fat thermometer is an aid in making fruit products without added pectin.

Other kitchen equipment that may be useful includes a quart measure, measuring cup and spoons, paring and utility knives, food chopper, masher, reamer, grater, bowls, wire basket, colander, long-handled spoon, ladle, clock with second hand, and household scale.

Containers

Jelly glasses or canning jars may be used as containers for jellied fruit products. Be sure all jars and closures are perfect. Discard any with cracks or chips; defects prevent airtight seals.

For jellies to be sealed with paraffin, use glasses or straight-sided containers that will make an attractive mold.

For jams, preserves, conserves, and marmalades, use canning jars with lids that can be tightly sealed and processed. Paraffin tends to loosen and break the seal on these products.

Get glasses or jars ready before you start to make the jellied product. Wash containers in warm, soapy water and rinse with hot water. Sterilize jelly containers in boiling water for 10 minutes. Keep all containers hot—either in a slow oven or in hot water—until they are used. This will prevent containers from breaking when filled with hot jelly or jam.

Wash and rinse all lids and bands. Metal lids with sealing compound may need boiling or holding in boiling water for a few minutes—follow the manufacturer's directions. Use new lids; bands and jars may be reused.

If you use porcelain-lined zinc caps, have clean, new rings of the right size for jars. Wash rings in hot, soapy water. Rinse well.

Making and storing jellied fruit products

Directions for making different kinds of jellied fruit products are given in this publication. The formulas selected take into account the natural pectin and acid content of the specified fruit.

Tips on jellied fruit products

For freshness of flavor. To have jellied fruit products at their best, make up only the quantity that can be used within a few months; they lose flavor in storage.

For softer or firmer products. If fruit with average jellying properties is used, the jellied products made according to directions in this publication should be medium firm for their type. However, because various lots of fruit differ in composition, it is not possible to develop formulas that will always give exactly the same results.

If the first batch from a particular lot of fruit is too soft or too firm, adjust the proportions of fruit or the cooking time for the next batch.

In products made with added pectin—

For a softer product, use ¼ to ½ cup *more* fruit or juice.

For a firmer product, use ¼ to ½ cup *less* fruit or juice.

In products made without added pectin—

For a softer product, *shorten* the cooking time.

For firmer product, *lengthen* the cooking time.

Using canned, frozen, or dried fruits. Any fresh fruit may be canned or frozen as fruit or juice and used in jellied products later. Both fruit and juice should be canned or frozen unsweetened; if sweetened—the amount of sugar should be noted and subtracted from the amount in the jelly or jam recipe. Fruit should be canned in its own juice or with only a small amount of water. If you plan to use canned or frozen fruit without added pectin, it is best to use part underripe fruit, especially for jelly.

Unsweetened commercially canned or frozen fruit or juice can also be used in jellied products. Concentrated frozen juices make very flavorful jellies. Commercially canned or frozen products are made from fully ripe fruit, and require added pectin if used for jelly.

Dried fruit may be cooked in water until tender and used to make jams and conserves, with or without added pectin as required.

Filling and sealing containers

Prepare canning jars and lids or jelly glasses as directed.

To seal with lids.—Use only standard home canning jars. For jars with two-piece lids: Use new lids; bands may be reused. Fill hot jars to ⅛ inch of top with hot jelly or fruit mixture. Wipe jar rim clean, place hot metal lid on jar with sealing compound next to glass, screw metal band down firmly, and stand jar upright to cool. For jars with porcelain-lined zinc caps: Place wet rubber ring on shoulder of empty jar. Fill jar to ⅛ inch of top, screw cap down tight to complete seal, and stand jar upright to cool.

Work quickly when packing and sealing jars. To keep fruit from floating to the top, gently shake jars of jam occasionally as they cool.

To seal with paraffin.—Use this method only with jelly. Pour hot jelly mixture immediately into hot containers to within ½ inch of top. Cover with hot paraffin. Use only enough paraffin to make a layer ⅛ inch thick. A single thin layer—which can expand or contract readily—gives a better seal than one thick layer or two thin layers. Prick air bubbles in paraffin. Bubbles cause holes as paraffin hardens; they may prevent a good seal. A double boiler is best for melting paraffin and keeping it hot without reaching smoking temperature.

To process jams, conserves, marmalades, and preserves.—Processing of these products is recommended in warm or humid climates. Inexpensive enamelware canners may be purchased at most hardware or variety stores. However, any large metal container may be used if it—

- Is deep enough to allow for 1 or 2 inches of water above the tops of the jars, plus a little extra space for boiling.
- Has a close-fitting cover.
- Has a wire or wood rack with partitions to keep jars from touching each other or the bottom or sides of the container.

Put filled home canning jars into a water bath canner or a container filled with hot water. Add hot water if needed to bring water an inch or two over tops of jars. Bring water to a rolling boil and boil gently for 5 minutes.

Remove jars from canner after processing. Cool away from drafts before storing.

Storing jellied fruit products

Let products stand undisturbed overnight to avoid breaking gel. Cover jelly glasses with metal or paper lids. Label with name, date, and lot number if you make more than one lot a day. Store in a cool, dry place; the shorter the storage time, the better the eating quality of the product.

Uncooked jams (P. 205) may be held up to 3 weeks in a refrigerator; for longer storage, they should be placed in a freezer.

Jellies

Jelly is clear and bright with the natural color and flavor of the fruit from which it is made. It is tender yet firm enough to hold its shape when cut.

When making jelly, with or without added pectin, it is best to prepare small cooking lots, as indicated in the recipes that follow. Increasing the quantities given is not recommended.

To prepare fruit

Approximate amounts of fruits needed to yield the amount of juice called for are given in each recipe. However, the exact amount will vary with juiciness of the particular lot of fruit used.

Wash all fruits in cold running water, or wash them in several changes of cold water, lifting them out of the water each time. Do not let fruit stand in water.

Prepare fruit for juice extraction as directed in the recipe; the method differs with different kinds of fruit. Juicy berries may be crushed and the juice pressed out without heating. For firm fruits, heating is needed to help start the flow of juice, and usually some water is added when the fruit is heated.

To extract juice

Put the prepared fruit in a damp jelly bag, fruit press, or a double layer of damp cheesecloth to extract the juice. The clearest jelly comes from juice that has dripped through a jelly bag without pressing. But a greater yield of juice can be obtained by twisting the bag of fruit tightly and squeezing or pressing, or by using a fruit press. Pressed juice should be re-strained through a double thickness of damp cheesecloth or a damp jelly bag; the cloth or bag should not be squeezed.

To make jelly

With added pectin. In this publication some of the recipes have been developed with powdered pectin, others with liquid pectin. Because of differences between the two forms, each should be used only in recipes worked out for that form.

The order in which the ingredients are combined depends on the form of pectin. Powdered pectin is mixed with the unheated fruit juice. Liquid pectin is added to the boiling juice and sugar mixture.

Boiling time is the same with either form of pectin; a 1-minute boiling period is recommended. Accurate timing is important. Time should not be counted until the mixture has reached a full rolling boil—one that cannot be stirred down.

For best flavor, use fully ripe fruit when making jelly with added pectin.

Without added pectin. Jellies made without added pectin require less sugar per cup of fruit juice than do those with added pectin, and longer boiling is necessary to bring the mixture to the proper sugar concentration. Thus the yield of jelly per cup of juice is less.

It is usually best to have part of the fruit underripe when no pectin is added, because underripe fruit has a higher pectin content. The use of one-fourth underripe and three-fourths fully ripe fruit is generally recommended to assure sufficient pectin for jelly.

To test for pectin in fruit juice

A rough estimate of the amount of pectin in fruit juice may be obtained through use of denatured alcohol or a jelmeter.

Alcohol test. Add 1 tablespoon cooked, cooled fruit juice to 1 tablespoon denatured alcohol. Stir slightly to mix. Juices rich in pectin will form a solid jelly-like mass. Juices low in pectin will form small particles of jelly-like material.

NOTE: *Denatured alcohol is poisonous. Do not taste the tested juice. Wash all utensils used in this test thoroughly.*

Jelmeter test. A jelmeter is a graduated glass tube with an opening at each end. The rate of flow of fruit juice through this tube gives a rough estimate of the amount of pectin in the juice.

If a test indicates that the juice is low in pectin, use a recipe calling for the addition of powdered or liquid pectin.

To test for doneness

The biggest problem in making jelly without added pectin is to know when it is done. It is particularly important to remove the mixture from the heat before it is overcooked. Although an undercooked jelly can sometimes be recooked to make a satisfactory product (see p.211), there is little that can be done to improve an overcooked mixture. Signs of overcooking are a change in color of mixture and a taste or odor of caramelized sugar.

Three methods that may be used for testing doneness of jelly made at home are described below. Of these, the temperature test probably is the most dependable.

Temperature test. Before cooking the jelly, take the temperature of boiling water with a jelly, candy, or deep-fat thermometer. Cook the jelly mixture to a temperature 8° F. higher than the boiling point of water. At that point the concentration of sugar will be such that the mixture should form a satisfactory gel.

It is necessary to find out at what temperature water boils in your locality because the boiling point differs at different altitudes. And, because the boiling point at a given altitude may change with different atmospheric conditions, the temperature of boiling water should be checked shortly before the jelly is to be made.

For an accurate thermometer reading, have the thermometer in a vertical position and read it at eye level. The bulb of the thermometer must be completely covered with the jelly mixture, but must not touch the bottom of the kettle.

Spoon or sheet test. Dip a cool metal spoon in the boiling jelly mixture. Then raise it at least a foot above the kettle, out of the steam, and turn the spoon so the sirup runs off the side. If the sirup forms two drops that flow together and fall off the spoon as one sheet, the jelly should be done. This test has been widely used; however, it is not entirely dependable.

Refrigerator test. Pour a small amount of boiling jelly on a cold plate, and put it in the freezing compartment of a refrigerator for a few minutes. If the mixture gels, it should be done. During this test, the jelly mixture should be removed from the heat.

Apple Jelly

without added pectin

4 cups apple juice (about 3 pounds apples and 3 cups water)
2 tablespoons strained lemon juice, if desired
3 cups sugar

• **To prepare juice.** Select about one-fourth underripe and three-fourths fully ripe tart apples. Sort, wash, and remove stem and blossom ends; do not pare or core. Cut apples into small pieces. Add water, cover, and bring to boil on high heat. Reduce heat and simmer for 20 to 25 minutes, or until apples are soft. Extract juice.
• **To make jelly.** Measure apple juice into a kettle. Add lemon juice and sugar and stir well. Boil over high heat to 8° F. above the boiling point of water, or until jelly mixture sheets from a spoon.

Remove from heat; skim off foam quickly. Pour jelly immediately into hot containers and seal.

Makes 4 or 5 eight-ounce glasses.

Blackberry Jelly

with powdered pectin

3½ cups blackberry juice (about 3 quart boxes berries)
1 package powdered pectin
4½ cups sugar

• **To prepare juice.** Sort and wash fully ripe berries; remove any stems or caps. Crush berries and extract juice.
• **To make jelly.** Measure juice into kettle. Add pectin and stir

well. Place on high heat and, stirring constantly, bring quickly to a full rolling boil that cannot be stirred down.

Add sugar, continue stirring, and heat again to a full rolling boil. Boil hard for 1 minute.

Remove from heat; skim off foam quickly. Pour jelly immediately into hot containers and seal.

Makes 5 or 6 eight-ounce glasses.

Blackberry Jelly

with liquid pectin

4 cups blackberry juice (about 3 quart boxes berries)
7½ cups sugar
1 bottle liquid pectin

• **To prepare juice.** Sort and wash fully ripe berries; remove any stems or caps. Crush berries and extract juice.

• **To make jelly.** Measure juice into a kettle. Stir in sugar. Place on high heat and, stirring constantly, bring quickly to a full rolling boil that cannot be stirred down.

Add pectin and heat again to a full rolling boil. Boil hard for 1 minute.

Remove from heat; skim off foam quickly. Pour jelly immediately into hot containers and seal.

Makes 8 or 9 eight-ounce glasses.

Blackberry Jelly

without added pectin

8 cups blackberry juice (about 5 quart boxes and 1½ cups water)
6 cups sugar

• **To prepare juice.** Select about one-fourth underripe and three-fourths ripe berries. Sort and wash; remove any stems or caps. Crush berries, add water, cover and bring to boil on high heat. Reduce heat and simmer for 5 minutes. Extract juice.

• **To make jelly.** Measure juice into a kettle. Add sugar and stir well. Boil over high heat to 8° F. above the boiling point of water, or until jelly mixture sheets from a spoon.

Remove from heat; skim off foam quickly. Pour jelly immediately into hot containers and seal.

Makes 7 or 8 eight-ounce glasses.

Orange Jelly

made from frozen concentrated juice

3¼ cups sugar
1 cup water
3 tablespoons lemon juice
½ bottle liquid pectin
1 six-ounce can (¾ cup) frozen concentrated orange juice

Stir the sugar into the water. Place on high heat and, stirring constantly, bring quickly to a full rolling boil that cannot be stirred down. Add lemon juice. Boil hard for 1 minute.

Remove from heat. Stir in pectin. Add thawed concentrated orange juice and mix well.

Pour jelly immediately into hot containers and seal.

Makes 4 or 5 eight-ounce glasses.

How to make jelly with liquid pectin

Strawberry Jelly

Select fully ripe sound strawberries. About 3 quart boxes are needed for each batch of jelly. Sort the berries. Wash about 1 quart at a time by placing berries in a wire basket and moving the basket up and down several times in cold water. Drain the berries.

(78430–B)

Remove caps and crush the berries. Place crushed berries, a small amount at a time, in a damp jelly bag or double thickness of cheesecloth held in a colander over a bowl.

(78431–B)

Bring the edges of the cloth together and twist tightly. Press or squeeze to extract the juice. Strain the juice again through two thicknesses of damp cheesecloth without squeezing.

(78432–B)

Measure 4 cups of juice into a large kettle. Add 7½ cups of sugar to the juice; stir to dissolve the sugar.

Place the kettle over high heat and, stirring constantly, bring the mixture quickly to a full rolling boil that cannot be stirred down.

(78433–B)

Add 1 bottle of liquid pectin. Again, bring to a full rolling boil and boil hard for 1 minute.

Remove from heat and skim off foam quickly. If allowed to stand, the jelly may start to "set" in the kettle.

(78434–B)

Pour jelly immediately into hot glasses to ½ inch of top. Cover each glass with a ⅛ inch layer of paraffin. Cool glasses on a metal rack or folded cloth, then cover with metal or paper lids, label, and store in a cool, dry place.

(78436–B)

How to make jelly without added pectin

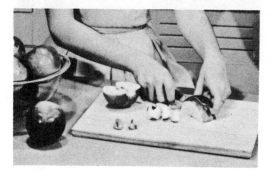

Apple Jelly

Use tart, firm apples. It takes about 3 pounds for a batch of jelly; about one-fourth of them should be underripe. Sort and wash the apples. Remove stems and blossom ends and cut apples into small pieces. Do not pare or core.

(9953–D)

Put apples into a kettle. Add 1 cup water per pound of apples. Cover, bring to boil on high heat. Reduce heat and simmer until apples are tender, about 20 to 25 minutes, depending on the firmness or ripeness of the fruit.

(78437–B)

Put cooked apples into a jelly bag and allow to drip, or press to remove juice. Strain pressed juice through two thicknesses of damp cheesecloth without squeezing.

(9954–D)

Measure 4 cups of the apple juice into a large kettle. Add 3 cups of sugar and 2 tablespoons of lemon juice, if desired. Stir to dissolve the sugar.

(78438–B)

Place on high heat and boil rapidly to 8° F. above the boiling point of water, or until jelly mixture sheets from a spoon. Remove from heat. Skim off foam.

(78439–B)

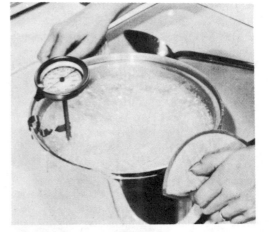

Pour jelly immediately into hot containers.

Fill glasses to ½ inch of top and cover with a ⅛-inch layer of paraffin.

Or fill canning jars (right) to ⅛ inch of top; wipe rims of jars. Place clean, hot metal lid on, with sealing compound next to glass. Screw metal band down tight.

Cool jars on a metal rack or folded cloth. Then label and store in a cool, dry place.

(78440–B)

Cherry Jelly

with powdered pectin

3½ cups cherry juice (about 3 pounds or 2 quart boxes sour cherries and ½ cup water)
1 package powdered pectin
4½ cups sugar

• **To prepare juice.** Select fully ripe cherries. Sort, wash, and remove stems; do not pit. Crush cherries, add water, cover, bring to boil on high heat. Reduce heat and simmer for 10 minutes. Extract juice.

• **To make jelly.** Measure juice into a kettle. Add pectin and stir well. Place on high heat and, stirring constantly, bring quickly to a full rolling boil that cannot be stirred down.

Add sugar, continue stirring, and heat again to a full rolling boil. Boil hard for 1 minute.

Remove from heat; skim off foam quickly. Pour jelly immediately into hot containers and seal.

Makes about 6 eight-ounce glasses.

Cherry Jelly

with liquid pectin

3 cups cherry juice (about 3 pounds or 2 quart boxes sour cherries and ½ cup water)
7 cups sugar
1 bottle liquid pectin

• **To prepare juice.** Select fully ripe cherries. Sort, wash, and remove stems; do not pit. Crush cherries, add water, cover, bring to boil quickly. Reduce heat and simmer 10 minutes. Extract juice.

• **To make jelly.** Measure juice into a kettle. Stir in sugar. Place on high heat and, stirring constantly, bring quickly to a full rolling boil that cannot be stirred down.

Add pectin; heat again to full rolling boil. Boil hard 1 minute.

Remove from heat; skim off foam quickly. Pour jelly immediately into hot containers and seal.

Makes about 8 eight-ounce glasses.

Grape Jelly

with liquid pectin

4 cups grape juice (about 3½ pounds Concord grapes and ½ cup water)
7 cups sugar
½ bottle liquid pectin

• **To prepare juice.** Sort, wash, and remove stems from fully ripe grapes. Crush grapes, add water, cover, and bring to boil on high heat. Reduce heat and simmer for 10 minutes. Extract juice (p. 185).

To prevent formation of tartrate crystals in the jelly, let juice stand in a cool place overnight, then strain through two thicknesses of damp cheesecloth to remove crystals.

• **To make jelly.** Measure juice into a kettle. Stir in sugar. Place on high heat and, stirring constantly, bring quickly to a full rolling boil that cannot be stirred down.

Add pectin and heat again to a full rolling boil. Boil hard for 1 minute.

Remove from heat; skim off foam quickly. Pour jelly immediately into hot containers and seal.

Makes 8 or 9 eight-ounce glasses.

Grape Jelly

made from frozen concentrated juice

6½ cups sugar
2½ cups water
1 bottle liquid pectin
3 six-ounce cans (2¼ cups) frozen concentrated grape juice

Stir sugar into water. Place on high heat and, stirring constantly, bring quickly to a full rolling boil that cannot be stirred down. Boil hard for 1 minute.

Remove from heat. Stir in pectin. Add thawed concentrated grape juice and mix well. Pour jelly immediately into hot containers and seal.

Makes about 10 eight-ounce glasses.

Grape Jelly

with powdered pectin

5 cups grape juice (about 3½ pounds Concord grapes and 1 cup water)
1 package powdered pectin
7 cups sugar

● **To prepare juice.** Sort, wash, and remove stems from fully ripe grapes. Crush grapes, add water, cover, and bring to boil on high heat. Reduce heat and simmer for 10 minutes. Extract juice (p. 185). To prevent formation of tartrate crystals in the jelly, let juice stand in a cool place overnight, then strain through two thicknesses of damp cheesecloth to remove crystals that have formed.

● **To make jelly.** Measure juice into a kettle. Add pectin and stir well. Place on high heat and, stirring constantly, bring quickly to a full rolling boil that cannot be stirred down.

Add sugar, continue stirring, and bring again to a full rolling boil. Boil hard for 1 minute.

Remove from heat; skim off foam quickly. Pour jelly immediately into hot containers and seal.

Makes 8 or 9 eight-ounce glasses.

Crabapple Jelly

without added pectin

4 cups crabapple juice (about 3 pounds crabapples and 3 cups water)
4 cups sugar

● **To prepare juice.** Select firm, crisp crabapples, about one-fourth underripe and three-fourths fully ripe. Sort, wash, and remove stem and blossom ends; do not pare or core. Cut crabapples into small pieces. Add water, cover, and bring to boil on high heat. Reduce heat and simmer for 20 to 25 minutes, or until crabapples are soft. Extract juice.

● **To make jelly.** Measure juice into a kettle. Add sugar and stir well. Boil over high heat to 8° F. above the boiling point of water, or until mixture sheets from a spoon.

Remove from heat; skim off foam quickly. Pour jelly immediately into hot containers and seal.

Makes 4 or 5 eight-ounce glasses.

Mint Jelly

with liquid pectin

1 cup chopped mint leaves and tender
  stems
1 cup water
½ cup cider vinegar
3½ cups sugar
5 drops green food coloring
½ bottle liquid pectin

• **To prepare mint.** Wash and chop mint. Pack solidly in a cup.
• **To make jelly.** Measure mint into a kettle. Add vinegar, water, and sugar; stir well. Place on high heat and, stirring constantly, bring quickly to a full rolling boil that cannot be stirred down.

Add food coloring and pectin; heat again to a full rolling boil. Boil hard for ½ minute.

Remove from heat. Skim. Strain through two thicknesses of damp cheesecloth. Pour jelly immediately into hot containers and seal.

Makes 3 or 4 eight-ounce glasses.

Mixed Fruit Jelly

with liquid pectin

2 cups cranberry juice (about 1 pound cranberries and 2 cups water)
2 cups quince juice (about 2 pounds quince and 4 cups water)
1 cup apple juice (about ¾ pound apples and ¾ cup water)
7½ cups sugar
½ bottle liquid pectin

• **To prepare fruit.** Sort and wash fully ripe cranberries. Add water, cover, and bring to a boil on high heat. Reduce heat and simmer for 20 minutes. Extract juice.

Sort and wash quince. Remove stem and blossom ends; do not pare or core. Slice very thin or cut into small pieces. Add water, cover, and bring to a boil on high heat. Reduce heat and simmer for 25 minutes. Extract juice.

Sort and wash apples. Remove stem and blossom ends; do not pare or core. Cut into small pieces. Add water, cover, and bring to a boil on high heat. Reduce heat and simmer 20 minutes. Extract juice.

NOTE: These juices may be prepared when the fruits are in season and then frozen or canned until the jelly is made.

• **To make jelly.** Measure juices into a kettle. Stir in sugar. Place on high heat and, stirring constantly, bring quickly to a full rolling boil that cannot be stirred down.

Add pectin and return to a full rolling boil. Boil hard for 1 minute.

Remove from heat; skim off foam quickly. Pour jelly immediately into hot containers and seal.

Makes 9 or 10 eight-ounce glasses.

Plum Jelly

with liquid pectin

4 cups plum juice (about 4½ pounds plums and ½ cup water)
7½ cups sugar
½ bottle liquid pectin

• **To prepare juice.** Sort and wash fully ripe plums and cut in pieces; do not peel or pit. Crush fruit, add water, cover, and bring to boil over high heat. Reduce heat and simmer for 10 minutes. Extract juice.

• **To make jelly.** Measure juice into a kettle. Stir in sugar. Place on high heat and, stirring constantly, bring quickly to a full rolling boil that cannot be stirred down.

Add pectin; bring again to full rolling boil. Boil hard 1 minute.

Remove from heat; skim off foam quickly. Pour jelly immediately into hot containers and seal.

Makes 7 or 8 eight-ounce glasses.

Plum Jelly

with powdered pectin

5 cups plum juice (about 4½ pounds plums and 1 cup water)
1 package powdered pectin
7 cups sugar

• **To prepare juice.** Sort and wash fully ripe plums and cut in pieces; do not peel or pit. Crush fruit, add water, cover, and bring to boil on high heat. Reduce heat and simmer for 10 minutes. Extract juice.

• **To make jelly.** Measure juice into a kettle. Add pectin and stir well. Place on high heat and, stirring constantly, bring quickly to a full rolling boil that cannot be stirred down.

Add sugar, continue stirring, and heat again to a full rolling boil. Boil hard for 1 minute.

Remove from heat; skim off foam quickly. Pour jelly immediately into hot containers and seal.

Makes 7 or 8 eight-ounce glasses.

Quince Jelly

without added pectin

3¾ cups quince juice (about 3½ pounds quince and 7 cups water)
¼ cup lemon juice
3 cups sugar

• **To prepare juice.** Select about one-fourth underripe and three-fourths fully ripe quince. Sort, wash, and remove stems and blossom ends; do not pare or core. Slice quince very thin or cut into small pieces. Add water, cover, and bring to boil on high heat. Reduce heat and simmer for 25 minutes. Extract juice (p. 185).

To make jelly. Measure quince juice into a kettle. Add lemon juice and sugar and stir well. Boil over high heat to 8° F. above the boiling point of water, or until jelly mixture sheets from a spoon.

Remove from heat; skim off foam quickly. Pour jelly immediately into hot containers and seal.

Makes about 4 eight-ounce glasses.

Strawberry Jelly

with liquid pectin

Follow directions for blackberry jelly with liquid pectin, page 188.

Strawberry Jelly

with powdered pectin

Follow directions for blackberry jelly with powdered pectin, page 187.

Spiced Orange Jelly

with powdered pectin

2 cups orange juice (about 5 medium oranges)
⅓ cup lemon juice (about 2 medium lemons)
⅔ cup water
1 package powdered pectin
2 tablespoons orange peel, finely chopped
1 teaspoon whole allspice
½ teaspoon whole cloves
4 sticks cinnamon, 2 inches long
3½ cups sugar

Mix orange juice, lemon juice, and water in a large saucepan. Stir in pectin.

Place orange peel, allspice, cloves, and cinnamon sticks loosely in a clean white cloth; tie with a string and add to fruit mixture.

Place on high heat and, stirring constantly, bring quickly to a full rolling boil that cannot be stirred down.

Add sugar, continue stirring, and heat again to a full rolling boil. Boil hard for 1 minute.

Remove from heat. Remove spice bag and skim off foam quickly. Pour jelly immediately into hot containers and seal (p. 183).

Makes 4 eight-ounce glasses.

Jams

Jam is smooth and thick and has the natural color and flavor of the fruit from which it is made. It has a softer consistency than jelly.

On the following pages are directions for making jams from various fruits and combinations of fruits.

Because the products contain fruit pulp or pieces of fruit, they tend to stick to the kettle during cooking and require constant stirring to prevent scorching.

To help prevent fruit from floating in jam, remove cooked mixture from heat and stir gently at frequent intervals for 5 minutes.

With added pectin

For jams, as for jellies, the method of combining ingredients varies with the form of pectin used. Powdered pectin is mixed with the unheated crushed fruit; liquid pectin is added to the cooked fruit and sugar mixture immediately after it is removed from the heat.

Cooking time is the same for all the products—1 minute at a full boil. The full-boil stage is reached when bubbles form over the entire surface of the mixture.

With added pectin, jams can be made without cooking from some fresh or frozen fruits.

Without added pectin

Jams made without added pectin require longer cooking than those with added pectin. The most reliable way to judge doneness is to use a thermometer. Before making the product, take the temperature of boiling water. Cook the mixture to a temperature 9° F. higher than the boiling point of water. It is important to stir the mixture thoroughly just before taking the temperature, to place the thermometer vertically at the center of kettle, and to have the bulb covered with fruit mixture but not touching the bottom of the kettle. Read the thermometer at eye level.

If you have no thermometer, cook products made without added pectin until they have thickened somewhat. In judging thickness allow for the additional thickening of the mixture as it cools. The refrigerator test suggested for jelly may be used (see 187).

Blackberry Jam

with powdered pectin

6 cups crushed blackberries (about 3 quart boxes berries)
1 package powdered pectin
8½ cups sugar

● **To prepare fruit.** Sort and wash fully ripe berries; remove any stems or caps. Crush berries. If they are very seedy, put part or all of them through a sieve or food mill.

● **To make jam.** Measure crushed berries into a kettle. Add pectin and stir well. Place on high heat and, stirring constantly, bring quickly to a full boil with bubbles over the entire surface.

Add sugar, continue stirring, and heat again to a full bubbling boil. Boil hard for 1 minute, stirring constantly. Remove from heat; skim.

Fill and seal containers.

Process 5 minutes in boiling water bath.

Makes 11 or 12 half-pint jars.

Blackberry Jam

with liquid pectin

Follow directions for strawberry jam with liquid pectin, page 204. Put very seedy blackberries through a sieve or food mill.

How to make jam with powdered pectin

Peach Jam

Sort and wash fully ripe peaches. Remove stems, skins, and pits.

(78442–B)

Crush or chop the peaches. A stainless steel potato masher is useful for this purpose.

(78443–B)

Measure 3¾ cups of crushed peaches into a large kettle.

(78444–B)

Add one package of powdered pectin and ¼ cup of lemon juice. Stir well to dissolve the pectin. Place on high heat and, stirring constantly, bring quickly to a full boil with bubbles over the entire surface.

(9955–D)

Stir in 5 cups of sugar, continue stirring, and heat again to a full bubbling boil. Boil hard for 1 minute, stirring constantly to prevent sticking.

Remove jam from heat and skim and stir alternately for 5 minutes to help prevent fruit from floating.

(78445–B)

Pour the jam into hot glasses to ⅛ inch of top. Process 5 minutes in boiling water bath (p. 5). Cool glasses on a metal rack or folded cloth, then cover them with metal or paper lids. After cooling, label and store in a cool, dry place.

(9956–D)

Cherry Jam

with liquid pectin

4½ cups ground or finely chopped pitted
  cherries (about 3 pounds or 2 quart boxes
  sour cherries)
7 cups sugar
1 bottle liquid pectin

- **To prepare fruit.** Sort and wash fully ripe cherries; remove stems and pits. Grind cherries or chop fine.
- **To make jam.** Measure prepared cherries into a kettle. Add sugar and stir well. Place on high heat and, stirring constantly, bring quickly to a full boil with bubbles over the entire surface. Boil hard for 1 minute, stirring constantly.

Remove from heat and stir in the pectin. Skim.

Fill and seal containers.

Process 5 minutes in boiling water bath.

Makes about 8 half-pint jars.

Cherry Jam

with powdered pectin

4 cups ground or finely chopped pitted
  cherries (about 3 pounds or 2 quart boxes
  sour cherries)
1 package powdered pectin
5 cups sugar

- **To prepare fruit.** Sort and wash fully ripe cherries; remove stems and pits. Grind cherries or chop fine.
- **To make jam.** Measure prepared cherries into a kettle. Add pectin and stir well. Place on high heat and, stirring constantly, bring quickly to a full boil with bubbles over the entire surface.

Add sugar, continue stirring, and heat again to a full bubbling boil. Boil hard for 1 minute, stirring constantly. Remove from heat; skim.

Fill and seal containers.

Process 5 minutes in boiling water bath.

Makes 6 half-pint jars.

Mint–Pineapple Jam

with liquid pectin

1 20-oz. can crushed pineapple
¾ cup water
¼ cup lemon juice
7½ cups sugar
1 bottle liquid pectin
½ teaspoon mint extract
Few drops green coloring

Place crushed pineapple in a kettle. Add water, lemon juice, and sugar and stir well. Place on high heat and, stirring constantly, bring quickly to a full boil with bubbles over the entire surface. Boil hard for 1 minute, stirring constantly. Remove from heat; add pectin, flavor extract, and coloring. Skim.

Fill and seal containers.

Process 5 minutes in boiling water bath.

Makes 9 or 10 half-pint jars.

Variation. Use 10 drops oil of spearmint instead of extract.

Ginger-Peach Jam

Use either of the peach jam recipes (p. 202). Add 1 to 2 ounces of finely chopped candied ginger, as desired, to crushed peaches before adding pectin.

Fig Jam

with liquid pectin

4 cups crushed figs (about 3 pounds figs)
½ cup lemon juice
7½ cups sugar
½ bottle liquid pectin

● **To prepare fruit.** Sort and wash fully ripe figs; remove stem ends. Crush or grind fruit.

● **To make jam.** Place crushed figs into a kettle. Add sugar and stir well. Place on high heat and, stirring constantly, bring quickly to a full boil with bubbles over the entire surface. Boil hard for 1 minute, stirring constantly.

Remove from heat. Stir in pectin. Skim.

Fill and seal containers.

Process 5 minutes in boiling water bath.

Makes about 9 half-pint jars.

Peach Jam

with liquid pectin

4¼ cups crushed peaches (about 3½ pounds peaches)
¼ cup lemon juice
7 cups sugar
½ bottle liquid pectin

● **To prepare fruit.** Sort and wash fully ripe peaches. Remove stems, skins, and pits. Crush peaches.

● **To make jam.** Measure crushed peaches into a kettle. Add lemon juice and sugar and stir well. Place on high heat and, stirring constantly, bring quickly to a full boil with bubbles over the entire surface. Boil hard for 1 minute, stirring constantly.

Remove from heat; stir in pectin. Skim.

Fill and seal containers.

Process 5 minutes in boiling water bath.

Makes about 8 half-pint jars.

Peach Jam

with powdered pectin

3¾ cups crushed peaches (about 3 pounds peaches)
¼ cup lemon juice
1 package powdered pectin
5 cups sugar

● **To prepare fruit.** Sort and wash fully ripe peaches. Remove stems, skins, and pits. Crush peaches.

● **To make jam.** Measure crushed peaches into a kettle. Add lemon juice and pectin; stir well. Place on high heat and, stirring constantly, bring quickly to a full boil with bubbles over the entire surface.

Add sugar, continue stirring, and heat again to a full bubbling boil. Boil hard for 1 minute, stirring constantly. Remove from heat; skim.

Fill and seal containers.

Process 5 minutes in boiling water bath.

Makes about 6 half-pint jars.

Pineapple Jam

with liquid pectin

1 20-ounce can crushed pineapple
3 tablespoons lemon juice
3¼ cups sugar
½ bottle liquid pectin

Combine pineapple and lemon juice in a kettle.

Add sugar and stir well.

Place on high heat and, stirring constantly, bring quickly to a full boil with bubbles over the entire surface. Boil hard for 1 minute, stirring constantly.

Remove from heat; stir in pectin. Skim.

Let stand for 5 minutes.

Fill and seal containers.

Process 5 minutes in boiling water bath.

Makes 4 or 5 half-pint jars.

Rhubarb–Strawberry Jam

with liquid pectin

1 cup cooked red-stalked rhubarb (about 1 pound rhubarb and ¼ cup water)
2½ cups crushed strawberries (about 1½ quart boxes)
6½ cups sugar
½ bottle liquid pectin

● **To prepare fruit.** Wash rhubarb and slice thin or chop; do not peel. Add water, cover, and simmer until rhubarb is tender (about 1 minute).

Sort and wash fully ripe strawberries; remove stems and caps. Crush berries.

● **To make jam.** Measure prepared rhubarb and strawberries into a kettle. Add sugar and stir well. Place on high heat and, stirring constantly, bring quickly to a full boil with bubbles over the entire surface. Boil hard for 1 minute, stirring constantly.

Remove from heat and stir in pectin. Skim.

Fill and seal containers.

Process 5 minutes in boiling water bath.

Makes 7 or 8 half-pint jars.

Plum Jam

with liquid pectin

4½ cups crushed plums (about 2½ pounds plums)
7½ cups sugar
½ bottle liquid pectin

● **To prepare fruit.** Sort fully ripe plums, wash, cut into pieces, and remove pits. If flesh clings tightly to pits, cook plums slowly in a small amount of water for a few minutes until they are softened, then remove pits. Crush fruit.

● **To make jam.** Measure crushed plums into a kettle. Add sugar and stir well. Place on high heat and, stirring constantly, bring quickly to a full boil with bubbles over the entire surface. Boil hard for 1 minute, stirring constantly.

Remove from heat and stir in pectin. Skim.

Fill and seal containers.

Process 5 minutes in boiling water bath.

Makes about 8 half-pint jars.

Plum Jam

with powdered pectin

6 cups crushed plums (about 3½ pounds plums)
1 package powdered pectin
8 cups sugar

● **To prepare fruit.** Sort fully ripe plums, wash, cut into pieces, and remove pits. If flesh clings tightly to pits, cook plums slowly in a small amount of water for a few minutes until they are softened, then remove pits. Crush fruit.

● **To make jam.** Measure crushed

plums into a kettle. Add pectin and stir well. Place on high heat and, stirring constantly, bring quickly to a full boil with bubbles over the entire surface.

Add sugar, continue stirring, and heat again to a full bubbling boil. Boil hard for 1 minute. Remove from heat; skim.

Fill and seal containers.

Process 5 minutes in boiling water bath.

Makes about 9 half-pint jars.

Spiced Blueberry–Peach Jam

without added pectin

4 cups chopped or ground peaches (about 4 pounds peaches)
4 cups blueberries (about 1 quart fresh blueberries or 2 ten-ounce packages of unsweetened frozen blueberries)
2 tablespoons lemon juice
½ cup water
5½ cups sugar
½ teaspoon salt
1 stick cinnamon
½ teaspoon whole cloves
¼ teaspoon whole allspice

● **To prepare fruit.** Sort and wash fully ripe peaches; peel and remove pits. Chop or grind peaches.

Sort, wash, and remove any stems from fresh blueberries. Thaw frozen berries.
● **To make jam.** Measure fruits into a kettle; add lemon juice and water. Cover, bring to a boil, and simmer for 10 minutes, stirring occasionally.

Add sugar and salt; stir well. Add spices tied in cheesecloth. Boil rapidly, stirring constantly, to 9° F. above the boiling point of water, or until the mixture thickens.

Remove from heat; take out spices. Skim.

Fill and seal containers.

Process 5 minutes in boiling water bath.

Makes 6 or 7 half-pint jars.

Strawberry Jam

with liquid pectin

4 cups crushed strawberries (about 2 quart boxes strawberries)
7 cups sugar
½ bottle liquid pectin

● **To prepare fruit.** Sort and wash fully ripe strawberries; remove stems and caps. Crush berries.
● **To make jam.** Measure crushed strawberries into a kettle. Add sugar and stir well. Place on high heat and, stirring constantly, bring quickly to a full boil with bubbles over the entire surface. Boil hard for 1 minute, stirring constantly.

Remove from heat and stir in pectin. Skim.

Fill and seal containers.

Process 5 minutes in boiling water bath.

Makes 8 or 9 half-pint jars.

Strawberry Jam

with powdered pectin

5½ cups crushed strawberries (about 3 quart boxes strawberries)
1 package powdered pectin
8 cups sugar

● **To prepare fruit.** Sort and wash fully ripe strawberries; remove stems and caps. Crush berries.
● **To make jam.** Measure crushed strawberries into a kettle. Add

pectin and stir well. Place on high heat and, stirring constantly, bring quickly to a full boil with bubbles over the entire surface.

Add sugar, continue stirring, and heat again to a full bubbling boil. Boil hard for 1 minute, stirring constantly. Remove from heat; skim.

Fill and seal containers.

Process 5 minutes in boiling water bath.

Makes 9 or 10 half-pint jars.

Tutti-Frutti Jam

with powdered pectin

3 cups chopped or ground pears (about 2 pounds pears)
1 large orange
¾ cup drained crushed pineapple
¼ cup chopped maraschino cherries (3-ounce bottle)
¼ cup lemon juice
1 package powdered pectin
5 cups sugar

• **To prepare fruit.** Sort and wash ripe pears; pare and core. Chop or grind the pears.

Peel orange, remove seeds, and chop or grind pulp.

• **To make jam.** Measure chopped pears into a kettle. Add orange, pineapple, cherries, and lemon juice. Stir in pectin. Place on high heat and, stirring constantly, bring quickly to a full boil with bubbles over the entire surface.

Add sugar, continue stirring, and heat again to a full bubbling boil. Boil hard for 1 minute, stirring constantly. Remove from heat; skim.

Fill and seal containers.

Process 5 minutes in boiling water bath.

Makes 6 or 7 half-pint jars.

Uncooked Berry Jam

with powdered pectin

2 cups crushed strawberries or blackberries (about 1 quart berries)
4 cups sugar
1 package powdered pectin
1 cup water

• **To prepare fruit.** Sort and wash fully ripe berries. Drain. Remove caps and stems; crush berries.

• **To make jam.** Place prepared berries in a large mixing bowl. Add sugar, mix well, and let stand for 20 minutes, stirring occasionally.

Dissolve pectin in water and boil for 1 minute. Add pectin solution to berry-and-sugar mixture; stir for 2 minutes.

Pour jam into freezer containers or canning jars, leaving ½ inch space at the top. Cover containers and let stand at room temperature for 24 hours or until jam has set.

Makes 5 or 6 half-pint jars.

• **To store.** Store uncooked jams in refrigerator or freezer. They can be held up to 3 weeks in a refrigerator or up to a year in a freezer. If kept at room temperature they will mold or ferment in a short time. Once a container is opened, jam should be stored in the refrigerator and used within a few days.

NOTE: If jam is too firm, stir to soften. If it tends to separate, stir to blend. If it is too soft, bring it to a boil. It will thicken on cooling.

Conserves, marmalades, preserves

Conserves are jam-like mixtures of two or more fruits plus nuts or raisins or both. They are rich in flavor and have a thick, but not sticky or gummy, consistency.

Marmalade is a mixture of fruits, usually including citrus, suspended in a clear, translucent jelly. The fruit is cut in small pieces or slices.

Preserves contain large or whole pieces of fruit saturated by a clear sirup of medium to thick consistency. The tender fruit retains its original size, shape, flavor, and color.

On the following pages are directions for making conserves, marmalades, and preserves from various fruits and combinations of fruits.

Because the products contain fruit pulp or pieces of fruit, they tend to stick to the kettle during cooking and require constant stirring to prevent scorching.

With added pectin

When powdered pectin is used in making conserves and marmalades, combine powdered pectin with unheated crushed fruit. Mix well. Bring to a full boil with bubbles over the entire surface. Add sugar and boil hard for 1 minute.

Without added pectin

Conserves, marmalades, and preserves made without added pectin require longer cooking than those with added pectin. The most reliable way to judge doneness is to use a thermometer. Before making the product, take the temperature of boiling water. Cook the mixture to a temperature 9° F. higher than the boiling point of water. It is important to stir the mixture thoroughly just before taking the temperature, to place thermometer vertically at the center of kettle, to have bulb covered with fruit mixture but not touching the bottom of the kettle. Read the thermometer at eye level.

If you have no thermometer, cook products made without added pectin until they have thickened somewhat. In judging thickness allow for the additional thickening of the mixture as it cools. The refrigerator test suggested for jelly may be used (see 187).

Apple Conserve

with powdered pectin

4½ cups finely chopped red apples (about 3
   pounds apples)
½ cup water
¼ cup lemon juice
½ cup raisins
1 package powdered pectin
5½ cups sugar
½ cup chopped nuts

• **To prepare fruit.** Select tart apples. Sort and wash apples. Remove stem and blossom ends and core; do not pare. Chop apples fine.

• **To make conserve.** Combine apples, water, lemon juice, and raisins in a kettle. Add pectin and stir well. Place on high heat and, stirring constantly, bring quickly to a full boil with bubbles over the entire surface.

Add sugar, continue stirring, and heat again to a full bubbling boil. Boil hard for 1 minute, stirring constantly. Add nuts.

Remove from heat. If desired, add 3 or 4 drops of red food coloring. Skim.

Fill and seal containers.

Process 5 minutes in boiling water bath.

Makes 6 or 7 half-pint jars.

Apple Marmalade

without added pectin

8 cups thinly sliced apples (about 3 pounds)
1 orange
1½ cups water
5 cups sugar
2 tablespoons lemon juice

• **To prepare fruit.** Select tart apples. Wash, pare, quarter, and core the apples. Slice thin.

Quarter the orange, remove any seeds, and slice very thin.

• **To make marmalade.** Heat water and sugar until sugar is dissolved. Add the lemon juice and fruit. Boil rapidly, stirring constantly, to 9° F. above the boiling point of water, or until the mixture thickens. Remove from heat; skim.

Fill and seal containers.

Process 5 minutes in boiling water bath.

Makes 6 or 7 half-pint jars.

Damson Plum–Orange Conserve

with powdered pectin

3½ cups finely chopped damson plums
   (about 1½ pounds plums)
1 cup finely chopped oranges (1 or 2
   oranges)
Peel of ½ orange
2 cups water
½ cup seedless raisins
1 package powdered pectin
7 cups sugar
½ cup chopped nuts

• **To prepare fruit.** Sort and wash plums; remove pits. Chop plums fine.

Peel and chop oranges. Shred peel of ½ orange very fine. Combine orange and peel, add the water, cover, and simmer for 20 minutes.

• **To make conserve.** Measure chopped plums into a kettle. Add orange, raisins, and pectin and stir well. Place on high heat and, stirring constantly, bring quickly to a full boil with bubbles over the entire surface.

Add sugar, continue stirring, and heat again to a full bubbling boil. Boil hard for 1 minute, stirring constantly. Stir in nuts. Remove from heat; skim.

Fill and seal containers.

Process 5 minutes in boiling water bath.

Makes 8 or 9 half-pint jars.

Apricot–Orange Conserve

without added pectin

3½ cups chopped drained apricots (about 2 20-oz. cans of unpeeled apricots or 1 pound dried apricots)
1½ cups orange juice (3 or 4 medium-size oranges)
Peel of ½ orange, shredded very fine
2 tablespoons lemon juice
3¼ cups sugar
½ cup chopped nuts

• **To prepare dried apricots.** Cook apricots uncovered in 3 cups water until tender (about 20 minutes); drain and chop.

• **To make conserve.** Combine all ingredients except nuts. Cook to 9° F. above the boiling point of water, or until thick, stirring constantly. Add nuts; stir well. Remove from heat; skim.

Fill and seal containers.

Process 5 minutes in boiling water bath.

Makes about 5 half-pint jars.

Grape Conserve

without added pectin

4½ cups grapes with skins removed (about 4 pounds Concord grapes)
1 orange
4 cups sugar
1 cup seedless raisins
½ teaspoon salt
Skins from grapes
1 cup nuts, chopped fine

• **To prepare fruit.** Sort and wash grapes; remove from stems. Slip skins from grapes; save skins. Measure skinned grapes into a kettle and boil, stirring constantly, for about 10 minutes, or until seeds show. Press through a sieve to remove seeds.

Chop orange fine without peeling it.

• **To make conserve.** Add orange, sugar, raisins, and salt to sieved grapes. Boil rapidly, stirring constantly, until the mixture begins to thicken (about 10 minutes).

Add grape skins and boil, stirring constantly, to 9° F. above the boiling point of water (about 10 minutes). Do not overcook; the mixture will thicken more on cooling. Add nuts and stir well. Remove from heat; skim.

Fill and seal containers.

Process 5 minutes in boiling water bath.

Makes 8 or 9 half-pint jars.

Citrus Marmalade

without added pectin

¾ cup grapefruit peel (½ grapefruit)
¾ cup orange peel (1 orange)
⅓ cup lemon peel (1 lemon)
1 quart cold water
Pulp of 1 grapefruit
Pulp of 4 medium-size oranges
⅓ cup lemon juice
2 cups boiling water
3 cups sugar

• **To prepare fruit.** Wash and peel fruit. Cut peel into thin strips. Add cold water and simmer in a covered pan until tender (about 30 minutes). Drain.

Remove seeds and membrane from peeled fruit. Cut fruit into small pieces.

- **To make marmalade.** Add boiling water to peel and fruit. Add sugar and boil rapidly to 9° F. above the boiling point of water (about 20 minutes), stirring frequently. Remove from heat; skim.

Fill and seal containers.

Process 5 minutes in boiling water bath.

Makes 3 or 4 half-pint jars.

Cranberry Marmalade

with powdered pectin

2 oranges
1 lemon
3 cups water
1 pound cranberries (about 4 cups)
1 box powdered pectin
7 cups sugar

- **To prepare fruit.** Peel oranges and lemon; remove half of white part of rinds. Finely chop or grind the remaining rinds. Put in large saucepan.

Add water, bring to a boil. Cover and simmer 20 minutes, stirring occasionally.

Chop peeled fruit. Sort and wash fully ripe cranberries. Add fruit to rind; cover and cook slowly 10 minutes longer.

- **To make marmalade.** Measure 6 cups of fruit into a large kettle. Add water to make 6 cups if necessary. Add pectin and stir well. Place on high heat and, stirring constantly, bring quickly to a full boil with bubbles over the entire surface.

Add sugar, continue stirring, and heat again to a full rolling boil. Boil hard for 1 minute, stirring constantly. Remove from heat; skim.

Fill and seal containers.

Process 5 minutes in boiling water bath.

Makes 10 or 11 half-pint jars.

Peach-Orange Marmalade

without added pectin

5 cups finely chopped or ground peaches (about 4 pounds peaches)
1 cup finely chopped or ground oranges (about 2 medium-size oranges)
Peel of 1 orange, shredded very fine
2 tablespoons lemon juice
6 cups sugar

- **To prepare fruit.** Sort and wash fully ripe peaches. Remove stems, skins, and pits. Finely chop or grind the peaches.

Remove peel, white portion, and seeds from oranges. Finely chop or grind the pulp.

- **To make marmalade.** Measure the prepared fruit into a kettle. Add remaining ingredients and stir well. Boil rapidly, stirring constantly, to 9° F. above the boiling point of water, or until the mixture thickens. Remove from heat; skim.

Fill and seal containers.

Process 5 minutes in boiling water bath.

Makes 6 or 7 half-pint jars.

Tomato Marmalade

without added pectin

3 quarts ripe tomatoes (about 5½ pounds tomatoes)
3 oranges
2 lemons
4 sticks cinnamon
1 tablespoon whole cloves
6 cups sugar
1 teaspoon salt

- **To prepare fruit.** Peel tomatoes; cut in small pieces. Drain. Slice oranges and lemons very thin; quarter the slices. Tie cinnamon and cloves in a cheesecloth bag.

● **To make marmalade.** Place tomatoes in a large kettle. Add sugar and salt; stir until dissolved. Add oranges, lemons, and spice bag. Boil rapidly, stirring constantly, until thick and clear (about 50 minutes). Remove from heat; skim.

Fill and seal containers.

Process 5 minutes in boiling water bath.

Makes about 9 half-pint jars.

Strawberry Preserves

6 cups prepared strawberries (about 2 quart boxes strawberries)
4½ cups sugar

● **To prepare fruit.** Select large, firm, tart strawberries. Wash and drain berries; remove caps.

● **To make preserves.** Combine prepared fruit and sugar in alternate layers and let stand for 8 to 10 hours or overnight in the refrigerator or other cool place.

Heat the fruit mixture to boiling, stirring gently. Boil rapidly, stirring as needed to prevent sticking.

Cook to 9° F. above the boiling point of water, or until the sirup is somewhat thick (about 15 or 20 minutes). Remove from heat; skim.

Fill and seal containers.

Process 5 minutes in boiling water bath.

Makes about 4 half-pint jars.

Questions and answers

High quality in jellied fruit products depends on so many complex factors that it is seldom possible to give just one answer to questions about problems in making these products. Using recipes from a reliable source—and following directions accurately—is the surest aid to success but does not guarantee it; it is impossible to assure uniform results because fruit varies widely in jellying quality.

The answers given here to questions commonly asked by homemakers who have had unsatisfactory results in making jellies and jams suggest possible reasons for lack of success.

Q. **What makes jelly cloudy?**

A. One or more of the following may cause cloudy jelly: Pouring jelly mixture into glasses too slowly. Allowing jelly mixture to stand before it is poured. Juice was not properly strained and so contained pulp. Jelly set too fast—usually the result of using too-green fruit.

Q. Why do crystals form in jelly?

A. Crystals throughout the jelly may be caused by too much sugar in the jelly mixture, or cooking the mixture too little, too slowly, or too long. Crystals that form at the top of jelly that has been opened and allowed to stand are caused by evaporation of liquid. Crystals in grape jelly may be tartrate crystals (see recipe for grape jelly).

Q. What causes jelly to be too soft?

A. One or more of the following may be the cause: Too much juice in the mixture. Too little sugar. Mixture not acid enough. Making too big a batch at one time.

Q. What can be done to make soft jellies firmer?

A. Soft jellies can sometimes be improved by recooking according to the directions given below. It is best to recook only 4 to 6 cups of jelly at one time.

To remake with powdered pectin. Measure the jelly to be recooked. For each quart of jelly measure ¼ cup sugar, ¼ cup water, and 4 teaspoons powdered pectin. Mix the pectin and water and bring to boiling, stirring constantly to prevent scorching. Add the jelly and sugar. Stir thoroughly. Bring to a full rolling boil over high heat, stirring constantly. Boil mixture hard for ½ minute. Remove jelly from the heat, skim, pour into hot containers, and seal.

To remake with liquid pectin. Measure the jelly to be recooked. For each quart of jelly measure ¾ cup sugar, 2 tablespoons lemon juice, and 2 tablespoons liquid pectin. Bring jelly to boiling over high heat. Quickly add the sugar, lemon juice, and pectin and bring to a full rolling boil; stir constantly. Boil mixture hard for 1 minute. Remove jelly from the heat, skim, pour into hot containers, and seal.

To remake without added pectin. Heat the jelly to boiling and boil for a few minutes. Use one of the tests described on pages 7 and 8 to determine just how long to cook it. Remove jelly from the heat, skim, pour into hot containers, and seal.

Q. What makes jelly sirupy?

A. Too little pectin, acid, or sugar. A great excess of sugar can also cause sirupy jelly.

Q. What causes weeping jelly?

A. Too much acid. Layer of paraffin too thick. Storage place was too warm or storage temperature fluctuated.

Q. What makes jelly too stiff?

A. Too much pectin (fruit was not ripe enough or too much added pectin was used). Overcooking.

Q. What makes jelly tough?

A. Mixture had to be cooked too long to reach jellying stage, a result of too little sugar.

Q. What makes jelly gummy?

A. Overcooking.

Q. What causes fermentation of jelly?

A. Too little sugar, or improper sealing.

Q. Why does mold form on jelly or jam?

A. Because an imperfect seal has made it possible for mold and air to get into the container.

Q. What causes jelly or jam to darken at the top of the container?

A. Storage in too warm a place. Or a faulty seal that allows air to leak in.

Q. What causes fading?

A. Too warm a storage place or too long storage. Red fruits such as strawberries and raspberries are especially likely to fade.

Q. Why does fruit float in jam?

A. Fruit was not fully ripe, was not thoroughly crushed or ground, was not cooked long enough, or was not properly packed in glasses or jars. To prevent floating fruit, follow directions on page 200.(If glasses are used, stir jam before packing; if canning jars are used, shake jars gently after packing.)

Making Pickles and Relishes at Home

Pickle products truly add spice to meals or snacks. The skillful blending of spices, sugar, and vinegar with fruits and vegetables gives crisp, firm texture and pungent, sweet-sour flavor.

Pickles and relishes contribute some nutritive value, contain little or no fat, and, except for the sweet type, are low in calories.

Although food markets today offer a wide variety of pickles and relishes, many homemakers like to make their own pickle products when garden vegetables and fresh fruits are in abundant supply.

This bulletin gives specific directions for selecting and preparing pickling ingredients and for processing pickles and relishes. Included are basic recipes for the old-time favorites, such as pickled peaches, picalilli, and sauerkraut; and for the newer fresh-pack or quick-process dills, sweet gherkins, crosscut pickle slices, and skilled green beans. Spices in these basic recipes can be increased or decreased to please family tastes.

Common causes of poor-quality pickles and spoilage in sauerkraut are pointed out.

Classes and Characteristics

Pickle products are classified on the basis of ingredients used and the method of preparation. There are four general classes.

Brined Pickles

Brined pickles, also called fermented pickles, go through a curing process of about 3 weeks. Dilled cucumbers and sauerkraut belong in this group. Other vegetables, such as green tomatoes, may also be cured in the same way as cucumbers. Curing changes cucumber color from a bright green to an olive or yellow green. The white interior of the fresh cucumber becomes uniformly translucent. A desirable flavor is developed during curing without being excessively sour, salty, or spicy. Cucumber dills may be flavored with garlic, if desired. The skin of the pickle is tender and firm, but not hard, rubbery, or shriveled. The inside is tender and firm, not soft or mushy.

Good sauerkraut (brined cabbage) has a pleasant tart and tangy flavor, and is free from any off-flavors or off-odors. It is crisp and firm in texture and has a bright, creamy-white color. The shreds are uniformly cut (about the thinness of a dime) and are free from large, coarse pieces of leaves or core.

Fresh-pack Pickles

Fresh-pack or quick-process pickles, such as crosscut cucumber slices and whole cucumber dills, sweet gherkins, and dilled green beans, are brined for several hours or overnight, then drained and combined with boiling-hot vinegar, spices, and other seasonings. These are quick and easy to prepare. They have a tart, pungent flavor. Seasonings can be selected to suit individual family preferences. Fresh-pack whole cucumbers are olive green, crisp, tender, and firm.

Fruit Pickles

Fruit pickles are usually prepared from whole fruits and simmered in a spicy, sweet-sour sirup. They should be bright in color, of uniform size, and tender and firm without being watery. Pears, peaches, and watermelon rind are prepared this way.

Relishes

Relishes are prepared from fruits and vegetables which are chopped, seasoned, and then cooked to desired consistency. Clear, bright color and uniformity in size of pieces make an attractive product. Relishes accent the flavor of other foods. They may be quite hot and spicy. Relishes include piccalilli, pepper-onion, tomato-apple chutney, tomato-pear chutney, horseradish, and corn relish.

BN—20906

A choice of pickles and relishes.

Ingredients for Successful Pickling

Satisfactory pickle products can be obtained only when good-quality ingredients are used and proper procedures are followed. Correct proportions of fruit or vegetable, sugar, salt, vinegar, and spices are essential. Alum and lime are not needed to make pickles crisp and firm if good-quality ingredients and up-to-date procedures are used.

Use tested recipes. Read the complete recipe before starting preparation. Make sure necessary ingredients are on hand. Measure or weigh all ingredients carefully.

Fruits and Vegetables

Selection.—Select tender vegetables and firm fruit. Pears and peaches may be slightly underripe for pickling. Use unwaxed cucumbers for pickling whole. The brine cannot penetrate waxed cucumbers. Sort for uniform size and select the size best suited for the recipe being followed.

Use fruits and vegetables as soon as possible after gathering from the orchard or garden, or after purchasing from the market. If the fruits and vegetables cannot be used immediately, refrigerate them, or spread them where they will be well ventilated and cool. This is particularly important for cucumbers because they deteriorate rapidly, especially at room temperatures.

Do not use fruits or vegetables that show even slight evidence of mold. Proper processing kills potential spoilage organisms, but does not destroy the off-flavor that may be produced by mold growth in the tissue.

Preparation.—Wash fruits and vegetables thoroughly in cold water, whether they are to be pared or left unpared. Use a brush and wash only a few at a time. Wash under running water or through several changes of water. Clinging soil may contain bacteria that are hard to destroy. Lift the fruits or vegetables out of the water each time, so soil that has been washed off will not be drained back over them. Rinse pan thoroughly between washings. Handle gently to avoid bruising.

Be sure to remove all blossoms from cucumbers. They may be a source of the enzymes responsible for softening of the cucumbers during fermentation.

Salt

Use pure granulated salt if available. Un-iodized table salt can be used, but the materials added to the salt to prevent caking may make the brine cloudy. Do not use iodized table salt; it may darken pickles.

Vinegar

Use a high-grade cider or white distilled vinegar of 4- to 6-percent acidity (40 to 60 grain). Vinegars of unknown acidity should not be used. Cider vinegar, with its mellow acid taste, gives a nice blending of flavors, but may darken white or light-colored fruits and vegetables. White distilled vinegar has a sharp, pungent, acetic acid taste and is desirable when light color is important, as with pickled pears, onions, and cauliflower.

Do not dilute the vinegar unless the recipe so specifies. If a less sour product is preferred, add sugar rather than decrease vinegar.

Sugar

Either white granulated or brown sugar may be used. White sugar gives a product with a lighter color, but brown sugar may be preferred for color.

Spices

The general term "spices" includes the sweet herbs and the pungent spices. Herbs are the leaves of aromatic plants grown in the Temperate Zone, and spices are the stems, leaves, roots, seeds, flowers, buds, and bark of aromatic plants grown in the tropics.

Use fresh spices for best flavor in pickles. Spices deteriorate and quickly lose their pungency in heat and humidity. If they cannot be used immediately, they should be stored in an airtight container in a cool place.

Equipment for Successful Pickling

Equipment of the right kind, size, and amount saves time and energy. Read the complete recipe before you start preparation and make sure you have the utensils and tools you need ready for use.

Utensils

For heating pickling liquids, use utensils of unchipped enamelware, stainless steel, aluminum, or glass. Do not use copper, brass, galvanized, or iron utensils; these metals may react with acids or salts and cause undesirable color changes in the pickles or form undesirable compounds.

For fermenting or brining, use a crock or stone jar, unchipped enamel-lined pan, or large glass jar, bowl, or casserole. Use a heavy plate or large glass lid, which fits inside the container, to cover vegetables in the brine. Use a weight to hold the cover down and keep vegetables below the surface of the brine. A glass jar filled with water makes a good weight.

Small utensils that add ease and convenience to home pickling include: Measuring spoons, large wood or stainless-steel spoons for stirring, measuring cups, sharp knives, large trays, tongs, vegetable peelers, ladle with lip for pouring, slotted spoon, footed colander or wire basket, large-mouthed funnel, food chopper or grinder, and wooden cutting board.

Water-Bath Canner

Any large metal container may be used for a water-bath canner if it—

● Is deep enough to allow for 1 or 2 inches of water above the tops of the jars, plus a little extra space for boiling.

● Has a close-fitting cover.

● Is equipped with a wire or wood rack with partitions to keep jars from touching each other and falling against the sides of the canner.

A steam-pressure canner can serve as a water bath. To use it for this purpose, set the cover in place without fastening it. Be sure the petcock is wide open so that steam escapes and pressure is not built up.

Glass Jars and Lids

Select jars and lids that are free of cracks, chips, rust, dents, or any defect that may prevent airtight seals and cause needless spoilage. Be sure to use the right kind of jar closure for the type of jar.

Do not use jars and lids from commercially canned foods. They are designed for use on special packing machines and are not suitable for home canning.

Wash glass jars in hot, soapy water. Rinse thoroughly with hot water.

Wash and rinse lids and bands. Metal lids with sealing compounds may need boiling or holding in boiling water for a few minutes until they are used. Follow the manufacturer's directions.

Use clean, new rubber rings of the right size for the jars. Do not test by stretching. Dip rubber rings in boiling water before putting them on the jars.

Scales

Household scales will be needed if the recipes specify ingredients by weight. They are necessary in making sauerkraut to insure correct proportions of salt and shredded cabbage.

BN—20543

A selection of jars and lids suitable for pickles and relishes is shown here. Jar types, from left to right, wide-mouth pint, regular pint, regular quart, 1½ pint with flared sides, wide-mouth quart, pint with flared sides, and ½ pint with flared sides. The closures, from left to right, flat metal lid with sealing compound, and metal screw band to fit regular jar; flat metal lid with sealing compound, and metal screw band to fit wide-mouth jar; and porcelain-lined zinc cap with shoulder rubber ring to fit regular jar.

Procedures for Successful Pickling

To insure acceptable quality and bacteriological safety of the finished pickle product, you must follow recommended procedures. Ingredients, time, and money may be wasted if you use outdated or careless canning procedures.

Filling Jars

Fill the jars firmly and uniformly with the pickle product. Avoid packing so tightly that the brine or sirup is prevented from filling around and over the product. Be sure to leave head space at the top of the jar, as recommended in recipe.

Wipe the rim and threads of the jar with a clean, hot cloth to remove any particles of food, seeds, or spices. Even a small particle may prevent an airtight seal.

When a porcelain-lined zinc cap with shoulder rubber ring is used, put the wet rubber ring on the jar shoulder before filling the jar. Do not stretch the rubber ring more than necessary. After filling the jar, wipe the rubber ring and jar rim and threads clean.

Closing Jars

The two-piece metal cap (flat metal lid and metal screw band) is the most commonly used closure. To use this type of closure, place the lid on the jar with the sealing compound next to the glass. Screw the metal band down tight by hand to hold the sealing compound against the glass. When band is screwed tight, this lid has enough "give" to let air escape during processing. Do not tighten screw band further after processing.

When using a porcelain-lined zinc cap with shoulder rubber ring, screw the cap down firmly against the wet rubber ring, then turn it back one-fourth inch. Immediately after processing and removal of the jar from the canner, screw the cap down tight to complete the seal.

If liquid has boiled out of a jar during processing, do not open it to add more liquid, because spoilage organisms may enter. Seal the jar just as it is.

Heat Treatment

Pickle products require heat treatment to destroy organisms that cause spoilage, and to inactivate enzymes that may affect flavor, color, and texture. Adequate heating is best achieved by processing the filled jars in a boiling-water bath.

Heat processing is recommended for all pickle products. There is always danger of spoilage organisms entering the food when it is transferred from kettle to jar. This is true even when the utmost caution is observed and is the reason open-kettle canning is not recommended.

Pack pickle products into glass jars according to directions given in the recipe. Adjust lids. Immerse the jars into actively boiling water in canner or deep kettle. Be sure the water comes an inch or two above the jars tops; add boiling water if necessary, but do not pour it directly on the jars. Cover the container with a close-fitting lid and bring the water back to boiling as quickly as possible. Start to count processing time when water returns to boiling, and continue to boil gently and steadily for the time recommended for the food being canned. Remove jars immediately and complete the seals if necessary. Set jars upright, several inches apart, on a wire rack to cool.

Processing procedures for fermented cucumbers and fresh-pack dills are slightly different from the usual water-bath procedures. For these products, start to count the processing time as soon as the filled jars are placed in the actively boiling water. This prevents development of a cooked flavor and a loss of crispness.

Processing times as given in the recipes are for altitudes less than 1,000 feet above sea level. At altitudes of 1,000 feet or above, you need to increase recommended processing times as follows:

Altitude (Feet)	Increase in processing time (minutes)
1,000	1
2,000	2
3,000	3
4,000	4
5,000	5
6,000	6
7,000	7
8,000	8
9,000	9
10,000	10

Cooling the Canned Pickles

Cool the jars top side up, on a wire rack, several inches apart to allow for free circulation of air. Keep the jars out of a draft. Do not cover.

Cool for 12 to 24 hours; remove metal screw bands carefully; then check jars for an airtight seal. If the center of the lid of the two-piece metal cap has a slight dip or stays down when pressed, the jar is sealed. Another test is to tap the center of the lid with a spoon. A clear, ringing sound means a good seal. A dull note, however, does not always mean a poor seal. Check for airtight seal by turning jar partly over. If there is no leakage, the jar may be stored.

If the porcelain-lined zinc cap with rubber ring has been used, check for airtight seal by turning the jar partly over. If there is no leakage, the seal is tight.

If a jar shows signs of leakage or a poor seal, use the product right away, or recan it. To recan, empty the jar, repack in another clean jar, and reprocess the product as before.

The metal screw bands from the two-piece metal caps may be used again. Remove them from the jars as soon as jars are cool. Sticking bands may be loosened by covering with a hot, damp cloth for a short time.

The metal lids from the two-piece metal caps may be used only one time.

Storing the Canned Pickles

Wipe the jars with a clean, damp cloth, and label with name of product and date.

Store the canned pickles in a dark,

dry, cool place where there is no danger of freezing. Freezing may crack the jars or break the seals, and let in bacteria that cause spoilage. Protect from light to prevent bleaching and possible deterioration of flavor.

Always be on the alert for signs of spoilage. Before opening a jar, examine it closely. A bulging lid or leakage may mean that the contents are spoiled.

When a jar is opened, look for other signs of spoilage, such as spurting liquid, mold, disagreeable odor, change in color, or an unusual softness, mushiness, or slipperiness of the pickle product. *If there is even the slightest indication of spoilage, do not eat or even taste the contents.* Dispose of the contents so that they cannot be eaten by humans or animals.

After emptying the jar of spoiled food, wash the jar in hot, soapy water and rinse. Boil in clean water for 15 minutes.

BN—20539

Heat-processed, brined dill pickles, ready for serving. Processing the pickles in a boiling-water bath destroys yeasts and molds in the jar and helps to preserve good texture and flavor in the pickles during storage for several months.

Recipes

VOLUME EQUIVALENTS

1 gallon = 4 quarts
1 quart = 4 cups
1 pint = 2 cups
1 cup = 16 tablespoons
1 tablespoon = 3 teaspoons

Brined dill pickles

Yield: 9 to 10 quarts

Cucumbers, 3 to 6 inches in length	20 pounds (about ½ bushel)
Whole mixed pickling spice	¾ cup
Dill plant, fresh or dried	2 to 3 bunches
Vinegar	2½ cups
Salt, pure granulated	1¾ cups
Water	2½ gallons

Cover cucumbers with cold water. Wash thoroughly, using a vegetable brush; handle gently to avoid bruising. Take care to remove any blossoms. Drain on rack or wipe dry.

Place half the pickle spices and a layer of dill in a 5-gallon crock or jar. Fill the crock with cucumbers to within 3 or 4 inches of the top. Place a layer of dill and remaining spices over the top of cucumbers. (Garlic may be added, if desired.) Thoroughly mix the vinegar, salt, and water and pour over the cucumbers.

Cover with a heavy china or glass plate or lid that fits inside the crock.

Use a weight to hold the plate down and keep the cucumbers under the brine. A glass jar filled with water makes a good weight. Cover loosely with clean cloth. Keep pickles at room temperature and remove scum daily when formed. Scum may start forming in 3 to 5 days. Do not stir pickles, but be sure they are completely covered with brine. If necessary, make additional brine, using original proportions specified in recipe.

In about 3 weeks the cucumbers will have become an olive-green color and should have a desirable flavor. Any white spots inside the fermented cucumbers will disappear in processing.

The original brine is usually cloudy as a result of yeast development during the fermentation period. If this cloudiness is objectionable, fresh brine may be used to cover the pickles when packing

How to make
Brined Dill Pickles

DN–2049

Wash cucumbers thoroughly with a brush. Use several changes of cold water. Take care to remove all blossoms. Drain on rack.

DN–2048

Place half of the spices and a layer of dill on the bottom of a 5-gallon jar or crock. Fill the cucumbers to 3 or 4 inches from top. Cover with remaining dill and add rest of spices. Mix salt, vinegar, and water and pour over cucumbers.

DN–2047

Use a heavy plate or glass lid which fits inside the container to cover cucumbers. Use a weight to hold the cover down and keep the cucumbers under the brine. A glass jar filled with water makes a good weight.

DN–2044

Bubbles and the formation of scum indicate active fermentation. Scum should be removed daily.

DN–2046

After 3 weeks of fermentation the dills are ready for processing. Cloudiness of the brine results from yeast development during fermentation. Strain the brine before using.

DN–2045

Pack pickles firmly into clean, hot quart jars. Do not wedge tightly. Add several pieces of the dill to each jar. Cover with boiling brine to ½ inch of top of jar; adjust lids. Place jars in boiling water and process for 15 minutes. Start to count processing time as soon as hot jars are placed into the actively boiling water.

DN–2043

Remove jars from the canner and complete seals if necessary. Set jars upright, several inches apart, on a wire rack to cool. Cloudiness of brine is typical when the original fermentation brine is used as the covering liquid.

them into jars; in making fresh brine use ½ cup salt and 4 cups vinegar to 1 gallon of water. The fermentation brine is generally preferred for its added flavor and should be strained before heating to boiling.

Pack the pickles, along with some of the dill, into clean, hot quart jars; add garlic, if desired. Avoid too tight a pack. Cover with boiling brine to ½ inch of the top of the jar. Adjust jar lids.

Process in boiling water for 15 minutes [1] (start to count the processing time as soon as hot jars are placed into the actively boiling water).

Remove jars and complete seals if necessary. Set jars upright, several inches apart, on a wire rack to cool.

Fresh-pack dill pickles

Yield: 7 quarts

Cucumbers, 3 to 5 inches in length, packed 7 to 10 per quart jar	17 to 18 pounds
5-percent brine (¾ cup pure granulated salt per gallon of water)	About 2 gallons
Vinegar	6 cups (1½ quarts)
Salt, pure granulated	¾ cup
Sugar	¼ cup
Water	9 cups (2¼ quarts)
Whole mixed pickling spice	2 tablespoons
Whole mustard seed	2 teaspoons per quart jar
Garlic, if desired	1 or 2 cloves per quart jar
Dill plant, fresh or dried	3 heads per quart jar
Or	
Dill seed	1 tablespoon per quart jar

Wash cucumbers thoroughly; scrub with vegetable brush; drain. Cover with the 5-percent brine (¾ cup salt per gallon of water). Let set overnight; drain.

Combine vinegar, salt, sugar, water, and mixed pickling spices that are tied in a clean, thin, white cloth; heat to boiling. Pack cucumbers into clean, hot quart jars. Add mustard seed, dill plant or seed, and garlic to each jar; cover with boiling liquid to within ½ inch of top of jar. Adjust jar lids.

Process in boiling water for 20 minutes [1] (start to count the processing time as soon as hot jars are placed into the actively boiling water).

Remove jars and complete seals if necessary. Set jars upright, several inches apart, on a wire rack to cool.

---

[1] Processing time is given for altitudes less than 1,000 feet above sea level. At altitudes of 1,000 feet or above, see table on page 219.

Sweet gherkins

Yield: 7 to 8 pints

Cucumbers, 1 ½ to 3 inches in length_____	5 quarts (about 7 pounds)
Salt, pure granulated_____	½ cup
Sugar_____	8 cups (2 quarts)
Vinegar_____	6 cups (1 ½ quarts)
Turmeric_____	¾ teaspoon
Celery seed_____	2 teaspoons
Whole mixed pickling spice_____	2 teaspoons
Stick cinnamon _____	8 1-inch pieces
Fennel (if desired)_____	½ teaspoon
Vanilla (if desired)_____	2 teaspoons

First day

Morning.—Wash cucumbers thoroughly; scrub with vegetable brush; stem ends may be left on if desired. Drain cucumbers; place in large container and cover with boiling water.

Afternoon (6 to 8 hours later).—Drain; cover with fresh, boiling water.

Second day

Morning.—Drain; cover with fresh, boiling water.

Afternoon.—Drain; add salt; cover with fresh, boiling water.

Third day

Morning.—Drain; prick cucumbers in several places with table fork. Make sirup of 3 cups of the sugar and 3 cups of the vinegar; add turmeric and spices. Heat to boiling and pour over cucumbers. (Cucumbers will be partially covered at this point.)

Afternoon.—Drain sirup into pan; add 2 cups of the sugar and 2 cups of the vinegar to sirup. Heat to boiling and pour over pickles.

Fourth day

Morning.—Drain sirup into pan; add 2 cups of the sugar and 1 cup of the vinegar to sirup. Heat to boiling and pour over pickles.

Afternoon.—Drain sirup into pan; add remaining 1 cup sugar and the vanilla to sirup; heat to boiling. Pack pickles into clean, hot pint jars and cover with boiling sirup to ½ inch of top of jar. Adjust jar lids.

Process for 5 minutes [1] in boiling water (start to count processing time as soon as water returns to boiling). Remove jars and complete seals if necessary. Set jars upright, several inches apart, on a wire rack to cool.

---

[1] Processing time is given for altitudes less than 1,000 feet above sea level. At altitudes of 1,000 feet or above, see table on page 219.

How to make
Crosscut Pickle Slices

DN–2054

Wash cucumbers thoroughly. Slice unpeeled cucumbers into 1/8- to 1/4-inch crosswise slices. Wash and remove skins from onions; slice into 1/8-inch slices.

DN–2053

Combine cucumber and onion slices with peeled garlic cloves. Add salt and mix thoroughly. Cover with crushed ice or ice cubes. Allow to stand 3 hours. Drain thoroughly; remove garlic cloves.

DN–2052

Combine sugar, spices, and vinegar; heat to boiling. Add drained cucumber and onion slices and heat 5 minutes.

Pack loosely into clean, hot pint jars to ½ inch of top of jar; adjust lids. Process in boiling water for 5 minutes. Start to count processing time as soon as water in canner returns to boiling.

Remove jars and complete seals if necessary. Set jars upright, several inches apart, on a wire rack or folded towel to cool.

Crosscut pickle slices

Yield: 7 pints

Cucumbers, medium size (about 6 pounds), sliced___	4 quarts
Onions (12 to 15 small white, about 1 pound), sliced_	1 ½ cups
Garlic cloves_____	2 large
Salt _____	⅓ cup
Ice, crushed or cubes_____	2 quarts (2 trays)
Sugar_____	4 ½ cups
Turmeric_____	1 ½ teaspoons
Celery seed_____	1 ½ teaspoons
Mustard seed _____	2 tablespoons
Vinegar, white_____	3 cups

Wash cucumbers thoroughly, using a vegetable brush; drain on rack. Slice unpeeled cucumbers into ⅛-inch to ¼-inch slices; discard ends. Add onions and garlic.

Add salt and mix thoroughly; cover with crushed ice or ice cubes; let stand 3 hours. Drain thoroughly; remove garlic cloves.

Combine sugar, spices, and vinegar; heat just to boiling. Add drained cucumber and onion slices and heat 5 minutes.

Pack hot pickles loosely into clean, hot pint jars to ½ inch of top. Adjust jar lids.

Process in boiling water for 5 minutes [1] (start to count processing time as soon as water in canner returns to boiling). Remove jars and complete seals if necessary. Set jars upright to cool.

Note: Sugar may be reduced to 4 cups, if a less sweet pickle is desired.

Tomato-apple chutney

Yield: 7 pints

Tomatoes (about 6 pounds), pared, chopped_____	3 quarts
Apples (about 5 pounds), pared, chopped_____	3 quarts
Raisins, seedless, white_____	2 cups
Onions (4 to 5 medium), chopped_____	2 cups
Green peppers (2 medium), chopped_____	1 cup
Brown sugar_____	2 pounds
Vinegar, white_____	1 quart
Salt_____	4 teaspoons
Ground ginger_____	1 teaspoon
Whole mixed pickling spice_____	¼ cup

Combine all ingredients except the whole spices. Place spices loosely in a clean, white cloth; tie with a string, and add to tomato-

----

[1] Processing time is given for altitudes less than 1,000 feet above sea level. At altitudes of 1,000 feet or above, see table on page 219.

apple mixture. Bring to a boil; cook slowly, stirring frequently, until mixture is thickened (about 1 hour). Remove spice bag.

Pack the boiling-hot chutney into clean, hot pint jars to ½ inch of the top of the jar. Adjust jar lids.

Process in boiling water for 5 minutes [1] (start to count processing time when water in canner returns to boiling). Remove jars and complete seals if necessary. Set jars upright, several inches apart, on a wire rack to cool.

Tomato-pear chutney

Yield: 3 to 4 jars (½ pint each)

Tomatoes, quartered, fresh or canned	2½ cups
Pears, diced, fresh or canned	2½ cups
Raisins, seedless, white	½ cup
Green pepper (1 medium), chopped	½ cup
Onions (1 or 2 medium), chopped	½ cup
Sugar	1 cup
Vinegar, white	½ cup
Salt	1 teaspoon
Ground ginger	½ teaspoon
Mustard, powdered, dry	½ teaspoon
Cayenne pepper	⅛ teaspoon
Pimiento, canned, chopped	¼ cup

When fresh tomatoes and pears are used, remove skins; include sirup when using canned pears.

Combine all ingredients except pimiento. Bring to a boil; cook slowly until thickened (about 45 minutes), stirring occasionally. Add pimiento and boil 3 minutes longer.

Pack the boiling-hot chutney into clean, hot jars, filling to the top. Seal tightly. *Store in refrigerator.*

If extended storage without refrigeration is desired, this product should be processed in boiling water. Pack the boiling-hot chutney into clean, hot jars to ½ inch of top of jar. Adjust jar lids. Process in boiling water for 5 minutes [1] (start to count processing time when water in canner returns to boiling). Remove jars and complete seals if necessary. Set jars upright, several inches apart, on a wire rack to cool.

Note: If a less spicy chutney is preferred, the amount of cayenne pepper may be reduced or omitted.

[1] Processing time is given for altitudes less than 1,000 feet above sea level. At altitudes of 1,000 feet or above, see table on page 219.

Dilled green beans
Yield: 7 pints

Green beans, whole	4 pounds (about 4 quarts)
Hot red pepper, crushed	¼ teaspoon per pint jar
Whole mustard seed	½ teaspoon per pint jar
Dill seed	½ teaspoon per pint jar
Garlic	1 clove per pint jar
Vinegar	5 cups (1 ¼ quarts)
Water	5 cups (1 ¼ quarts)
Salt	½ cup

Wash beans thoroughly; drain and cut into lengths to fill pint jars. Pack beans into clean, hot jars; add pepper, mustard seed, dill seed, and garlic.

Combine vinegar, water and salt; heat to boiling. Pour boiling liquid over beans, filling to ½ inch of top of jar. Adjust jar lids.

Process in boiling water for 5 minutes [1] (start to count processing time as soon as water in canner returns to boiling). Remove jars and complete seals if necessary. Set jars upright, several inches apart, on a wire rack to cool.

Pickled peaches
Yield: 7 quarts

Sugar	3 quarts
Vinegar	2 quarts
Stick cinnamon	7 2-inch pieces
Cloves, whole	2 tablespoons
Peaches, small or medium size	16 pounds (about 11 quarts)

Combine sugar, vinegar, stick cinnamon, and cloves. (Cloves may be put in a clean cloth, tied with a string, and removed after cooking, if not desired in packed product.) Bring to a boil and let simmer covered, about 30 minutes.

Wash peaches and remove skins; dipping the fruit in boiling water for 1 minute, then quickly in cold water makes peeling easier. To prevent pared peaches from darkening during preparation, immediately put them into cold water containing 2 tablespoons each of

salt and vinegar per gallon. Drain just before using.

Add peaches to the boiling sirup, enough for 2 or 3 quarts at a time, and heat for about 5 minutes. Pack hot peaches into clean, hot jars. Continue heating in sirup and packing peaches into jars. Add 1 piece of stick cinnamon and 2 to 3 whole cloves (if desired) to each jar. Cover peaches with boiling sirup to

[1] Processing time is given for altitudes less than 1,000 feet above sea level. At altitudes of 1,000 feet or above, see table on page 219.

½ inch of top of jar. Adjust jar lids.

Process in boiling water for 20 minutes [1] (start to count processing time after water in canner returns to boiling). Remove jars and complete seals if necessary. Set jars upright, several inches apart, on a wire rack to cool.

Pickled pears
Yield: 7 to 8 pints

Sugar	2 quarts
Vinegar, white	1 quart
Water	1 pint
Stick cinnamon	8 2-inch pieces
Cloves, whole	2 tablespoons
Allspice, whole	2 tablespoons
Seckel pears	8 pounds (4 or 5 quarts)

Combine sugar, vinegar, water, and stick cinnamon; add cloves and allspice that are tied in a clean, thin white cloth. Bring to a boil and simmer, covered, about 30 minutes.

Wash pears, remove skins, and all of blossom end; the stems may be left on if desired. To prevent peeled pears from darkening during preparation, immediately put them into cold water containing 2 tablespoons each of salt and vinegar per gallon. Drain just before using.

Add pears to the boiling sirup and continue simmering for 20 to 25 minutes. Pack hot pears into clean, hot pint jars; add one 2-inch piece cinnamon per jar and cover with boiling sirup to ½ inch of top of jar. Adjust jar lids.

Process in boiling water for 20 minutes [1] (start to count processing time as soon as water in canner returns to boiling). Remove jars and complete seals if necessary. Set jars upright, several inches apart, on a wire rack to cool.

Kieffer pears are also frequently used for making fruit pickles.

To pickle Kieffer pears: Use 12 pounds Kieffer pears and reduce vinegar to 3 cups in recipe above. Wash the pears, peel, cut in halves or quarters, remove hard centers and cores. Boil pears for 10 minutes in water to cover. Use 1 pint of this liquid in place of the pint of water in recipe above. Finish in the same way as Seckel pears. Makes about 8 pints.

---

[1] Processing time is given for altitudes less than 1,000 feet above sea level. At altitudes of 1,000 feet or above, see table on page 219.

Watermelon pickles
Yield: 4 to 5 pints

Watermelon rind (about 6 pounds, unpared, or ½ large melon)	3 quarts
Salt	¾ cup
Water	3 quarts
Ice cubes	2 quarts (2 trays)
Sugar	9 cups (2¼ quarts)
Vinegar, white	3 cups
Water	3 cups
Whole cloves	1 tablespoon (about 48)
Stick cinnamon	6 1-inch pieces
Lemon, thinly sliced, with seeds removed	1

Pare rind and all pink edges from the watermelon. Cut into 1-inch squares or fancy shapes as desired. Cover with brine made by mixing the salt with 3 quarts cold water. Add ice cubes. Let stand 5 or 6 hours.

Drain; rinse in cold water. Cover with cold water and cook until fork tender, about 10 minutes (do not overcook). Drain.

Combine sugar, vinegar, water, and spices (tied in a clean, thin white cloth). Boil 5 minutes and pour over the watermelon with spices; add lemon slices. Let stand overnight.

Heat watermelon in sirup to boiling and cook until watermelon is translucent (about 10 minutes). Pack hot pickles loosely into clean, hot pint jars. To each jar add 1 piece of stick cinnamon from spice bag; cover with boiling sirup to ½ inch of top of jar. Adjust jar lids.

Process in boiling water for 5 minutes [1] (start to count processing time when water in canner returns to boiling). Remove jars and complete seals if necessary. Set jars upright, several inches apart, on a wire rack to cool.

The sugar may be reduced to 8 cups, if a less sweet pickle is desired.

Note: Red or green coloring may be added to the sirup, if desired. Keep watermelon rind in plastic bags in refrigerator until enough rinds for one recipe are collected.

---

[1] Processing time is given for altitudes less than 1,000 feet above sea level. At altitudes of 1,000 feet or above, see table on page 219.

Sauerkraut
Yield: 16 to 18 quarts

Cabbage _____ About 50 pounds
Salt, pure granulated_____ 1 pound (1½ cups)

Remove the outer leaves and any undesirable portions from firm, mature, heads of cabbage; wash and drain. Cut into halves or quarters; remove the core. Use a shredder or sharp knife to cut the cabbage into thin shreds about the thickness of a dime.

In a large container, thoroughly mix 3 tablespoons salt with 5 pounds shredded cabbage. Let the salted cabbage stand for several minutes to wilt slightly; this allows packing without excessive breaking or bruising of the shreds.

Pack the salted cabbage firmly and evenly into a large clean crock or jar. Using a wooden spoon or tamper or the hands, press down firmly until the juice comes to the surface. Repeat the shredding, salting, and packing of cabbage until the crock is filled to within 3 or 4 inches of the top.

Cover cabbage with a clean, thin, white cloth (such as muslin) and tuck the edges down against the inside of the container. Cover with a plate or round paraffined board that just fits inside the container so that the cabbage is not exposed to the air. Put a weight on top of the cover so the brine comes to the cover but not over it. A glass jar filled with water makes a good weight.

A newer method of covering cabbage during fermentation consists of placing a plastic bag filled with water on top of the fermenting cabbage. The water-filled bag seals the surface from exposure to air, and prevents the growth of film yeast or molds. It also serves as a weight. For extra protection, the bag with the water in it can be placed inside another plastic bag.

Any bag used should be of heavyweight, watertight plastic and intended for use with foods.

The amount of water in the plastic bag can be adjusted to give just enough pressure to keep the fermenting cabbage covered with brine. See illustration on page 25.

Formation of gas bubbles indicates fermentation is taking place. A room temperature of 68° to 72° F. is best for fermenting cabbage. Fermentation is usually completed in 5 to 6 weeks.

To store: Heat sauerkraut to simmering (185° to 210° F.). Do not boil. Pack hot sauerkraut into clean, hot jars and cover with hot juice to ½ inch of top of jar. Adjust jar lids. Process in boiling-water bath, 15 minutes for pints, and 20 minutes for quarts.[1] Start to count processing time as soon as hot jars are placed into the actively boiling water.

Remove jars and complete seals if necessary. Set jars upright, several inches apart, to cool.

---

[1] Processing time is given for altitudes less than 1,000 feet above sea level. At altitudes of 1,000 feet or above, see table on page 219.

How to make Sauerkraut

DN–2042

Remove the outer leaves from firm, mature heads of cabbage; wash and drain. Remove core or cut it into thin shreds.

DN–2041

Shred cabbage and weigh 5 pounds. Accuracy in weighing is important to insure correct proportion of cabbage to salt.

DN–2040

Measure 3 tablespoons pure granulated salt and sprinkle over 5 pounds shredded cabbage.

DN–2061

Allow the salted cabbage to stand a few minutes to wilt slightly. Mix well, with clean hands or a spoon, to distribute salt uniformly.

DN–2039

Pack the salted cabbage into container. Press firmly with wooden spoon, tamper, or with hands until the juices drawn out will just cover the shredded cabbage.

DN–2060

Place a water-filled plastic bag on top of the cabbage. A water-filled plastic bag fits snugly against the cabbage and against the sides of the container and prevents exposure to air.

DN–2062

When fermentation is complete, remove from container and heat in kettle to simmering temperature. Pack hot sauerkraut into clean, hot jars; cover with hot juice, filling to ½ inch of top of jar. Adjust lids. Place jars in boiling-water bath and process 15 minutes for pints and 20 minutes for quarts. Start to count the processing time as soon as hot jars are placed into the actively boiling water.

Remove jars from the canner and complete seals if necessary. Set jars upright, several inches apart, on a wire rack to cool.

DN–2063

Relishes for which ingredients are available throughout the year can be made up in small quantities for use within a period of 3 or 4 weeks. For such products, the boiling water-bath process may be omitted *but they must be stored in the refrigerator.* Recipes for two relishes that can be made in this way appear on this page.

Horseradish relish

Grated horseradish _____ 1 cup
Vinegar, white _____ ½ cup
Salt _____ ¼ teaspoon

Wash horseradish roots thoroughly and remove the brown, outer skin. (A vegetable peeler is useful in removal of outer skin.) The roots may be grated, or cut into small cubes and put through a food chopper or a blender.

Combine ingredients. Pack into clean jars. Seal tightly. *Store in refrigerator.*

Pepper-onion relish

Yield: 5 jars (½ pint each)

Onions (6 to 8 large), finely chopped _____ 1 quart
Sweet red peppers (4 or 5 medium), finely chopped _____ 1 pint
Green peppers (4 or 5 medium), finely chopped _____ 1 pint
Sugar _____ 1 cup
Vinegar _____ 1 quart
Salt _____ 4 teaspoons

Combine all ingredients and bring to a boil. Cook until slightly thickened (about 45 minutes), stirring occasionally. Pack the boiling-hot relish into clean, hot jars; fill to top of jar. Seal tightly. *Store in refrigerator.*

If extended storage without refrigeration is desired, this product should be processed in a boiling-water bath. Pack the boiling-hot relish into clean, hot jars to ½ inch of top of jar. Adjust jar lids. Process in boiling water for 5 minutes [1] (start to count processing time when water in canner returns to boiling).

Remove jars and complete seals if necessary. Set jars upright, several inches apart, on a wire rack to cool.

---

[1] Processing time is given for altitudes less than 1,000 feet above sea level. At altitudes of 1,000 feet or above, see table on page 219.

Piccalilli
Yield: 4 pints

Green tomatoes (about 16 medium), chopped___	1 quart
Sweet red peppers (2 to 3 medium), chopped___	1 cup
Green peppers (2 to 3 medium), chopped_____	1 cup
Onions (2 to 3 large), chopped_____	1½ cups
Cabbage (about 2 pounds), chopped_____	5 cups (1¼ quarts)
Salt_____	⅓ cup
Vinegar_____	3 cups
Brown sugar_____	2 cups, firmly packed
Whole mixed pickling spice_____	2 tablespoons

Combine vegetables, mix with salt, let stand overnight. Drain and press in a clean, thin, white cloth to remove all liquid possible.

Combine vinegar and sugar. Place spices loosely in a clean cloth; tie with a string. Add to vinegar mixture. Bring to a boil.

Add vegetables, bring to a boil, and simmer about 30 minutes, or until there is just enough liquid to moisten vegetables. Remove spice bag. Pack hot relish into clean, hot pint jars. Fill jars to ½ inch of top. Adjust lids.

Process in boiling water for 5 minutes [1] (start to count processing time as soon as water in canner returns to boiling).

Remove jars and complete seals if necessary. Set jars upright on a wire rack to cool.

Corn relish
Yield: 7 pints

Corn, whole kernel_____	2 quarts
Use fresh (16 to 20 medium-size ears) or frozen (whole kernel, six 10-ounce packages)	
Sweet red peppers (4 to 5 medium) diced_____	1 pint
Green peppers (4 to 5 medium), diced_____	1 pint
Celery (1 large bunch), chopped_____	1 quart
Onions (8 to 10 small, ¾ pound) chopped or sliced_____	1 cup
Sugar_____	1½ cups
Vinegar_____	1 quart
Salt_____	2 tablespoons
Celery seed_____	2 teaspoons
Mustard, powdered dry_____	2 tablespoons
Turmeric_____	1 teaspoon

Fresh corn.—Remove husks and silks. Cook ears of corn in boiling water for 5 minutes; remove and

[1] Processing time is given for altitudes less than 1,000 feet above sea level. At altitudes of 1,000 feet or above, see table on page 219.

plunge into cold water. Drain; cut corn from cob. Do not scrape cob.

Frozen corn.—Defrost overnight in refrigerator or for 2 to 3 hours at room temperature. Place containers in front of a fan to hasten defrosting.

Combine peppers, celery, onions, sugar, vinegar, salt, and celery seed. Cover pan until mixture starts to boil, then boil uncovered for 5 minutes, stirring occasionally. Mix dry mustard and turmeric and blend with liquid from boiling mixture; add, with corn, to boiling mixture. Return to boiling and cook for 5 minutes, stirring occasionally.

This relish may be thickened by adding ¼ cup flour blended with ½ cup water at the time the corn is added for cooking. Frequent stirring will be necessary to prevent sticking and scorching.

Pack loosely while boiling hot into clean, hot pint jars, filling to ½ inch of top. Adjust jar lids.

Process in boiling water for 15 minutes [1] (start to count processing time as soon as water in canner returns to boiling). Remove jars and complete seals if necessary. Set jars upright, several inches apart, on a wire rack to cool.

Common Causes of Poor-Quality Pickles

Shriveled Pickles

Shriveling may result from using too strong a vinegar, sugar, or salt solution at the start of the pickling process. In making the very sweet or very sour pickles, it is best to start with a dilute solution and increase gradually to the desired strength.

Overcooking or overprocessing may also cause shriveling.

Hollow Pickles

Hollowness in pickles usually results from—

• Poorly developed cucumbers.

• Holding cucumbers too long before pickling.

• Too rapid fermentation.

• Too strong or too weak a brine during fermentation.

Soft or Slippery Pickles

These generally result from microbial action which causes spoilage. Once a pickle becomes soft it cannot be made firm. Microbial activity may be caused by—

• Too little salt or acid.

• Cucumbers not covered with brine during fermentation.

• Scum scattered throughout the brine during fermentation period.

• Insufficient heat treatment.

• A seal that is not airtight.

• Moldy garlic or spices.

Blossoms, if not entirely removed from the cucumbers before fermentation, may contain fungi or yeasts

[1] Processing time is given for altitudes less than 1,000 feet above sea level. At altitudes of 1,000 feet or above, see table on page 219.

responsible for enzymatic softening of pickles.

Dark Pickles

Darkness in pickles may be caused by—

- Use of ground spices.
- Too much spice.
- Iodized salt.
- Overcooking.
- Minerals in water, especially iron.
- Use of iron utensils.

Common Causes of Spoilage in Sauerkraut

Off-flavors and off-odors develop when there is spoilage in sauerkraut. Spoilage in sauerkraut is indicated by undesirable color, off-odors, and soft texture.

Soft Kraut

Softness in sauerkraut may result from—

- Insufficient salt.
- Too high temperatures during fermentation.
- Uneven distribution of salt.
- Air pockets caused by improper packing.

Pink Kraut

Pink color in kraut is caused by growth of certain types of yeast on the surface of the kraut. These may grow if there is too much salt, an uneven distribution of salt, or if the kraut is improperly covered or weighted during fermentation.

Rotted Kraut

This condition in kraut is usually found at the surface where the cabbage has not been covered sufficiently to exclude air during fermentation.

Dark Kraut

Darkness in kraut may be caused by—

- Unwashed and improperly trimmed cabbage.
- Insufficient juice to cover fermenting cabbage.
- Uneven distribution of salt.
- Exposure to air.
- High temperatures during fermentation, processing, and storage.
- Long storage period.